Diversity Perspectives for Social Work Practice

Diversity Perspectives for Social Work Practice

Editors:

Joseph Anderson

Robin Wiggins Carter

Boston   New York   San Francisco
Mexico City   Montreal   Toronto   London   Madrid   Munich   Paris
Hong Kong   Singapore   Tokyo   Cape Town   Sydney

Series Editor: Patricia Quinlin
Editorial Assistant: Annemarie Kennedy
Production Administrator: Marissa Falco
Electronic Composition: Publishers' Design and Production Services, Inc.
Composition and Prepress Buyer: Linda Cox
Manufacturing Buyer: JoAnne Sweeney
Cover Administrator: Kristina Mose-Libon

For related titles and support materials, visit our online catalog at www.ablongman.com

Library of Congress Cataloging-in-Publication Data
Diversity perspectives for social work practice / edited by Joseph Anderson, Robin Wiggins Carter. — 1st ed.
        p.   cm.
    Includes index.
    ISBN 0-205-34065-2 (pbk.)
    1. Social work with minorities. 2. Social service and race relations. 3. Multiculturalism.
    I. Anderson, Joseph, 1941–   II. Carter, Robin Wiggins.
    HV3176.D594 2002
    362.84—dc21   2002023222

Printed in the United States of America

10 9 8 7 6 5 4 3   RRD-IN   07 06 05

Greetings! I am pleased to see we are different. May we together become greater than the sum of both of us.

—Vulcan Greeting, *Star Trek*

People connect on the basis of being similar and grow on the basis of being different.

—Virginia Satir, *Conjoint Family Therapy*

. . . Everything now . . . is in our hands; we have no right to assume otherwise. If we—and now I mean the relatively conscious whites and relatively conscious blacks, who must, like lovers, insist on, or create, the consciousness of others—do not falter in our duty now, we may be able, handful that we are, to end the racial nightmare, and achieve our country, and change the history of the world. If we do not now dare everything, the fulfillment of that prophecy, re-created from the Bible in song by a slave, is upon us: "God gave Noah the rainbow sign, No more water, the fire next time!"

—James Baldwin, *The Fire Next Time*

. . . at the treaty of Lancaster, in Pennsylvania, anno 1744, between the Government of Virginia, and the Six Nations . . . the Commissioners from Virginia acquainted the Indians by a Speech, that there was at Williamsburg, a College with a Fund for Educating Indian youth; and that, if the Six Nations would send down half a dozen of their young lads to that College, the Government would take care that they should be well provided for, and instructed in all the Learning of the White People. [The Indians' spokesperson replied:]

. . . we know . . . that you highly esteem the kind of Learning taught in those Colleges, and that the Maintenance of our young Men, while with you, would be very expensive to you. We are convinc'd, therefore, that you mean to do us Good by your Proposal; and we thank you heartily.

But you, who are wise, must know that different nations have different Conceptions of things; and you will therefore not take it amiss, if our Ideas of this kind of Education happen not to be the same as yours. We have had some Experience of it; Several of our young People were formerly brought up at the Colleges of the Northern Provinces; they were instructed in all your Sciences; but, then they came back to us, they were bad Runners, ignorant of every means of living in the Woods, unable to bear either Cold or Hunger, knew neither how to build a Cabin, take a Deer, or kill an Enemy, spoke our Language imperfectly, were therefore neither fit for Hunters, Warriors, nor Counsellors; they were totally good for nothing.

We are however not the less oblig'd by your kind Offer, tho' we decline accepting it; and, to show our grateful Sense of it, if the Gentlemen of Virginia will send us a Dozen of their Sons, we will take great Care of their Education, instruct them in all we know, and make Men of them.

—Benjamin Franklin, *Remarks Concerning the Savages of North America*

Contents

Dedication

To our families: Wandarah, Bailey, Sean, Caitlin, Stephen, Simone, and Brent, and to our diverse colleagues and students who provide support and challenge to our ongoing professional development.

Preface

Social workers, in the context of their practice and their central values and ethics, must develop competencies for working with and on behalf of diverse populations. This book contributes to preparation for this practice. It presents perspectives and conceptual frameworks for understanding ethnocultural differences, the dynamics and consequences of oppression, and diversity in relation to vulnerable or at-risk populations.

This book covers substantive knowledge. It also provides direction on how to learn continually about diversity and its meanings and consequences for individuals, families, groups, organizations, and communities that we serve. It organizes the presentation of these social work-derived diversity frameworks in a manner designed to aid the reader's comparative and critical analysis and synthesis.

Following the schema developed by one of the editors and introduced in Chapter 1, the book presents an overview and analysis of twelve relatively distinct frameworks. These include the central, or core, frameworks of the (1) *strengths perspective* and the (2) *empowerment approach*; the ethnocultural frameworks of (3) *ethnic-sensitive social work practice* and (4) *value orientation*; the oppression frameworks of (5) *people of color*, (6) *dual perspective*, (7) *ethnic-centric*, and (8) *social justice*; and the vulnerable life situations' (9) *ethnographic*, (10) *communication*, (11) *feminist*, and (12) *constructivist* frameworks. The book concludes with consideration of these frameworks and diversity content in general in social work education and practice. Thus, the diversity content in this text derives from diverse frameworks.

The content also evolves from a diversity of authors. Among them are women and men, African Americans, Latinos, Asian Americans, Native Americans, and Caucasians; Protestants, Catholics, Jews, and Buddhists; and those with diverse sexual orientations. Their teaching areas cover practice, diversity, human behavior in the social environment, and/or policy.

One thing the editors and authors have in common is their affiliation with a single social work program, California State University, Sacramento. This is no accident. Most faculty who contributed to this book have published some of the earliest as well as more recent work on several of these diversity frameworks and on other diversity issues and content. They develop and teach curricula to prepare students for competent diversity practice in one of the most diverse social work programs in the nation. Also in common, and evident in this text, is their commitment to diversity competence in social work's contribution to the pluralistic community of the future.

The editors especially acknowledge our colleagues at California State, Sacramento, for their scholarly and thoughtful contributions to this book. Their work is truly the heart of this work. Special encouragement, patience, and support for this project came initially from Judy Fifer and more recently from Pat Quinlin and Alyssa Pratt at Allyn & Bacon. The editors are grateful for the collaborative and encouraging manner in which they worked with us.

1

Introduction and Organization: Diversity Perspectives

Joseph Anderson

The organization and writing of this book come at the birth of a new century—a critical era. Whatever the projections for the future, there is a central recognition that the promises and problems of diversity will be confronted in all their natural and socially constructed forms. The Chinese appear quite accurate in using two graphic characters to represent the concept of crisis, the root from which the English language derives its term "critical." One character stands for opportunity and the other for danger. This current critical period, then, presents a potential turning point in human history and in growth through diversity.

Social Work and Diversity

Social work needs to be at the heart (if not a large part of the heart itself) of turning the corner toward enhancing well-being and accomplishing social justice—the two tests that society and the social work profession must pass in addressing diversity issues and the potentials and obstacles in evolving as a healthy global community. The NASW Code of Ethics clearly defines social work's diversity-related mission and ethical obligation to serve both individuals and society. The code calls for using knowledge, values, and skills to understand and respect difference, to protect and empower those most vulnerable to marginalization and oppression as a result of their difference, to change discriminatory practices, and to promote social justice in all social work. It conceives this practice as beneficial both to individuals and society in their inevitable interdependence.

Social Work Education and Diversity

The 1994 Curriculum Policy Statement of the Council on Social Work Education (CSWE) required educators to provide educational objectives and content regarding human diversity, social and economic justice, and populations-at-risk. These accreditation standards, separating these three closely related areas, reflect the current state of our social work knowledge base regarding diversity. Building this knowledge base both within and outside the social work profession has been fraught with ideological differences—and, of course, conflicts—many of which appear in this book, some readily and others more subtly. Often, ideological conflicts evolve from the lack of acknowledgement that different theories serve different purposes. These theoretical frameworks spotlight different parts of the stage in the overall diversity drama.

Webster's simplest definition of ideology is "visionary theorizing." Despite any ideological differences, it is safe to say this book's authors and other social work professionals, for the most part, have their "eye on the prize," envisioning the diversity mission as central to the professional function of facilitating contexts for self-actualization of each and all to the greatest extent possible. On this common ground stand the passion and vision of those who commit their work to increasing diversity competence.

The authors of this text are among those who believe that social workers in the twenty-first century will need to practice with consciousness, commitment, confidence, and competence on behalf of diverse populations. Such practice will require not only substantive knowledge but also the ability to "learn how to learn" about diversity's meaning and consequences for individuals, families, groups, organizations, and communities. In professional education, much of this learning evolves from the development and use of conceptual frameworks.

Conceptual Frameworks

Conceptual frameworks are theoretical perspectives and formulations constructed to interpret, explain, and resolve particular challenges faced in practice. Theoretical models direct attention to particular practice dynamics; relate concepts with one another to interpret these dynamics; and provide guidelines or principles for responding to these dynamics consistent with professional purposes and values (Anderson, 1981). A major task of professional education is the student's development of conceptual frameworks that establish a basis for practice competence and a foundation from which to build ongoing competence development. This learning is akin to what Bruner (1966) called "cognitive structuring." Such inquiry applies general principles to specific problems and draws general principles from these problem-solving experiences. In this sense, conceptual frameworks, such as those discussed in this text, serve as a "working heuristic of discovery" (Bruner, 1966, p. 618).

Perspectives and Frameworks in Text

This book organizes the presentation of social work-derived diversity frameworks to aid students' comparative and critical analysis and synthesis and to provide a springboard for further study and development of their own and the profession's knowledge base for practice. This book presents an overview and analysis of twelve relatively distinct frameworks created to serve objectives within three overarching perspectives—*ethnocultural diversity, oppression*, and *vulnerable life situations*—and it connotes their differences and their over-laps. Figure 1.1 depicts the overall conceptual framework for this text. The circles represent the three separate and overlapping perspectives. Within the circles and their overlaps are placed the specific frameworks covered in subsequent chapters.

Central Frameworks

At the core of this diagram and integrating the three major perspectives are the *strengths perspective* and the *empowerment approach*. All of the discrete conceptual frameworks are consistent with a vision to base social work practice on a strengths perspective (rather than a deficit, pathological, problem-in-person-not-in-system orientation) (Saleebey, 1997) and to infuse diversity practice with significant assumptions, principles, and concepts from this perspective. Chapter 2 covers the *strengths perspective* as applied to diversity (Wright & Anderson, 1998). All of the frameworks also, to some degree, advocate for making empow-erment (Gutierrez, 1990; Parsons, 1991) a central aim of social work practice and for incor-porating essential principles and concepts from the empowerment approach (Lee, 1994; Gutierrez, Parsons, & Cox, 1998) into diversity practice. Chapter 3 reviews the *empower-ment approach* and its core principles and concepts (Anderson, 1997).

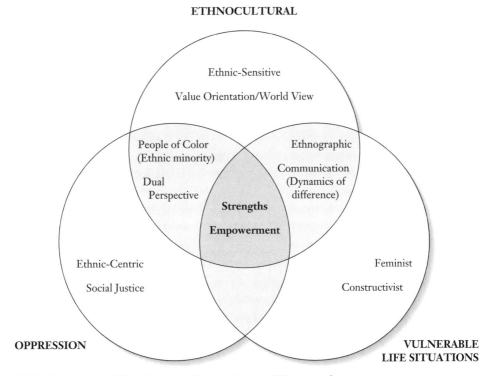

FIGURE 1.1 *Social Work Diversity Perspectives and Frameworks*

Ethnocultural Perspective and Frameworks

Parts II and III address the *ethnocultural diversity perspective* (Lister, 1987). The common defining element of frameworks within this perspective is the relationship of ethnicity to culture. Ethnicity here refers to self-conscious collectivities of people who, on the basis of a common heritage or subculture, maintain a distinct identity among themselves and in relation to other groups in a diverse, multicultural society. This discernment of difference affects their sense of personal identity, loyalty and belonging. Diversity of ethnic groups evolves from perceived or actual cultural differences that are socialized into particular value orientations and normative dispositions for behaviors. Two of the predominant frameworks for sensitizing social workers to (and, we hope, not stereotyping) ethnocultural differences are *ethnic-sensitive social work practice* (Devore & Schlesinger, 1999; Cox & Ephross, 1998) and *value orientation* (DuBray, 2000; Anderson, 1992, 1997) or *cultural world view* (Dana, 1993; Anderson, 1997). Part III presents the ethnic-sensitive practice framework in Chapter 4 and the value orientation/world view framework in Chapter 5.

Oppression Perspective and Frameworks

Overlapping the ethnocultural perspective are two frameworks within the *oppression perspective*. The common defining element of frameworks within the oppression perspective is the combination of prejudice and power. The 1997 *Social Work Encyclopedia* defines *Oppressions* as follows: "Simply stated, oppression is an institutionalized, unequal power relationship—prejudice plus power" (Wambach & Van Soest, 1997, p. 243). The predominant oppression frameworks in social work have evolved primarily from concerns about ethnics of color. Frameworks that overlap with the ethnocultural perspective entail a combination of concepts to understand and appreciate members of these groups through their distinguishing cultural heritage and their survival and growth in the face of oppression and marginalization. These frameworks all include recognition of the use and abuse of power by a Eurocentric sociopolitical and cultural power structure that idealizes, favors, and grants privileges to those who are white and devalues, exploits, and deprives of privileges those who are nonwhite (Pinderhughes, 1994). Part III includes frameworks in this overlap: the *people of color* (*ethnic minority*) framework (Lum, 1996, 1999) covered in Chapter 6, and the *dual perspective* framework (Chestang, 1980; Norton, 1978; Anderson, 1988) covered in Chapter 7.

More centrally addressing oppression in practice is the *ethnic-centered* framework, as developed, for instance, in the Afrocentric perspective (Scheile, 1996, 1999). This perspective shifts the center from which to view ethnics of color toward their intra- and inter-group relations and away from the marginalized position that dominant social work perspectives, and dominant cultural world views, have historically constructed these groups. Part IV presents this ethnic-centered framework in Chapter 8.

The contributors and frameworks represented in this book value social justice in social work practice. Chapter 9 more predominately addresses oppression and injustice through the social justice framework (Gil, 1994). At its core, this framework requires continual development of critical consciousness on the part of practitioners, service consumers, and society, and it is grounded in three fundamental values: self-determination, distributive justice, and inclusion (Swenson, 1998; Prillettensky & Gonich, 1994).

Vulnerable Life Situations Perspective and Frameworks

Also overlapping the ethnocultural perspective are two frameworks within the *vulnerable life situations perspective*. Victims of both ethnic exclusion and all forms of oppression become vulnerable to disempowering life situations. Thus, all three circles in Figure 1.1 overlap at points; however, the *ethnographic* framework (Bein & Lum, 1999; Green, 1999; Anderson, 1997) covered in Part V, Chapter 10, and the *communication* or "dynamics of difference" (Gudykunst, 1998) framework covered in Chapter 11 have in common with frameworks in the ethnocultural diversity perspective their focus on how the strengths and sufferings affect the vulnerable life situations of particular people and how those people's experience of and response to the immediate dynamics of difference affect the helping and situational context. In short, these frameworks are designed to discover how those we serve define themselves ethnoculturally and how they can identify for practitioners the differences that have affected their past and current life situations. The ethnographic and communication frameworks shift our focus from examining the "culture in the group" to discovering the "culture in the person" (Anderson, 1997).

Many people with cultural and other diversities come to us in social work because of vulnerabilities specifically related to their socially constructed devalued roles and statuses. Part VI discusses frameworks addressing the needs and issues of some of these groups (the Council on Social Work Education in the Curriculum Policy Statement identifies them as "populations-at-risk": people of color, women, and gay and lesbian persons) and includes the *feminist* framework (Bricker-Jenkins & Lockett, 1995) covered in Chapter 12 and the *constructivist* framework (Laird, 1998) covered in Chapter 13.

We hope the perspectives and frameworks in this book collectively contribute to social work students' developing a more comprehensive and differentiated knowledge base as they learn to practice with and on behalf of diverse populations. Part VII, the last part of this text, considers the collective curricular implications of all the perspectives and frameworks in Chapter 14 and a summary and conclusion in Chapter 15.

To promote understanding of each chapter's unique contribution as well as the comparative and critical analysis and synthesis, contributing scholars followed a common outline for each chapter:

1. A summary of the framework's major precursors, developers, and contributions;
2. A presentation defining the framework's core concepts and their interrelationships within the model;
3. A development of five to ten principles or guidelines for applying the framework in social work practice, with particular attention to foundation or generalist practice;
4. An example of the framework's application to a particular practice situation;
5. An assessment of the framework's major contributions and limitations as applied to practice;
6. A selection of key annotated sources for further study of the framework; and

7. Discussion questions to promote critical thinking for learning about and using the framework.

Conclusion

This book presents diversity perspectives and conceptual frameworks as a central part of a knowledge foundation for social work practice. For pedagogical purposes, it covers the perspectives and frameworks in separate parts and chapters while recognizing their overlaps and the value of their integrative use in competent practice. Each chapter covers and emphasizes the coherence and contribution of one framework. Each distinct framework also has its limitations to illuminate and inform practice with the multidimensions of diverse individuals, families, groups, organizations, and communities. The authors hope that students learning about similarities and differences in applying these frameworks can then use them differentially and more integratively in their practice. The authors also hope the perspectives and frameworks discussed here can lead students to develop basic skills for working with persons of any cultural background.

Among the skills that the authors promote are:

- The knowledge of one's own and one's client's specific values, beliefs and cultural practices;
- The ability to respect and appreciate the values, beliefs and practices of all clients, including those who are culturally different, and to perceive such individuals through the cultural lenses of their clients instead of their own;
- The ability to be comfortable with difference in others and thus not trapped in anxiety or defensive behaviors;
- The ability to control—or even change—assumptions, stereotypes, and false beliefs, and therefore feel less need for defensive behavior;
- The ability to think flexibly and to recognize that one's own way of thinking is not the only way;
- The ability to behave flexibly, demonstrated by a readiness to engage in extra time, effort, and energy (Pinderhughes, 1994, p. 266) required to sort through general knowledge about a cultural group and to see specific ways in which knowledge applies or does not apply to a given client;
- A critical consciousness to understand the causes, consequences, and dynamics of all forms of oppression;
- The ability to let others teach us about the differences that make a difference for them;
- The ability to facilitate personal, interpersonal, and political empowerment; and
- The use of self to envision and enable social and economic justice for the benefit of individuals, society, and the global community.

References

Anderson, J. (1981). *Social work methods and processes*. Belmont, CA: Wadsworth.

Anderson, J. (1988). *Foundations of social work practice*. New York: Springer.

Anderson, J. (1997). *Social work with groups*. New York: Longman.

Anderson, J. D. (1992). Family-centered practice in the 1990's: A multicultural perspective. *Journal of Multicultural Social Work, 1*, 17–30.

Baldwin, J. (1963). *The fire next time*. New York: W.W. Norton.

Bein, A., & Lum, D. (1999). Inductive learning. In D. Lum, *Culturally competent practice* (pp. 145–122). Pacific Grove, CA: Brooks/Cole.

Bricker-Jenkins, M., & Lockett, P. W. (1995). Women: Direct practice. In R. L. Edwards (Ed.), *Encyclopedia of social work* (19th ed.) (pp. 2529–2539). Washington, D.C.: NASW Press.

Bruner, J. S. (1966). *Toward a theory of instruction*. Cambridge, MA: Harvard University Press.

Chestang, L. W. (1980). Competencies and knowledge in clinical social work: A dual perspective. In P. A. Ewalt (Ed.), *Toward a definition of clinical social work* (pp. 12–27). Washington, D.C.: NASW Press.

Council on Social Work Education (1994). *Handbook on accreditation standards*. Alexandria, VA: Council on Social Work Education.

Cox, C. B., & Ephross, P. H. (1998). *Ethnicity and social work practice*. New York: Oxford.

Dana, R. H. (1993). *Multicultural assessment perspectives for professional psychology*. Boston: Allyn & Bacon.

Devore, W., & Schlesinger, E. (1999). *Ethnic-sensitive social work practice* (5th ed.). Boston: Allyn & Bacon.

DuBray, W. (2000). *Mental health interventions with people of color*. Belmont, CA: Wadsworth.

Gil, D. G. (1994). Confronting social injustice and oppression. In F. G. Reamer (Ed.), *The foundation of social work knowledge, 23* (pp. 1–263). New York: Columbia University Press.

Green, J. (1999). *Cultural awareness in the human services*. Boston: Allyn & Bacon.

Gudykunst, W. B. (1998). *Bridging differences: Effective intergroup communication* (2nd ed.). Thousand Oaks, CA: Sage.

Gutierrez, L. M., Parsons, R. J., & Cox, E. O. (1998). *Empowerment in social work practice: A sourcebook*. Pacific Grove, CA: Brooks/Cole.

James Madison University Political Science Department (n.d.) *Benjamin Franklin on Native Americans*. Retrieved January 12, 2002 from http://www.jmu.edu/madison/franklinatamer.htm.

Laird, J. (1998). Theorizing culture: Narrative ideas and practice principles. In M. McGolrich (Ed.), *Revisioning family therapy: Race, culture and gender in clinical practice* (pp. 20–36). New York: Guilford.

Lee, J. A. B. (1994). *The empowerment approach to social work practice*. New York: Columbia University Press.

Lister, L. (1987). Ethnocultural content in social work. *Journal of Social Work Education, 23*, 31–39.

Lum, D. (1996). *Social work and people of color: A process-stage approach* (4th ed.). Thousand Oaks, CA: Brooks/Cole.

Lum, D. (1999). *Culturally competent practice: A framework for growth and action*. Pacific Grove, CA: Brooks/Cole.

Norton, D. G. (1978). *The dual perspective: Inclusion of ethnic minority content in the social work curriculum*. New York: Council on Social Work Education.

Parsons, R. J. (1991). Empowerment: Purpose and practice principle in social work. *Social Work with Groups, 14*, 7–21.

Pinderhughes, E. (1994). Diversity and populations at risk: Ethnic minorities and people of color. In F. G. Reamer (Ed.), *The foundations of social work knowledge* (pp. 264–308). New York: Columbia University Press.

Prilletensky, I., & Gonick, L. (1994). The discourse of oppression in the social sciences: Past, present, and future. In E. Trickett, R. Watts and D. Birman (Eds.), *Human diversity: Perspectives on people in context* (pp. 145–177). San Francisco: Jossey-Bass.

Saleebey, D. (Ed.). (1997). *The strengths perspective in social work practice*. New York: Longman.

Scheile, J. H. (1996). Afrocentricity: An emerging paradigm in social work practice. *Social Work, 41,* 284–294.

Scheile, J. H. (1999). *The Afrocentric perspective in the human services*. Thousand Oaks, CA: Sage.

Swenson, C. R. (1998). Clinical social work's contribution to a social justice perspective. *Social Work, 43,* 539–550.

Wambach, K. G., & Van Soest, D. (1997). Oppression. In R. L. Edwards (Ed.), *Encyclopedia of social work* (19th ed. Supplement) (pp. 243–252).(1997). Washington, D.C.: NASW Press.

Wright, O. L., & Anderson, J. D. (1998). Clinical social work with urban African American families. *Families in Society, 79,* 197–206.

Part I

Central Frameworks

2

Strengths Perspective

Joseph Anderson

The strengths perspective, in conjunction with the closely related empowerment approach (Chapter 3), is a central (or core) framework for all social work practice with and on behalf of diverse populations. The strengths perspective in social work has a long, if checkered, history. At the turn of the century, Jane Addams's settlement-house movement promoted the "positive ideal of raising life to its highest values" (Addams, 1902, p. 32) in the United States. Addams believed in the strengths of people for democratic functioning and in the strengths of democracy for fostering individual self-actualization. Her "experiment in democracy," as she was fond of calling it, at Chicago's Hull House brought diverse neighborhood people together to develop and participate in self-determined programs.

The strengths perspective in direct practice had its earliest adherents in the "functional school" of social work. This approach assumed that mobilizing the creative will of individuals produced the strengths necessary for growth. Functional social workers conceived social work's purpose was to release individual human power for reaching personal potential and contributing to the common social good and conversely to release social power toward changing society so that it provides individuals with resources and opportunities for growth (Smalley, 1967). This orientation to human potential and strengths developed in opposition to the predominant "medical model" of practice, which tended to perceive individual problems as illnesses or other forms of deficit expected change, therefore, to be derived primarily from what social workers did to or for their clients.

Core Concepts

Currently, the strengths perspective encompasses a "collation of principles, ideas, and techniques" that enable "resources and resourcefulness of clients" (Saleebey, 1997, p. 15). Social work within the strengths perspective includes that which assumes and promotes competence in clients (Maluccio, 1981), emphasizes resilience in an individual's ecological context (Fraser, 1997), focuses on solutions rather than problems (de Shazer, 1985), and

11

uses strengths as the central organizing principle for practice (Saleebey, 1997; Rapp, 1998; Weick, et al., 1989). These humanistic views are considered especially consonant with social work's fundamental values regarding human worth and social justice.

> Focusing and building on client strengths is not only a counterweight to the previous deficit model. It is an imperative of the several values that govern our work and the operation of a democratic and pluralistic society, including distributive justice, equality, respect for dignity of the individual, and the search for maximum autonomy and maximum community. (Saleebey, 1997, p. 169)

The Code of Ethics for social workers states a responsibility to "understand culture and its function in human behavior and society, recognizing the strengths that exist in all cultures" (NASW, 1996, p. 9). The strengths perspective provides principles and concepts that respond to the inherent capacity of human beings for maximizing both their own autonomy and interdependence as well as to the resourcefulness of diverse cultures for fostering survival and growth among its members.

Core Principles for Practice

Several principles common to strength-based social work models combine to constitute the strengths perspective:

> *Humanistic:* Human beings are inherently self-actualizing. Even in the face of external obstacles, they strive for autonomy, self-determination, competence, and connection. This principle de-emphasizes pathology, especially psychopathology, and recognizes each person's potentialities, strengths, and latent and creative resources.
>
> *Phenomenological:* Understanding the meaning of human behavior and social functioning requires a frame of reference from the individual life experience. This principle suggests that from the individual's point of view, all behavior is purposeful. Culturally and socially different behavior is framed as a solution rather than a pathology and deemed functional by the person in the context of his or her experience.
>
> *Contextual:* Human beings organize their lives and develop their functional competence and potentialities in transaction with their ecosystem's demands and supports. This principle suggests that discovering, using, and creating strengths and other resources in one's environmental context, especially one's family and community, is vital to self-actualization and social competence.
>
> *Empowerment:* Self-actualization and social competence evolve from empowerment—the individual's ability to take charge of his or her life—and the underlying need and motivation for empowerment intensifies in persistent disempowering contexts. This principle posits that social work practice entailing cooperative, collaborative, empowering relationships between client and practitioner discovers and fosters strengths, expands learning based on these strengths, and challenges the tendency to blame social injustice for the client's sense of helplessness and powerlessness.

The Strengths Perspective and Diversity Frameworks

Applying the strengths perspective to diversity practice means acknowledging that each individual is (1) like no other in uniqueness; (2) like some others in cultural and other contexts; and (3) like all others in human spirit and potential. Acknowledging diverse strengths in practice requires, then, an ability to discover the unique resources of each individual, opportunities in the cultural context, and motivations and capacities for growth and change in human nature. Every client system has multidimensional strengths to foster further development of individual self-actualization and social well-being. While this chapter focuses on applying the strengths perspective to cultural diversity and pluralism, social work practice is also greatly informed by understanding and tapping the reservoir of strengths unique to each individual and universal to human nature and its potential.

Members of social and cultural groups that have survived a history of oppression in the United States very often evidence special adaptive strengths. These strengths generally evolve from three sources: (1) personal transformation qualities as a result of overcoming self-depreciating forces (Chestang, 1982); (2) family and community structures that develop self-esteem and provide a network of psychosocial and economic resources (Billingsley, 1992); and (3) survival determination and skills (Hopps, Pinderhughes, & Shankar, 1995). For example, ethnocultural frameworks in recent years identify strengths in these general areas for ethnic groups of color who have survived and evolved through the challenges of racism.

In reference to African Americans, for instance, scholars identify strengths as especially related to the "helping tradition" rooted in family and community (Billingsley, 1992; Hill, 1997; Martin & Martin, 1985; Wright & Anderson, 1998). This helping tradition emerged from the African American extended family and kinship system and includes mutual aid and relatively egalitarian social-class and gender relationships. There is also a strong focus on the nurturing and social development of children. This mutual-aid tradition transfers to other institutions in the African American community, through fictive kinship patterns and racial and religious consciousness (Hill, 1997; Lee, 1994). African American families and communities represent well how the strengths perspective's application to culturally diverse populations is especially necessary in relation to those who struggle with the devaluing forces of marginalization, discrimination, and oppression.

Marginalization results from a cultural perspective that views the center of power, strengths, and superiority as being among white, male, middle-class, heterosexual, able-bodied, mentally healthy, church-going Christians and ascribes any differences as "less-than" deviance (Van Voorhis, 1998). This view, historically embedded in our North American consciousness, attributes deficits to differences from this central standard. It constructs structural arrangements that benefit those privileged by birth through ascribed social status and systematically excludes those who differ from this central norm through discrimination and oppression.

This normative group need not represent a numerical majority. However, it maintains control through institutional and economic power and through violence (Pharr, 1988). When viewed from this dominant center of political, economic, and social power and resources, as well as cultural and linguistic dominance in a social structure, those not in this group are identified on the margin and lacking in power and resources (hooks, 1984). They are "part of the whole but outside the main body" (hooks, 1984, p. ix).

Forming an identity as a member of a marginalized group in such oppressive conditions can deter members from claiming and being proud of their differences (Collins, 1991; Gould, 1987; hooks; 1983). Such negative identity and self-image can lead to the denial of one's own perceptions, experiences, strengths, power, and opportunities in relationships with those at the center (Van Voorhis, 1998). Thus, social work practice requires (1) critical consciousness regarding the oppressor rooted deep within us all (Freire, 1970); (2) the affirmation of strengths; and (3) empowerment approaches. These components are most central to competency to develop and deliver services to individuals and groups who have been marginalized by oppressive structures because of their difference from the "center" in regard to color, ethnicity, gender, class, sexual orientation, disability, age, or some combination thereof.

The Strengths Perspective in Empowerment

Empowerment approaches to social work practice utilize three perspectives: the ecosystems perspective to understand how resources in the individual client's own context do or do not match their needs; the generalist perspective to identify ways to better match resources to needs; and the strengths perspective to discover solutions in the personal, interpersonal, and sociopolitical dimensions of clients' lives. In social work practice from an empowerment approach, empowerment informs both the means and ends of social work. It is "a process of increasing personal, interpersonal, or political power . . . [to] take action to improve . . . life situations" (Gutierrez, 1990, p. 149). It also involves "the creation of structural conditions under which people can choose to 'give to' their community as well as 'take from' their community" (Breton, 1994, p. 29).

Empowerment of marginalized diverse populations at personal, interpersonal and sociopolitical levels requires practitioners to work in strengths-oriented collaborative partnerships with client systems to facilitate

- positive perceptions of personal worth, efficacy, and autonomy toward achieving self-determined goals through using personal resources and skills,
- recognition, by oneself and others, that many of one's perceptions about oneself and the surrounding world, no matter how different, are indeed valid and legitimate to voice,
- connections between autonomous and interdependent individuals who can share the power of knowledge, caring, and action to achieve group goals,
- critical analysis of social, political, and economic systems and their affect on one's sense of dignity, and worth, and opportunities for individual and community development,
- knowledge and skill for developing social action strategies on behalf of one's own needs and goals and those of the people one cares about, and
- reflective and efficacious collaboration toward defining and attaining collective goals and achieving better balanced power relations in responsible social change (Anderson, 1997).

Thus, the strengths of diversity, when channeled into empowerment, are the antidote to social injustices; they facilitate development of social well-being for all in our underlying interdependence; and they expand shared power to create resources that facilitate development of the personal, interpersonal, and community dimensions of our lives.

Case Example

Ruth Parsons (1991, pp. 14–19) presents an especially relevant practice example of empowerment in work with a diverse population. It includes a strength-oriented generalist approach that addresses the personal, interpersonal, and political dimensions of Head Start mothers. A social worker assigned to a Head Start agency in an inner-city housing project was asked to intervene with mothers of children who were experiencing difficulty in the school program. Head Start staff indicated the mothers were single parents who seemed to have problems disciplining their children; the children presented problems in the classroom that concerned the teachers.

The social worker approached each woman individually to discuss her child, parenting issues, and any identified concerns regarding discipline. Although some women identified disciplining their children as a specific problem for them, others seemed to take parenting in stride along with other stress-producing situations. They particularly noted environmental conditions that contributed not only to parenting issues but also to concerns in their lives in general. The practitioner did not identify each woman as having a discipline problem. Instead, she asked each woman if she would like to be a part of a group of women like herself who had children in the Head Start center. The practitioner said the purpose of the group would be to share parenting hassles and solutions. Seven women agreed to come to the group and try it out.

The social worker was White, 29 years old, with no children of her own; she had training in group social work during her BSW and MSW education. She had three years of pre-MSW degree experience working with AFDC (Aid to Families with Dependent Children) mothers in Hispanic communities and two years of post-MSW experience, including group social work.

Initially, all but two of the group's seven members were Latina. One of the two White women was severely scarred from multiple birth defects and related surgeries; the other was illiterate. Ages among the women ranged from 30 to 45. All were single parents; two experienced intermittent involvement with their children's fathers. All were low income, living either on AFDC or at a similar subsistence level; all lived in public housing projects in the same neighborhood. A sixth Latina woman, Lupe, who was a teacher aide in Head Start, joined the group also. She identified with the other women being single parents living at a low level of economic security, as she had been in a similar situation. She suggested that her inclusion in the group would encourage the other women to participate; it did.

The social worker began the group by supporting the women for participating to "share common problems and common solutions about parenting." The practitioner clarified her expectations for the group and promoted the group's capacity for self-determination, indicating that the group would set its own goals and determine the activities for achieving them.

The social worker then reached for the commonality of group members, including the disciplinary concerns. While members talked about parenting issues, they also voiced many other concerns very early on about stresses associated with single parenthood, such as low incomes; housing problems (especially in the housing project itself); ex-husbands, boyfriends, and relationships with men in general; and feelings of anger about their lives. Anger seemed to stem from being left by the men to raise their children by themselves, with little or no support or economic base to do so. Quickly the group became a resource for venting and sharing these more intense and common needs. The group goals combined to create a group culture, with therapeutic norms for validating and supporting feelings and perceptions among the women.

The social worker reinforced these evolving norms to facilitate the supportive and validating environment of the group. The members quickly recognized that they had common feelings, problems, and experiences. They experienced other members and the social worker hearing then validating their feelings about their circumstances. The group's contracted goals expanded beyond dealing with parenting to include supporting each other in dealing with stresses of being poor and being single parents.

Initially members were reluctant to trust one another with confidentiality because of their close living proximity. They were also reluctant to trust the social worker, who represented a different ethnic group, social class, and lifestyle. Lupe helped allay some of this mistrust by serving as a bridge between the social worker and the group. The group, however, had to deal (directly, through concerns they expressed and less directly, through "testing out") with the social worker's stake in them. As their trust developed, they began to share their feelings, and they experienced being heard. When they resolved the initial trust issues, they were ready to assert more autonomy in setting goals and moved on to learning more specifically about the issues and solutions in the context of their situations.

The social worker collaborated in this work, sharing her expertise regarding income and other resources, knowledge about the housing project, and information about parenting techniques. As members developed more closeness in their shared support, understanding, and work, they voiced and focused on common problems. They targeted specific problems for work, and with the social worker they shared knowledge and skills toward resolving these problems.

As group members began to share both problems and expertise in an evolving mutual aid process, they identified many environmental conditions that were common to all of them. These included a teacher in the neighborhood school whose racist attitudes were a source of frustration and anger to their children and to them, a local grocery story owner who charged an exorbitant fee to cash monthly checks, the city recreation center director who dealt drugs at the center, broken-down equipment on the playground, poor lighting in the projects that made it unsafe for women and young girls to walk at night, and the project's housing manager who dealt unfairly and capriciously with residents. All these issues were integral to parenting, constituting the women's ecosystem and presenting major consequences for them, including issues around disciplining their children.

One by one, the group put these problems on the agenda. With much interdependence, group members and the social worker educated each other about the issues. As they developed action strategies to address the issues, they became more convinced that they could take effective action against and control of the problems that now controlled their daily lives.

The group did indeed intervene with the school system regarding the racist teacher. They intervened with the city regarding the recreation center director. They confronted the housing manager about his behavior; the housing office appointed a liaison to work directly with community residents to ensure more responsiveness to their concerns. When the local grocery store owner refused to lower his check-cashing fees, the women led a boycott against the store and organized transportation to a supermarket where they could buy groceries at a lower price and cash their checks for free.

As they experienced success and some failure, the group began to find that other groups and organizations, both within and outside of their community, were concerned with the same issues. They began to join forces. They joined the local community interagency citizens action council, which was concerned with the whole of the community. Through that council they became members of community project task forces. They engaged the community council's help in writing grants to fund playground equipment and street lighting. They joined with the community council to get a traffic light installed at the corner for protection of the children for crossing. They eventually began to serve on citywide task forces, as representatives from and a subgroup of the community action council.

One such project was to raise the awareness of counselors at the local community mental health center regarding a large number of depressed women in the community, some suicidal and abusive to their children. The group had observed that when these women went to the community mental health center for help, they rarely went back a second time. They asked counselors to come to the women's homes and to alter the services to fit the community's culture and needs. The women served as liaisons for the community mental health center, setting up meetings between women and the center counselors.

Although the women experienced success in working collaboratively with other community groups, they maintained their original group for support and for discussing personal and interpersonal concerns such as parenting and their relationships with men. Overall, the group's life was approximately three years in duration. Membership changed, but a core remained active throughout. Discipline of children was a running theme in the group's discussions; however, discipline was never viewed as a deficit internal to the members. It was consistently viewed holistically in its ecosystem context and as being related to many other parts of the group members' lives. The women's self-esteem, not only as parents but also as partners in relationships with men, improved remarkably—and consequently, so did their parenting skills!

Contributions and Limitations

A major contribution of the strengths perspective, as demonstrated in the case example above, is its significant shift from deficit models when viewing diversity within an ecosystems context. Deficit models serve primarily to justify the marginalization of those whose differences stand in contrast to historically dominant white, middle class, heterosexual males (Pinderhughes, 1994). The strengths perspective instead views the individual in his or her particular context as the central focus and conceives the functionality of adaptive strengths within this ecosystem niche (Rapp, 1998).

Closely related to this contribution is the strengths perspective's antidote to stigmatized labeling. As noted by Miley, O'Melia, & DuBois (1998),

> . . . The labels social workers use influence their sense of client's worth and even shape their ideas about what needs to be done. Pathological labels establish negative expectations that diminish the chances for positive change. Collectively, pejorative labels and stereotypes assign categorical meanings, block visions of potential, and constrict plans for service delivery and social policy. When social work practitioners shift their orientation to strengths, they escape the many pitfalls . . . (p. 82)

Among the other contributions of the strengths perspective in relation to diversity is its base for empowerment-oriented practice. Empowerment-based practice accentuates resiliency and examines sociopolitical rather than individual obstacles to self-actualization.

One of the most frequently acknowledged criticisms of the strengths perspective is its potential to romanticize those who are experiencing multiple problems as a result of oppressive social structures and practices as well as personal disorders. While the strengths perceptive does assess dysfunctional adaptation as well as strengths, it avoids the damage model that tends to blame victims rather than credit survivors.

Conclusion

The strengths perspective considers pluralism as the mark of health in diverse social systems and those whose differences have led to systemic discrimination and oppression as manifesting personal and ecosystems strengths necessary for their survival and growth. Practice with and on behalf of such a diversity of clients needs an awareness of not only the existing and potential sufferings and vulnerabilities that social and economic injustices create, but also the resiliency, resources, and strengths honed by individuals and their support systems to survive and grow amidst such challenges.

Sources for Further Study

deShazer, S. (1991). *Putting difference to work.* New York: W.W. Norton. This work explicates a solution-focused rather than a problem-solving approach to practice, especially in diversity practice.

Fraser, M. W. (Ed.). (1997). *Risk and resilience in childhood: An ecological perspective.* Washington, D.C.: NASW Press. The book defines resiliency in an ecosystems context. It identifies risk and protective (or strength and resource) factors in a variety of social work practice contexts. While it only peripherally considers application to diversity, much can be translated to identify the risk and protective factors of diverse populations.

Gutierrez, L. M., Parsons, R. J., & Cox, E. O. (1998). *Empowerment in social work practice. A sourcebook.* Pacific Grove, CA: Brooks/Cole. This book introduces principles and concepts for strengths-based empowerment practice. These practice perspectives and guidelines are especially applied to such diverse groups as women, communities of color, and lesbian and gay persons.

Maluccio, A. N. (Ed.). (1981). *Promoting competence in clients: A new/old approach to social work practice.* New York: The Free Press. This book is one of the earliest to promote a strengths-oriented paradigm as opposed to deficit models for social work practice. In particular, it relates coping patterns and resources to cultural strengths and resources within an ecological perspective.

Saleebey, D. (Ed.). (1997). *The strengths perspective in social work practice* (2nd ed.). New York: Longman. This book is the first and most developed source presenting the strengths perspective principles, concepts, and applications in social work. While dealing more generally with the perspective, it provides useful guidelines for application to practice with and on behalf of diverse populations.

Questions for Critical Thinking

1. How does the strengths perspective differ from more problem-focused models in relation to "blaming the victim" when considering practice with diverse populations who have experienced oppression?

2. What are the culturally based strengths for such ethnics of color as Latinos, African Americans, Native Americans, and Asian Americans?

3. How can the strengths perspective be applied in practice while addressing problems?

4. What is the connection of the strengths of diversity to a healthy pluralistic community?

5. What would be possible alternatives to the strengths perspective and the empowerment approach as core frameworks for social work practice with and on behalf of diverse populations?

References

Addams, J. (1902). *Democracy and social ethics*. New York: Macmillan.

Anderson, J. (1997). *Social work with groups: A process model*. New York: Longman.

Billingsley, A. (1992). *Climbing Jacob's ladder: The enduring legacy of African American families*. New York: Simon and Schuster.

Breton, M. (1994). On the meaning of empowerment and empowerment-oriented social work practice. *Social Work with Groups*, *17*, 23–37.

Chestang, L. (1982). *Character development in a hostile society*. Occasional paper. Chicago: University of Chicago Press.

Collins, P. H. (1991). *Black feminist thought*. New York: Routledge and Kegan Paul.

deShazer, S. (1985). *Keys to solution in brief therapy*. New York: W.W. Norton.

Fraser, M. W. (Ed.). (1997). *Risk and resilience in childhood: An ecological perspective*. Washington, D.C.: NASW Press.

Freire, P. (1970). *The pedagogy of the oppressed*. New York: Seabury.

Gould, K. (1987). Feminist principles and minority concerns: Contributions, problems, and solutions. *Affilia*, *2*, 6–19.

Gutierrez, L. (1990). Working with women of color: An empowerment perspective. *Social Work*, 35, 149–153.

Hill, R. B. (1997). *The strengths of African American families: Twenty-five years later*. Washington, D.C.: R & B Publishers.

hooks, b. (1983). Ain't I a Woman: Black women and feminism. *The Black Scholar*, *14*, 38–45.

hooks, b. (1984). *Feminist theory: From margin to center*. Boston: South End.

Hopps, J. G., Pinderhughes, E., & Shankar, R. (1995). *The power to care: Clinical practice effectiveness with overwhelmed clients*. New York: Free Press.

Lee, J. A. B. (1994). *The empowerment approach to social work practice*. New York: Columbia University Press.

Maluccio, A. N. (1981). *Promoting competence in clients: A new/old approach to social work practice*. New York: The Free Press.

Martin, J. M., & Martin, E. P. (1985). *The helping tradition in the black family and community*. Silver Spring, MD: NASW Press.

Miley, K. K., O'Melia, M., & DuBois, B. L. (1998). *Generalist social work practice: An empowering approach* (2nd ed.). Boston: Allyn & Bacon.

National Association of Social Workers. (1996). *Code of ethics*. Washington, D.C.: NASW Press.

Parsons, R. J. (1991). Empowerment: Purpose and practice principles in social work. *Social Work with Groups, 14*, 7–21.

Pinderhughes, E. (1994). Diversity and populations at risk: Ethnic minorities and people of color. In F. G. Reamer (Ed.), *The foundations of social work knowledge* (pp. 264–308). New York: Columbia University Press.

Pinderhughes, E. (1995). Empowering diverse families in the 21st century. *Families in Society, 76*, 131–140.

Rapp, C. A. (1998). *The strengths model*. New York: Oxford.

Saleebey, D. (Ed.). (1997). *The strengths perspective in social work practice* (2nd ed.). New York: Longman.

Smalley, R. (1967). *Theory for social work practice*. New York: Columbia University Press.

Van Voorhis, R. M. (1998). Culturally relevant practice: A framework for teaching the psychosocial dynamics of oppression. *Journal of Social Work Education, 34*, 121–134.

Weick, A., et al. (1989). A strengths perspective for social work practice. *Social Work, 89*, 350–354.

Weick, A., & Saleebey, D. (1995). Supporting family strengths: Orienting policy and practice toward the 21st century. *Families in Society, 76*, 141–149.

Wright, O. L., & Anderson, J. D. (1998). Clinical social work practice with urban African American families. *Families in Society, 79*, 192–205.

3

Empowerment Perspective

Krishna L. Guadalupe

When I dare to be powerful—to use my strengths in the service of my vision, then it becomes less and less important whether I am afraid.

—Audre Lorde

Much has been written about the importance of understanding "human diversity" as well as the use of "empowerment theory" for identifying intrapersonal, interpersonal, and social areas that need strengthening and/or attention while promoting change. Diversity and empowerment have become buzzwords used freely and often with ignorance to their multifaceted natures and their interdependence to a multidimensional set of variables. For instance, it is not uncommon to find the terms "human diversity" and "ethnic differences" used interchangeably in social science literature that explores variation based on race. Racial differences are rooted in biological characteristics such as skin color and features. However, ". . . while a biological term (race) takes on ethnic meaning if specific ways of living have evolved for members of that biological group" (Pinderhughes, 1994, p. 264). Race and ethnicity—a sense of group connectedness based on shared history, constructed social identity, biological relationship, culture, or some combination of these (Devore & Schlesinger, 1996)—are important pieces of the puzzle identified as "human diversity"; however, race and ethnicity are not a complete frame. Human diversity transcends group ethnicity, as evidenced by differences found among individuals sharing a specific ethnicity or biological characteristics. Furthermore, it is not unusual to read about empowerment theory and cultivate the notion that self-empowerment—a sense of self-confidence/control and ability to promote change internally and externally—is exclusively affiliated to institutional and societal transformation. Although institutional and social changes are important variables to encourage individual, group, or community empowerment, they cannot stand in isolation.

Throughout this chapter, readers are encouraged to examine the complexity of "human diversity." Readers are also exposed to an empowerment perspective and its affiliation to human diversity. This chapter exposes readers to an exploration of motivating principles for working with diverse populations in different social contexts, as well as the importance of ongoing professional self-evaluation. It is important for readers to keep in mind that the content in this chapter is influenced by the author's professional and personal paradigms and must not be taken as "absolute truth," but, rather, as one person's analysis intended to give a voice to the experience of many.

Human Diversity: A General Understanding

Human diversity evolves, in part, by powerful subjective experiences being interpreted differently by different people (Saleebey, 1994). Human diversity can be defined as the differences among humans based on a multidimensional set of variables, including individual, group, and community values, beliefs, religious/spiritual practices, age, gender, sexual orientation, race, ethnicity, socioeconomic status, social conditions/experiences, political structures, educational backgrounds, rituals/customs, mental/physical abilities, cultures, and languages, among others. In other words, human diversity can generally be defined as human differences, influenced by the interplay of cognitive, physical, social, and/or spiritual variables, to make each person unique and unduplicated.

An aspect of human diversity is that while some individuals, groups, or communities may differ, others may experience commonalities through a combination of some of the aforementioned diverse attributes. Understanding and speaking the same language/dialect, sharing similar sexual orientations, encountering physical/mental disabilities, experiencing a common history, ethnicity, culture, or events are a few examples of how various attributes of human diversity may be common experiences within specific groups of people. Thus, human commonalities exist within the context of human diversity and vice versa, neither being super-ordinal to the other (Guadalupe & Freeman, 1999).

Although human commonality must not be ignored, a focus on human diversity and its legitimacy is vital to preventing unique individual, group, and community experiences from being misunderstood, stereotyped, marginalized, ignored, underestimated, and/or disempowered. For instance, while all humans need food and fluids to stay alive, individuals follow slightly to vastly different diets that reflect their lifestyles, health conditions, and economic resources. Another example is that while humans create and use symbols (e.g., words, codes, signs) to create meaning, express ideas, and otherwise relate to one another (Allen, 1993; Bruner, 1990; Dean, 1993), symbols are likely to be shaped and interpreted differently, depending on such variables as the context in which they were used, the background of individuals who are using them, time, and the social conditions (Pozatek, 1994).

The human mind strives to understand the human condition through the exchange of individual and collective literature (White, 1991; White & Epston, 1990). In the case of human diversity—a vast, complex, and indefinable totality—it is important to recognize that the evolution of such understanding does not represent absolute truth, but rather a series of interpretations.

A review of literature on human diversity shows a number of trends:

- Terminology for aspects of human diversity (e.g., culture, ethnicity, race) is often used loosely and interchangeably, creating barriers to learning and understanding.
- Stereotypes are frequently perpetuated in content written about diverse populations.
- Cultural and social experiences are generally observed to affect the development of "self."
- Human diversity is often perceived as deviance rather than a strength.
- Coercive social power, power withheld by privileged groups, and control of production means have been observed to generate and reinforce forms of social injustice and oppressive force.
- Populations have been observed to demonstrate resiliency and strength while facing and overcoming adversity.
- Social movements have been shown to form with the ultimate goal of influencing the development of egalitarian societies.

The knowledge generated by empirical and conceptualized work regarding the effects that the aforementioned trends have in our lives is always changing. Unfortunately, the length and purpose of this chapter do not allow for a detailed exploration of the aforementioned trends. They are, however, by and large incorporated into the content that follows.

Honoring Human Diversity Through an Empowerment Theoretical Framework

While addressing human diversity, as a multidimensional whole or through one or a combination of its fragmented components (e.g., ethnicity, class, gender, sexual orientation, mental/physical disabilities, etc.), careful attention must be given to the guiding principles of the theory or theoretical frameworks and practice approaches being employed. Conscious and predetermined attention provided by theory is likely to raise understanding of possible outcomes while engaging in professional services within the context of human diversity. (Note: the terms *theory* and *theoretical frameworks* are used here interchangeably to encompass a set of principles used to conceptualize, describe, and rationalize professional involvement, while practice approaches are approaches generated from theory and theoretical frameworks to provide descriptive and specific guidelines and skills for assessment, provision of services, and evaluation.) Although awareness does not guarantee change (Cramer, 1997), it is an important ingredient for engaging in conscious decision-making. This author finds the following questions useful in selecting a theoretical framework that promotes a willingness and commitment to advocate for the well-being of individuals, groups, families, and communities while embracing and respecting human diversity. For instance, is the theory consistent in respecting and supporting human diversity? Does the theoretical framework uphold faith in the human spirit and potential for transcending adversity? Is the theoretical framework reliable in simultaneously considering the multidimensional set of variables interchangeably affecting the well-being of diverse individuals, families, small groups, and communities? Is the theory practice-oriented? In other words, does the theory incorporate a practice model(s) that assists in the process of strengthening professional competence while guiding professional engagement, assessment, planning, intervention, as well as evaluation? Positive answers to these questions would not necessarily imply that the theoretical framework does not have limitations, but rather that it provides a baseline from which to begin. For example, empowerment theory and practice have had their restrictions; however, the contributions made to the social work profession have transcended those limitations. As a continually evolving theoretical framework with various practice approaches, the empowerment theory has, in its basic beliefs, honored, encouraged, valued, and incorporated human diversity principles while advocating for social justice, individual and community well-being, as well as the development of an egalitarian society.

Empowerment has been a crucial word and theme used in political science, social work, psychology, psychiatry, sociology, health care, and public administration literature for the past several decades (Gutierrez, Parsons, & Cox, 1998; Pinderhughes, 1983; Simon, 1994; Solomon, 1976). The construction, deconstruction, and reconstruction of what is today known as the *empowerment movement* has been strengthened by contributions made by a variety of scholars, social reforms, struggles, other social movements, researchers, and practitioners from diverse social disciplines including the aforementioned ones. The endeavor for empowerment as an ideology has been ingrained throughout U.S. political and philosophical history. For instance, during the late 1800s personal and social circumstances were by and large influenced by poverty, racist and sexist oppression, massive immigration, exploitation of children, concentration of wealth in the hands of the elite, and economic recession, to mention only a few (Jansson, 2001; Wenocur & Reisch, 1989). Social reforms as well as the roots of the social work profession, evidenced by the development of the Charity Organization Societies and the Settlement House Movement, emerged as responses to those conditions. Those responses ". . . reflected differences in perspective, from a focus on social control of the poor to an emphasis on self-determination and [personal as well as social] empowerment" (Parsons, Gutierrez, & Cox, 1998).

The current focus on empowerment, as an ideology based on assumptions promoting hope for change, a process involving a series of proceedings and actions, and an outcome illustrated by effects and end results has been a continuous effort to promote social justice and the well-being of individuals, groups, and communities (Evans, 1992). Oppressive forces such as racism, sexism, classism, ageism, homophobia, and discrimination based on mental or physical disabilities historically have affected—and continue to influence—the dynamics of human interaction and the shape of our lives. Poverty, economic deprivation, hatred, and violence are some of oppression's effects. Thus, embracing and encouraging personal, group, and community empowerment while promoting change of oppressive forces is not only meaningful, but also vital in honoring the wisdom of human diversity.

Many social workers, researchers, practitioners, and writers have contributed to the on-going development as well as the reemergence of empowerment as a theoretical framework broken down into practice models. Furthermore, writers have defined *empowerment* in a variety of ways, reflecting their paradigms and experiences, making it difficult to provide a single definition that is inclusive and absolute. For example, while some scholars have focused on empowerment as a process concerning a series of decisions, proceedings, and actions, others have placed a greater emphasis on empowerment as an outcome or end result of an intervention. Nevertheless, Hasenfeld (1987) stresses that "the theory of empowerment is based on the assumption that the capacity of people to improve their lives is determined by their ability to control their environment, namely, by having power" (p. 478). This author supports the notion that having power needs to be coupled by an ability to influence change. Ng (1980) defines *power* as the potential to influence, and *influence* as power in motion.

The work by Barbara Solomon (1976) has been one of the most referenced historical writings of empowerment practice in the social work profession. In her writing, Solomon describes how historically ". . . black communities have been subjected to negative valuations [and stigmatization] from the larger society . . ." (p. 12), generally affecting individuals' and communities' sense of self, personal fulfillment, direction, usage of adequate resources, and illustration of competence while achieving life goals. According to Solomon, a phenomenon that can be observed is that negative valuations have had different effects on individuals within black communities. For instance, strong family and group relationships have served as a ". . . cushion or protective barrier against negative valuations . . ." (p. 21), through which some individuals and groups have been able to identify, confront, and transform adversity. However, the exposure to negative valuations and stigmatization for other individuals and groups ". . . has been so intense that they accept these valuations as 'right' or at least inevitable and therefore make no effort to exert power at all. . . . The powerlessness that they exhibit can be considered power absence rather than power failure" (p. 21).

Another way of interpreting this phenomenon is in terms of oppression internalized by individuals and illustrated through group consciousness (i.e., the development and maintenance of self-rejection and the acceptance of stigmatization generated during interaction with others). Internalized oppression seems to be an end result of outer negative variations believed as "truth" by individuals that prevents optimum expansion of inner personal resources. Therefore, according to Solomon, as a means for increasing inner and outer capacity to promote necessary change, social workers utilizing empowerment as a model for practice need to engage in a set of activities and utilization of skills that enhance, support, and facilitate intrapersonal, interpersonal, socioeconomic, and political power.

Social work scholars, researchers, and practitioners have expanded Solomon's (1976) initial work and contributions made by other individuals such as Paulo Freire (1973) in his book titled, *Pedagogy of the Oppressed*. Freire's emphasis on consciousness-raising as a key factor for promoting action and change has become a critical paradigm and principle in empowerment practice. Gutierrez (1990) points out that consciousness-raising needs to be incorporated as a goal within the process and outcome of empowerment practice in order to reduce self-blame, support self-efficacy, and promote personal responsibility to encourage change.

Throughout its evolution, empowerment practice has been stretched to incorporate empowerment issues, needs, and interventions within diverse contexts and experiences. These include empowerment practice with women (GlenMaye, 1998; Gutierrez, 1990), gays and lesbians (DeLois, 1998), individuals with disabilities (Manning, 1998; Renz-Beaulaurier, 1998), the homeless (Andrus & Ruhlin, 1998), youth (Rees, 1998), families (Hodges, Burwell, & Ortega, 1998), public housing (McGuire, 1994), and social service delivery (Cox & Randal Joseph, 1998; Gutierrez, Parsons, & Cox, 1998), to mention only a few. As observed by Lee (1996):

> There are two strong streams that feed into empowerment theory for social work practice. The first is such social/political/economic movements as decolonization, the African liberation movements, the women's movement, the gay rights movement, and the Black power and poor people's power movement. . . . The second human development/clinical theories from the helping professions related to releasing human potentialities. The empowerment approach seeks to channel the two streams into one mighty flow. (pp. 223–224)

In other words, empowerment practice seeks to recognize and incorporate the relationship that often exists between personal, social, and political powers affecting individuals, families, groups, and communities.

The notion of interdependence among those dimensions of empowerment practice is well supported by forerunners of empowerment as a theoretical framework and practice approach (Gutierrez, 1995, 1990; Gutierrez, Parsons, & Cox 1998; Krogsrud Miey, O'Melia, & Dubois, 2001; Lee, 1996, 1994; Mancoske & Hunzeker, 1989; Pinderhughes, 1989, 1983; Rappaport, 1987; Simon, 1994; Solomon, 1976). An empowerment lens advocates for interventions that can be used individually or simultaneously at the micro (with individuals, families, and small groups), meso (with organizations), and macro (with the larger socioeconomic and political structure) capacities. Rappaport (1987) stresses that "empowerment conveys both a psychological sense of personal control or influence and a concern with actual social influence, political power, and legal rights. It is a multilevel construct applicable to individual citizens as well as to organizations and neighborhoods: it suggests the study of people in context" (p. 12).

Although empowerment practice cannot be packaged into one absolute model due to considerations given to diverse contexts, social times, groups of people, communities, and/or social and cultural experiences, there are basic core assumptions and conditions, some already mentioned, that unify empowerment as a theoretical framework. As observed in the above discussion, a relationship is believed to exist among the ". . . personal (feelings and perceptions regarding the ability to influence and resolve one's own issues); interpersonal (experiences with others that facilitate problem resolution); and environmental (societal institutions that can facilitate or thwart self-help efforts)" (Parsons, Gutierrez, & Cox, 1998). Thus, an ecological view and multidimensional approach that integrates knowledge and skills to intervene at the intrapersonal (i.e., with self-efficacy, awareness, and acceptance issues, etc.), interpersonal (i.e., collective experiences), and political/community (i.e., political action/participation) levels are vital (Parsons, Gutierrez, & Cox, 1998).

Understanding of oppression, a by-product of stigmatization and social stratification shaped by coercive social power, control, privilege, and constructed hierarchies of differences (Appleby, Colon, & Hamilton, 2001) and oppressive forces is also central to empowerment practice. Social as well as internalized personal oppression supports individual, group, family, and community destruction as it breaks down self-determination and the spirit of human potential and prolongs self-defeating actions (Lee, 1996, 1994). Another core principle of empowerment practice is that individuals have the potential to change their conditions. As stressed by Lee (1996),

> . . . [people] are fully capable of solving immediate problems and moving beyond them to analyze institutionalized oppression and the structures that maintain it, as well as its effects

upon themselves. They are able to strengthen internal resources and work collaboratively in their families, groups, and communities to change and empower themselves in order to challenge the very conditions that oppress. The basic principle of this approach is that people empower themselves through individual empowerment work, empowerment-oriented group work, community action, and political knowledge and skill. The approach sees people as capable of praxis: action-reflection and action, action-in reflection, and dialogue. (p. 229)

As mentioned earlier consciousness-raising becomes vital in encouraging, supporting, and facilitating empowerment as a goal, process, and/or outcome. After exploring core principles that give focus to empowerment lenses, it becomes important to more directly address elements of empowerment practice within the context of human diversity, issues, and needs.

A Closer Look at Human Diversity Through an Empowerment Lens and Practice

In considering and promoting empowerment practice within the context of human diversity, a number of important concerns are raised: can the interlocking nature of individual narratives and collective experiences be taken into account without prioritizing one over the other through empowerment practice? Can empowerment practice assist in moving beyond "either/or" categories, which tend to focus exclusively on the effects that single entities such as class, race, ethnicity, gender, sexual orientation, or physical/mental ability have on human experiences, and which neglect the interplay of these in shaping individuals' and communities' experiences as a whole? How can empowerment practice assist practitioners to move beyond stereotypes, stigmatization, and marginalization of individuals, families, groups, or communities often cultivated through neglect of differences? What core knowledge, values, and skills of empowerment practice can assist in more appropriately addressing the previously mentioned concerns while continuing to honor and support personal, family, group, and/or community well-being? The above concerns support the establishment of some guiding principles for employing empowerment practice within the context of human diversity. Several standards are presented below.

Promotion of Optimal Health and Well-Being

Empowerment practice must incorporate its guiding principle regarding the encouragement and promotion of individual, family, group, and community optimal health and well-being at any given time. Thus, individual narratives and collective experiences need to be perceived as equally important, neither one being more or less significant. Ignoring collective experiences through exclusive focus on the individual narrative does not encourage a sense of community or personalization of social responsibility; that is, the collective consciousness needed to promote cooperative action to resist and modify oppressive forces such as sexism, racism, classism, ageism, and homophobia, among others. By the same token, single emphasis on the collective experience while neglecting the individual narrative is likely to reinforce marginalization of individual uniqueness and prolongation of oppressive forces in the name of collectivism.

In honoring a dual focus through the incorporation of individual and collective experience, empowerment practice acknowledges and begins where the client (i.e., individual, family, and community) is through active engagement in reflective listening. Reflective listening is defined here as one's ability to cognitively collect and organize information and verbally present back to the client with intention to seek clarification or simply to ensure the client of one's understanding. As assessment and interaction continue, educational didactics, movies, literature, and supportive systems (i.e., supportive community services, family members or friends, etc.) can be employed to enhance collective consciousness-raising.

Consideration of Multiple Dimensions

In applying empowerment as a practice model that incorporates core values, knowledge, and skills to promote change within the context of human diversity, issues, and needs, it is important to consider individuals, families, and communities as multidimensional (i.e., comprehensive entities being affected simultaneously by multiple variables including race, class, gender, sexual orientation, and physical or mental abilities. No single experience completes one's identity. No single variable can account for it all. Multiple experiences shape multiple identities. Andersen & Collins (2001) stress that although race affects group experiences and identities, exploration of race in isolation from its relationship with other social experiences such as class and gender allows for a palliative understanding of individuals, families, groups, and communities. Laird (1998) agrees as she points out that experiences such as gender, class, and ethnicity cannot stand alone. Laird's observation is reflected in human "code switching abilities," being able to perform competently within different contexts (i.e., a white middle-class woman, with children and a physical disability who considers herself a lesbian). Code switching is also demonstrated by the ability to engage in diverse communication styles to transmit the same message to different groups or types of people.

As emphasized earlier, empowerment is not something that can be given; instead encouragement and support are given as individuals and communities become empowered. The use of "either/or" categories can injure the empowerment process, as individual, family, and community experiences may be stereotyped, stigmatized, and marginalized through neglect of differences within and among groups of people (Guadalupe, 2000), and it illustrates promotion of disempowerment in the name of empowerment. This perspective must not go unnoticed if social workers strive to be holistic in their empowerment practice. Nonstereotypical assessment and interventions are vital in strengthening empowerment social work practice. Generalizations that lead to stereotypes (i.e., standardized categorization that neglects individual uniqueness and differences within and among groups of people regardless of information indicating otherwise) can harm the helping process. For instance, terminologies such as "people of color" and "White groups" have been used throughout diversity literature to classify individuals, groups, and communities.

An interesting observation can be made here. The aforementioned terminologies are misleading. They attempt to unify social adversities or privilege encountered by diverse groups while neglecting individual experience and difference among those being addressed. For instance, differences based on socioeconomic status, gender, sexual orientation, or physical or mental abilities within a specific ethnic or racial group add to the complexity of dynamics and interactions among group members. As observed by Andersen and Collins (2001),

> White women, for example may be disadvantaged because of gender, but privileged by race and perhaps (but not necessarily) by class. . . . For that matter, White Americans do not fit in "either/or" categories—either oppressor or oppressed. Isolating White Americans as if their experience stands alone ignores how White experience is intertwined with that of other groups. . . . Race, class, and gender are manifested differently, depending on their configuration with the others. . . . One might say Black men are privileged as men, this makes no sense when their race and gender and class are taken into account. Otherwise, how can we possibly explain the particular disadvantages African American men experience as men—in the criminal justice system, in education, and in the labor market? For that matter, how can we explain the experience that Native American women experience as Native American women—Disadvantage by the unique experiences that they have based on race, class, and gender—none of which is isolated from the effects of the others? (p. 5)

The neglect of unique experiences, reinforced by "either/or" categories, and the use of terminologies that do not recognize diversity within diversity prolong marginalization of experiences, which in turn promotes victimization instead of empowerment.

Promotion of Consciousness-Raising

Empowerment practice advocates for promoting consciousness-raising as a key factor for encouraging action and change (Gutierrez, 1995). Thus, while engaging in empowerment practice, awareness regarding the possible relationship between knowledge (i.e., the acquisition of information perceived as useful and important) and power (the potential to influence) must be gained and maintained. As emphasized by Dean (1993), knowledge is not discovered, but rather created through human interactions and agreements. It can be observed that historically within the United States, those who possess social authority to define people and experience (i.e., U.S. Bureau of the Census; U.S. Supreme Court; the elite with socioeconomic and political power) often bear some social power to control their lives (Jansson, 2001). Also, as supported by other authors (Allen, 1993; Bruner, 1990; Dean, 1993; Foucault, 1980; Pozatek, 1994; Saleebey, 1994), a relationship seems to exist between power, knowledge, and the creation of experience, whether or not such experience is influenced through external force and/or self-fulfilling prophesies. Knowing who defines whom and encouraging individuals, families, and communities to share their unique experiences as they begin to understand their potential and ability to promote change is important in empowerment practice within the context of human diversity. This principle directs empowerment practice beyond "linguistic imperialism"—a form of oppression that uses linguistic jargon to control people.

Acknowledgement of Many Ways of Knowing

While employing an empowerment lens, practitioners, scholars, and researchers need to acknowledge and honor the experience of "many ways of knowing," which affects many ways of feeling, acting, and being. For instance, some people visit traditional physicians when feeling physically sick while others rely on medicinal herbs or even spiritual practices. Some communities rely on concrete evidence of resources to feel empowered while others find reassurance and empowerment through meditation practices. For that matter, some individuals within the scientific culture use "facts" to teach children about astronomy while some Native Americans use storytelling. As knowing comes in many ways, so can empowerment practice be implemented in many ways.

The paradigm of many ways of knowing, feeling, acting, and being is reflected in the multiple frameworks used to describe human experiences embraced by the term "culture." For instance, while some writers define culture as a "totality" of learned behavior including beliefs, values, customs, and lifestyle (Boutte, 1999), others refer to culture in terms of a "process" by which collective experiences are arranged to meet a group's biological and psychosocial needs (Pinderhughes, 1994). These definitions reflect cultural experience as a product or outcome as well as a transactional process to accomplish a goal. Saleebey (1994) refers to culture as ". . . the mean by which we receive, organize, rationalize, and understand our particular experience in the world" (p. 352). Saleebey emphasizes that culture is based on subjective experiences likely to hold no "truth" within a different context. Saleebey states,

> Truth may be an irrelevant standard by which to judge a culture or microculture such as a group, family, or gang. . . . Truth by one culture's standards is fantasy or folly by another. Even the truths of a particular culture change and shift with the passage of time, the intermingling with other people, and the dynamism of the human-made and natural world. Whatever meanings a culture sustains are mostly expressed in two ways: (1) stories, narratives, and myths (individual and collective versions) and (2) nonverbal communication (the expressions of the body in context). (p. 352)

Honoring many ways of knowing as a guiding principle of empowerment practice can assist practitioners while sensitively exploring human diversity, its complexity, and its rewards. This principle can help practitioners to take off their professional masks and commit to entering the wisdom of uncertainty, in which the so-called "clients" become the "experts" in their own empowerment.

Trust in the Human Spirit

The final guiding principle suggested here for the use of empowerment practice within the context of human diversity emphasizes the importance of trust in the human spirit. The human spirit has demonstrated resilience in the face of adversity, including the negative effects of oppressive forces, through articulation of potential, modification of environment, ability to reflect and reenergize, capacity to interact within different contexts, and ability to overcome difficulty. Thus, trust in the human spirit to overcome adversity becomes vital in enhancing empowerment as a goal, process, and outcome. The power of vulnerability becomes even more obvious and personalized as we explore our own life struggles and successes.

This author is uncomfortable with some of the literature written in the name of empowerment that is constantly focused on "clients needing empowerment" due to their "problems." While empowerment as a theory and practice does deal with issues and needs based on power, powerlessness, and oppression, empowerment through the lens presented in this writing advocates for considering this observation *and* moving toward viewing and sustaining empowerment through daily interaction regardless of whether or not "problems" are encountered. It advocates for perceiving and acknowledging the spirit's inspiration, resiliency, and guidance as the essence of a person, family, or community.

Empowerment in Diversity Competence

Human diversity is non-static, constantly changing. Empowerment as a theoretical framework and practice is sensitive to the study of human diversity as it incorporates knowledge, values, and skills that are flexible and can be used while assessing and intervening at intrapersonal, interpersonal, and environmental and social levels. As emphasized by Gutierrez, DeLois, and GlenMaye (1995a),

> The goal of empowerment is to increase personal, interpersonal, or political power so the individuals, families, or communities can take action to improve their situations. Empowerment is a process that can take place on the individual, interpersonal, and community levels of intervention. It consists of the following subprocesses: development of group consciousness, reduction of self blame, assumption of personal responsibility for change, and enhancement of self-efficacy. Empowerment occurs through intervention methods that include basing the relationship on collaboration, trust, and shared power; utilizing small groups; accepting the client's definition of the problem; identifying and building upon the client's strengths; raising the client's consciousness of issues of class and power; actively involving the client in the change process; teaching specific skills; using mutual aid, self-help, or support groups; experiencing a sense of personal power within the helping relationship; and mobilizing resources or advocating for the client. (p. 535)

The word *client* is used to describe intervention with single individuals, families, small groups, or the community as a whole. Elements of empowerment such as self-efficacy (one's ability to create and regulate life events), personal responsibility (one's participation in sustaining oppressive forces or promoting their change), and group consciousness (a collective awareness of oppressive forces, their effects, and human potential and resiliency) require attention from both practitioner and client. Awareness of the interplay between self-efficacy, personal responsibility, and group consciousness becomes vital to helping clients claim their own power, remember that they are not alone in the process of change, and understand both self- and collective-reliance. For instance, oppressive forces create painful cognitive, emotional, and often physical scars, regardless of whether they are created through sexism, racism, or classism.

Consciousness-raising can become less fragmented and marginalized if the aforementioned elements of empowerment intervention are honored and supported. Subprocesses that need consideration in empowerment practice are understanding ongoing cognitive and social patterns that promote and sustain fear of change, internalized oppression based on self-rejection and distrust in one's potential and abilities, and external forces injuring empowerment as a process and outcome. Looking at core cultures and subcultures that promote, sustain, and perpetuate social norms can enhance empowerment intervention methods applied within a diversified society. Cultivating an understanding for what a society generally considers "normal" and "abnormal" is essential to promoting change within paradigms so that human diversity is no longer perceived as deviant and rejected for the notion that the more similar we are the better.

Empowerment intervention at the personal, interpersonal, or environmental levels can involve various strategies including, beginning where the client is, active/reflective listening, self-disclosure from the practitioner to build rapport and partnership, development of mutual understanding and agreement regarding needs and methods for achieving goals, and professional self-reflection and evaluation. Other empowerment intervention methods embody linking individuals, families, and communities with resources and supportive systems as well as advocating for needed social action and change. Linking individuals and communities with resources and other supportive systems reduces the sense of isolation and increases the potential for group consciousness (I/we are not alone) likely to promote social action toward necessary social change. Educational didactics, self-evaluation exercises and strategies, videos, written documentation, poetry, music, and mutual-aid groups can be used in consciousness-raising.

Understanding that empowerment practice is not based on sequential, linear thinking is important within the context of human diversity. Instead, it embraces transactions between person and environment, and vice versa. For instance, in confronting domestic violence against women, the practitioner can incorporate counseling skills (e.g., reflective listening and empathic responses) to provide intrapersonal support, find shelter resources to address interpersonal needs, and advocate for social change through political action to address environmental or social causes. For that matter, while lobbying for social policies that promote racial/ethnic/gender equality, practitioners may also work in small-group or community educational projects to address internalized oppression and stimulate a sense of empowerment. Overall, an ecological view that incorporates understanding historical and current social conditions, patterns of adaptation, forces that discourage or promote optimal health and well-being, and resources and strengths is important while identifying, cultivating, selecting, and promoting empowerment intervention methods within the context of human diversity (Germain, 1994; Germain & Gitterman, 1996).

The Shadow and Light of Social Service: A Look at Oneself

Encouraging and honoring empowerment in others requires that the practitioner, researcher, scholar, or educator engage in a similar process for himself or herself. One cannot promote that with which one cannot identify. Because empowerment is individualized, one needs a sense of what it tastes like through one's own interactions and experiences. Such exploration can assist a practitioner's understanding for what motivates social work and provide guidelines for engaging in the paradox of caring for self while serving others. Are "Shadows" (Straub, 2000) or "Lights" the baseline for service engagement? Subconscious need for approval, control, status, and power, as well as fear, shame, guilt, and addiction to social service (to avoid examining one's own pain and resiliency) reflects the "Shadows" that lead some to social work. How often do practitioners assume whole credit—"look how great I am"—when seeing success in clients' lives? The shadows of service are reflections of hidden masks buried in personal narratives. All practitioners have them; the important issue is how to be aware and guide oneself through cognitive, emotional, and/or physical healing (Kornfield, 2000). Unmasking the shadows of service requires honesty, humility, and trust in one's own power in the face of vulnerability; this is vital in empowerment practice to help others.

An exploration of one's own narrative is a prerequisite to conscious practice at any level and within any context. Cultivating understanding and acceptance of one's own wounds and shadows creates a place where reinforcement of the "Lights" of service can be embraced. Self-reflection; evaluation of strengths and areas that need improvement; a commitment to enhancing one's own empowerment through transforming destructive cognitive, emotional, and behavioral patterns; and finding resources and supportive systems to sustain awareness and commitment are attributes of "Lights" of service that guide conscious practice.

Empowerment as a process and outcome is strengthened through internal and external cleansing. Thus, personal discipline in self-evaluation, conscious regeneration, and commitment to changing patterns and behaviors that support oppressive forces will strengthen one's ability for professional service. "Walking the talk" through the Warrior's heart—responding skillfully to suffering—is the name of the plan (Guadalupe & Torres, 2001; Kornfield, 2000). Removing one's own masks becomes the first step toward closing the separation between those who heal and those who need healing and toward separating one's efforts to help others gain empowerment from one's own need for approval, control, status, and power. Being unaware of the power that shadows of service have limits a practitioner's professional competence, and it may likely cause clients additional suffering despite the practitioner's good intentions. Social workers have a personal and professional responsibility to recognize and commit to addressing their own "unfinished business"—their inner and outer dragons—through vision, hope, trust, and action—not cynicism. A practitioner's belief that he or she can make a difference through caring for oneself while connecting with and assisting in necessary societal transformation is important (Straub, 2000). This balance of social action and self-reflection creates a strong foundation for sociopolitical activism and respect for justice and equality. As once stated by Mahatma Gandhi, "action without contemplation is blind."

Professional competence can be enhanced by "Lights" of service that support cultivation and perpetuation of consciousness-based practice, or it can be damaged by "Shadows" of service leading to practices that are not based on consciousness. Wrestling with our "Shadows" of service while attempting to identify and sustain our "Lights" is not a simple, linear process, but rather a complex one. However, one can decide and take action toward maintaining a consciousness-based practice. Practitioners can raise their collective awareness through education and/or interaction with pain, suffering, and resiliency among themselves, families, colleagues, and communities to cultivate a mutual connection. Periods of silence to reflect and meditate can help to clarify and strengthen personal and professional vision. Meditation need not be used as a drug to numb people to experience, but rather as a tool to mindfully reawaken them to explore alternatives and actions to promote necessary change. Thich Nhat Hanh (1987) emphasizes that remaining unaware of internal and external pain and suffering through meditation is using meditation not to promote mindfulness needed to engage in appropriate action, but instead it is using meditation to create a state for attempting to escape. There is no where to go, but the present. Isolating oneself from one's own suffering can only prolong it. Other practices such as journal writing, poetry, and listening to heart-inspiring music can help to unfold and transform "unfinished business." As energy-draining cognitive, emotional, or behavioral patterns are released, space is created for cultivating individual and collective compassion. Intellectual knowledge of human diversity, issues, and needs does not automatically translate into compassionate action that promotes change for the better. The impact of social service can be strengthened through conscious investigation and transformation of internal "Shadows."

Conclusion

As emphasized throughout this writing, the total experience of human diversity is indefinable. Understanding is glimpsed through interactions, research, and conceptual interpretations. Empowerment as an ongoing and evolving philosophy, process, and outcome addresses specific dynamics created and reinforced through human interactions within the context of human diversity. Awareness of the interplay between intrapersonal, interpersonal, and environmental forces is important to consider in applying empowerment as a theory and practice with contextually diverse populations. Empowerment is individualized. It cannot be given, but rather encouraged and supported in others. Thus, personal and professional self-evaluation by researchers and educators, among other practitioners, is vital to avoiding engagement in satisfying their own needs in the name of servicing others. Individual and collective consciousness-raising can support ongoing development of visions and hopes for the future. Practitioners, researchers, and educators need to remember that our lives heavily depend on our cocreating experiences, meanings, interpretations, and effects.

The social work profession must honor transformation that emerges through the interplay of natural internal self-regeneration and constructed external protective factors, forces that support social functioning and preservation of well-being (Saleebey, 1997). Social workers must be careful not to engage in principles of a disease model in the name of empowerment by promoting the notion that changes are exclusively dependent on the knowledge and skills of "experts." Saleebey emphasizes, ". . . we have a native wisdom about what is right for us and what we should do when confronted with organismic or environmental challenges" (p. 10). Life transformations seem to be generated by an awareness of inner and outer barriers and a commitment to challenging and modifying them as well as through support and assistance from others, and vice versa. It seems important to remember that ultimately people cannot empower anyone outside of themselves. Instead, they can encourage, facilitate, and support others in gaining power through their actions and examples (Simon, 1994). As stressed by Lee (1996), "the empowerment process resides in the person, not the helper" (p. 224). Thus, in providing professional services through an empowerment approach a "dual focus" that honors natural, individual self-regeneration and external support is vital.

Questions for Critical Thinking

1. How would you define empowerment?

2. What affects your sense of empowerment or disempowerment?

3. What are some of the attributes of empowerment that you perceive as most significant or most important? Discuss.

4. What effect does your perception of empowerment have on your philosophy of life, decision-making process, and lifestyle?

5. What advantages and disadvantages do you perceive in addressing empowerment as an internal or external process and outcome?

6. Do you agree with the notion that permanent empowerment cannot solely occur through external political changes? Discuss.

7. Can intrapersonal changes be enough to sustain self-efficacy? Discuss.

8. What recommendations do you have to strengthen empowerment as a theory and practice within the context of human diversity?

Sources for Further Study

Gutierrez, L. M., Parsons, R. J., & Cox, E. O. (Eds.). (1998). *Empowerment in social work practice: A sourcebook*. Pacific Grove, CA: Brooks/Cole. This text examines core theoretical principles for empowerment-based interventions with diverse populations. Readers are exposed to a number of dimensions of empowerment practice including empowerment as a philosophy, concept, process, and outcome.

Lee, J. (1994). *The empowerment approach to social work practice*. New York: Columbia University Press. This text presents an overview of the history of empowerment practice, including dynamics and interventions observed during the roots of social work practice in the late 1800s. Empowerment-based practice, principles, concepts, and methodologies are explored through micro, meso, and macro lenses.

Solomon, B. (1976). *Black empowerment: Social work in oppressed communities*. New York: Columbia University Press. This text addresses social stigmatization and oppressive treatment historically experienced by African American communities. Solomon explores general effects of such experiences in African Americans' sense of self, personal fulfillment, and self-direction, to mention a few. Solomon exposes the reader to possible intrapersonal, interpersonal, and environmental outcomes when engaging in empowerment-based practice with African American communities.

References

Allen, J. A. (1993). The constructivist paradigms: Values and ethics. *Journal of Teaching in Social Work, 8*(1/2), 31–54.

Andersen, M. L., & Collins, P. H. (Eds.). (2001). *Race, class, and gender: An anthology* (4th ed.). Belmont, CA: Wadsworth/Thomson Learning.

Andrus, G., & Ruhlin, S. (1998). Empowerment practice with homeless people/families. In L. M. Gutierrez, R. J. Parsons, & E. O. Cox (Eds.), *Empowerment in social work practice: A sourcebook*. Pacific Grove, CA: Brooks/Cole.

Appleby, G. A., Colon, E., & Hamilton, J. (2001). *Diversity, oppression, and social functioning: Person-in-environment assessment and intervention*. Boston: Allyn & Bacon.

Boutte, G. (1999). *Multicultural education: Raising consciousness*. Belmont, CA: Wadsworth Publishing Company.

Bruner, J. (1990). *Acts of meaning*. Cambridge, MA: Harvard University Press.

Cox, E. O., & Randal Joseph, B. H. (1998). Social service delivery and empowerment: The administrator's role. In L. M. Gutierrez, R. J. Parsons, & E. O. Cox (Eds.), *Empowerment in social work practice: A sourcebook*. Pacific Grove, CA: Brooks/Cole.

Cramer, E. P. (1997). Effect of an educational unit about lesbian identity development and disclosure in a social work methods course. *Journal of Social Work Education, 33*(3), 461–472.

Dean, R. G. (1993). Teaching a constructivist approach to clinical practice. *Journal of Teaching in Social Work, 8*(1/2), 55–75.

DeLois, K. A. (1998). Empowerment practice with lesbians and gays. In L. M. Gutierrez, R. J. Parsons, & E. O. Cox (Eds.), *Empowerment in social work practice: A sourcebook*. Pacific Grove, CA: Brooks/Cole.

Devore, W., & Schlesinger, E. G. (1996). *Ethnic-sensitive social work practice* (4th ed.). Boston: Allyn & Bacon.

Evans, E. N. (1992). Liberation theology, empowerment theory, and social work practice with the oppressed. *International Social Work, 35*, 135–147.

Foucault, M. (1980). *Power/knowledge: Selected interviews and other writings*. New York: Pantheon.

Freire, P. (1973). *Pedagogy of the oppressed*. New York: Seabury.

Germain, C. B. (1994). Human behavior and the social environment. In E. G. Reamer (Ed.), *The foundation of social work knowledge* (pp. 88–121). New York: Columbia University Press.

Germain, C. B., & Gitterman, A. (1996). *The life model of social work practice: Advances in theory and practice* (2nd ed.). New York: Columbia University Press.

GlenMaye, L. (1998). Empowerment of women. In L. M. Gutierrez, R. J. Parsons, & E. O. Cox (Eds.), *Empowerment in social work practice: A sourcebook*. Pacific Grove, CA: Brooks/Cole.

Guadalupe, J. L., & Freeman, M. (fall, 1999). Common human needs in the context of diversity: Integrating schools of thought. *The Journal of Cultural Diversity, 6*(3), 85–92.

Guadalupe, J. L. (2000). *The challenge: Development of a curriculum to address diversity content without perpetuating stereotypes*. Ann Arbor, MI: UMI Company.

Gutierrez, L. M. (1990). Working with women of color: An empowerment perspective. *Social Work, 35*(2), 149–154.

Gutierrez, L. M. (1995). Understanding the empowerment process: Does consciousness make a difference? *Social Work Research, 19*(4), 229–237.

Gutierrez, L. M., Delois, K., & GlenMaye, L. (1995a). Understanding empowerment practice: Building on practitioner-based knowledge. *Families in Society, 76*(9), 534–542.

Gutierrez, L. M., Parsons, R. J., & Cox, E. O. (1998). Creating opportunities for empowerment-oriented programs. In L. M. Gutierrez, R. J. Parsons, & E. O. Cox (Eds.), *Empowerment in social work practice: A sourcebook*. Pacific Grove, CA: Brooks/Cole.

Hahn, T. N. (1987). *Being peace*. Berkeley, CA: Parallax Press.

Hasenfeld, Y. (1987). Power in social work practice. *Social Service Review, September*, 469–483.

Hodges, V. G., Burwell, Y., & Ortega, D. (1998). Empowering families. In L. M. Gutierrez, R. J. Parsons, & E. O. Cox (Eds.), *Empowerment in social work practice: A sourcebook*. Pacific Grove, CA: Brooks/Cole.

Jansson, B. S. (2001). *The reluctant welfare state: American social welfare policies, past, present, and future* (4th ed.). Belmont, CA: Brooks/Cole Thomson Learning.

Kornfield, J. (2000). *After the ecstasy the laundry: How the heart grows wise on the spiritual path*. New York: Bantam Books.

Krogsrud Miey, K., O'Melia, M., & Dubois, B. (2001). *Generalist social work practice: An empowering approach*. Boston: Allyn & Bacon.

Laird, J. (1998). Theorizing culture: Narrative ideas and practice principles. In M. McGoldrick (Ed.), *Revisioning family therapy: Race, culture, and gender in clinical practice* (pp. 20–36). New York: The Guilford Press.

Lee, J. A. B. (1994). *The empowerment approach to social work practice*. New York: Columbia University Press.

Lee, J. A. B. (1996). The empowerment approach to social work practice. In F. J. Turner (Ed.), *Social work treatment: Interlocking theoretical approaches*. New York: The Free Press.

Mancoske, R. J., & Hunzeker, J. M. (1989). *Empowerment based generalist practice: Direct services with individuals*. New York: Cummings and Hathaway.

Manning, S. S. (1998). Empowerment in mental health programs: Listening to the voices. In L. M. Gutierrez, R. J. Parsons, & E. O. Cox (Eds.), *Empowerment in social work practice: A sourcebook*. Pacific Grove, CA: Brooks/Cole.

McGuire, L. E. (1994). The division of housing project: Opportunity for empowerment practice with public housing residents. In L. M. Gutierrez & P. Nurius (Eds.), *Education and research for empowerment practice*. Seattle: Center for Policy and Practice Research.

Ng, S. H. (1980). *The social psychology of power*. New York: Academic Press.

Parsons, R. J., Gutierrez, L. M., & Cox, E. O. (1998). A model for empowerment practice. In L. M. Gutierrez, R. J. Parsons, & E. O. Cox (Eds.), *Empowerment in social work practice: A sourcebook*. Pacific Grove, CA: Brooks/Cole.

Pinderhughes, E. (1983). Empowerment: For our clients and for ourselves. *Social Casework, 64*, 312–314.

Pinderhughes, E. (1989). *Understanding race, ethnicity, and power: The key to efficacy in clinical practice*. New York: The Free Press.

Pinderhughes, E. (1994). Diversity and population at risk: Ethnic minorities and people of color. In E. G. Reamer (Ed.), *The foundation of social work knowledge* (pp. 264–308). New York: Columbia University Press.

Pozatek, E. (1994). The problem of certainty: Clinical social work in the postmodern era. *Social Work, 39*(4), 396–403.

Rappaport, J. (1987). Terms of empowerment/exemplars of prevention: Toward a theory for community psychology. *American Journal of Community Psychology, 15*(2), 121–144.

Rees, S. (1998). Empowerment of youth. In L. M. Gutierrez, R. J. Parsons, & E. O. Cox (Eds.), *Empowerment in social work practice: A sourcebook*. Pacific Grove, CA: Brooks/Cole.

Renz-Beaulaurier, R. (1998). Empowering people with disabilities: The role of choice. In L. M. Gutierrez, R. J. Parsons, & E. O. Cox (Eds.), *Empowerment in social work practice: A sourcebook*. Pacific Grove, CA: Brooks/Cole.

Saleebey, D. (1994). Culture, theory and narrative: The intersection of meanings in practice. *Social Work, 39*(4), 351–359.

Saleebey, D. (1997). *The strength perspective in social work practice*. White Plains, NY: Longman Publishing.

Simon, B. L. (1994). *The empowerment traditions in American social work*. New York: Columbia University Press.

Solomon, B. (1976). *Black empowerment: Social work in oppressed communities*. New York: Columbia University Press.

Straub, G. (2000). *The rhythm of compassion: Caring for self, connecting with society*. Boston: Tuttle Publishing.

Wenocur, S., & Reisch, M. (1989). *From charity to enterprise: The development of American social work in a market economy*. Chicago: University of Illinois Press.

White, M. (1991). Deconstruction and therapy. *Dulwich Centre Newsletter, 3*, 21–40.

White, M., & Epston, D. (1990). *Narrative means to therapeutic ends*. New York: Norton.

Part II

Ethnocultural Diversity Perspectives

4

Ethnic-Sensitive Social Work Practice Framework

Joseph Anderson

Major Precursors and Developers

Ethnic-sensitive practice represents the framework developed almost exclusively by Wynetta Devore and Elfriede Schlesinger, first conceptualized in *Ethnic-Sensitive Social Work Practice* (1981) and refined through four subsequent editions (1987, 1991, 1996, 1999) and two *Social Work Encyclopedia* articles (1987, 1994). Central to this model is the integration of the concepts of ethnicity, social class, and oppressed ethnic groups within a framework of principles and strategies for social work practice. Thus, Devore and Schlesinger draw greatly on the work of others, contributing their own synthesis of this work into a model for practice that is attuned to the values and dispositions related to the client's ethnic-group membership, social-class position, and oppression experiences.

Core Concepts

Major concepts incorporated from other theorists include the dual perspective (Chestang, 1980; Norton, 1978), biculturalism (deAndra, 1997; Ho, 1987), generalist practice with people of color (Lum, 1992), and ethclass (Gordon, 1973). The dual perspective and the closely related biculturalism construct (deAndra, 1997) illuminate how simultaneous membership in the core society and in the ethnic group, especially one that has experienced a history of oppression, affects people's behaviors and attitudes. This institutional oppression and its effect on human behavior in the social environment requires social work practice that is generalist in nature. Such practice involves a core problem-solving endeavor that simultaneously addresses individual and systemic concerns. Assessment for this generalist practice involves use of the concepts of ethclass and ethnic reality. Ethclass concerns the intersect of ethnicity and social class. This suggests that the differences in behavior, attitudes, and life chances of those within a particular social class result from ethnicity, and differences within those of similar ethnic-group membership result from social-class status. This "ethclass" position generates identifiable dispositions and behaviors. Devore and Schlesinger call these dispositions "ethnic reality" and view these as deeply ingrained feelings, beliefs, and actions in such areas as child-rearing, sexuality, gender roles, and spirituality. This ethnic reality especially evolves for oppressed ethnic groups of color. These are the groups to which ethnocultural ignorance is deemed particularly detrimental and to which the ethnic-sensitive social work practice framework especially applies.

Closely related to this framework are the other ethnocultural propositions of ethnic group difference (Cox & Ephross, 1998), especially those that relate ethnicity to family processes and dynamics and to practice with and on behalf of culturally diverse families (Anderson, 1991; Ho, 1987; McGoldrick, Giordano, & Pearce, 1982, 1996). The ethnic-sensitive social work practice model is distinguished from this related work by the incorporation of social class with ethnicity and the consideration of the generalist perspective and prevailing practice approaches as adapted to ethnic reality.

Core Principles for Practice

Ethnic-sensitive social work practice consists of three primary components: (1) A professional perspective conceptualized as "layers of understanding"; (2) A series of assumptions especially pertinent to ethnocultural competencies; and (3) Adaptation to the ethnoculture of prevailing practice principles and skills. The central values, knowledge, and skills of this framework address seven layers of understanding. These include

1. Social work values (including the value of cultural competence);
2. Knowledge of human behavior in the social environment (especially as biopsychosocial);
3. Knowledge of social welfare policies and services (with emphasis on exclusionary practices);
4. Self-awareness (including awareness of one's own ethnicity and how it influences practice);
5. Knowledge of the impact of ethnic reality (in the daily life of clients);
6. The route of the client to the social worker (from totally involuntary to totally voluntary); and
7. Adaptation and modification of strategies and skills (the application of prevailing social work approaches to specific ethnic realities).

The ethnic-sensitive social work practice framework's five central assumptions are (1) Individual and collective history have a bearing on problem generation and solution; (2) The present is most important; (3) Ethnicity is a source of cohesion, identity, and strength, as well as a source of strain, discordance, and strife. Social class is a major determinant of life's chances; (4) The social/societal context and resources needed to enhance quality of life make a major contribution to social functioning; and (5) Nonconscious phenomena affect individual functioning. From these assumptions evolve the two primary principles for ethnic-sensitive social work practice: (1) Simultaneous attention to micro (individual) and macro (systemic) issues; and (2) Adapting skills to ethclass needs and dispositions.

These layers of understanding, assumptions, and principles are incorporated into a paradigm for ethnic-sensitive generalist practice. This framework is based on the work of those who developed models that simultaneously attend to individual and systemic needs (Anderson, 1981, 1982; Wood & Middleman, 1989). These generalist frameworks suggest some combination of two or more of the following dimensions of practice: (1) Direct work with individuals and families in troublesome times; (2) Work with groups experiencing similar troubles; (3) Influencing informal and institutional systems, with concern for particular individuals, families, and communities and their particular issues; and (4) Influencing informal and institutional systems, with concern for particular individuals or families. This generalist framework for ethnic-sensitive practice can be organized into four quadrants as depicted in the following figure.

Case Example

Devore and Schlesinger (1999) use a variety of case studies to apply the concepts from the ethnic-sensitive practice framework. One such case for illuminating generalist practice is "The Sandra Miller Story."

Sandra Miller is a twenty-one-year-old African American single mother with four children. She has been able to complete only ninth grade, which limits her potential for employment. At present, she receives public welfare assistance for Edith, 13 months old, and herself.

She has two other daughters. Mandy, who is five, lives with her, and Jessica, who is three, lives with Sandra's parents who have custody. Although two-year-old Stella lives comfortably with her father's mother, Sandra wished to regain custody. Sandra and her

I	II
Work with individuals and families in troublesome times	Work with groups experiencing similar troubles
III	**IV**
Influencing informal and institutional systems on behalf of particular clients and their particular issues	Influencing informal and institutional systems on behalf of particular individuals or families

FIGURE 4.1 *Four Quadrants for Ethnic-Sensitive Generalist Practice*

young family were referred to the Catholic Youth Organization Protective Services Division by the local child protective agency. There has been evidence of domestic violence, with Sandra having been physically abused by her boyfriend.

Due to her youth, she has few skills that support her in child-care responsibilities. Appointments with the children's doctors are often missed. The tasks of motherhood overwhelm her. She wants to be a good mother but appears not to know what this takes.

In the generalist paradigm, Devore and Schlesinger (1999) suggest working with Sandra and including the grandparents as a resource in the change process (Quadrant 1); involving them in a single-mother support group and a grandparents support group (Quadrant 2); working with family violence prevention programs and community women's groups to address the domestic violence issues of Sandra and others (Quadrant 3); establishing grants to prepare welfare mothers for work and cooperating with African American churches to provide services to grandparents who are caring for grandchildren (Quadrant 4).

These strategies evolve from sensitive understanding for Sandra's ethclass reality as a young African American woman. For example, it includes the need for an empowerment-group experience (Gutierrez, 1990), for care in the African American community (McAdoo, 1993), for extended-family role flexibility (Harper & Lantz, 1996), and for church involvement as a resource for all three generations of this African American family (McAdoo, 1993).

Contributions and Limitations

Ethnic-sensitive practice, as the ethnocultural perspective generally, is among the most frequently taught frameworks in social work education (Gutierrez, Fredrickson, & Soffer, 1999). As one of the earlier models for diversity teaching, it appears useful in preparation for culturally sensitive social work practice. The model posits that group cultural differences create ethnic realities for members that can be understood best through knowledge of these differences. The strength of this framework relates to its sensitizing ability. When the application of the framework accurately illuminates ethnocultural norms that explain behaviors, practitioners can assess and intervene more effectively. This appears especially applicable to recent immigrant groups (Longres, 1992).

Conversely, if generalizations of group differences do not accurately describe the norms and behaviors of particular individuals and families within the group, the framework may not be applicable or it could erroneously stereotype those clients. This risk of being inaccurately stereotyped has increased for ethic groups that have been through more than one generation in this country.

Lorraine Gutierrez (2000) and her coauthors have identified the importance and the limitation of ethnocultural perspectives (such as the ethnic-sensitive approach for social work practice). With specific attention to social work on behalf of Latinos, they note,

> In developing our knowledge and skills, we must always consider how well students are incorporating knowledge and understanding of both the distinctive cultural patterns and disadvantaged social status of Latinos into their work. Until both are addressed, Latinos indi-

vidually and as a group will continue to experience the problems associated with poverty, discrimination, and lack of political influence. (p. 555)

The ethnic-sensitive practice approach proposes concepts for understanding distinctive cultural patterns among ethnic groups with specific attention to how disadvantaged social status affects these patterns. To the degree that this cultural understanding accurately reflects various ethclass realities, the model provides a useful conceptual framework for assessment and intervention on behalf of clients from different ethnic backgrounds.

The standpoint from which concepts on ethnic values and norms are applied can be an obstacle to this accuracy. If ethnic-sensitivity is approached from a Eurocentric rather than an ethnic-centric standpoint (see Chapter 9), non-European ethnic groups and their members may not be understood from the validity and integrity of their own history and strengths. (Schiele, 1999). This lack of understanding can be especially so when those of European descent study non-European groups such as African Americans, Asian Americans, Mexican Americans, Puerto Ricans, and Native Americans.

Sources for Further Study

Cox, Carol B. and Ephross, Paul H. *Ethnicity and Social Work Practice*. New York: Oxford, 1998. This small book highlights the immigration history of ethnic groups in the United States. It conceives ethnic identity as a lens through which clients view their ethclass reality and social work practitioners can view ethnic diversity in their work with individuals, families, groups, organizations, and communities. Ethnicity is also examined in reference to current and future trends and issues in social services, health care, and social policy.

Devore, Wynetta and Schlesinger, Elfriede G. *Ethnic-Sensitive Social Work Practice*. 5th ed. Boston: Allyn & Bacon, 1999. This is the fullest, most recent source of the ethnic-sensitive social work practice framework. It develops the concept of ethnic reality and relates this to the life course approaches to social work practice. It concludes with application of the principles of ethnic-sensitive social work practice as applied to case examples in generalist, direct, and macro practice and in practice with refugees and new immigrants, families, public welfare, and health care.

McAdoo, Harriette Pipes, ed. *Family Ethnicity: Strength in Diversity*. Newburg Park, CA: Sage, 1993. Contributors to this anthology in family ethnicity address the strengths of ethnocultural diversity for social work practice with and on behalf of families and their members. Each section focuses on aspects of the strengths in a different family ethnicity: African American, Mexican, and Spanish-Origin American, Native American, Muslim, and Asian American.

Mc Goldrick, Monica, Giordano, Joe, and Pearce, John K. *Ethnicity and Family Therapy*. 2nd ed. New York: Guilford, 1996. This anthology presents intervention strategies for practice with a vast array of ethnic families. Following a conceptual overview on ethnicity as related to race, class, and intergroup relations, several chapters each cover Native American families, families of African origin, Latino families, Asian American families, Middle Eastern families, Asian Indian families, families of European origin, Jewish families and Slavic families. In these paradigms of ethnic families, authors cover clinical questions such as cultural differences, attitudes toward problem solving, and family-role behavior.

Winkleman, Michael. *Ethnic Sensitivity in Social Work*. Dubuque, IA: Eddie Boners, 1999. This text includes two major sections. The first introduces core cultural diversity concepts toward a general cross-cultural orientation. The second covers special cultural orientations. The latter includes European Americans, Native Americans, African Americans, Hispanic Americans, and Asian and Pacific Americans. An epilogue suggests the current promises and obstacles to cultural and structural pluralism.

Questions for Critical Thinking

1. How might the concept of ethclass be applied to sensitize (suggest where to look) rather than stereotype (prescribe what to see) aspects of ethnic diversity?

2. To what degree does this model promote the dual perspective (see Chapter 7) to understand the behavior and norm dispositions of various ethnic group members?

3. How does ethnic reality fit with the concept of multicultural practice and its assumption that multiple cultural influences shape identities, values, and normative expectations?

4. How might practitioners develop approaches that are more responsive to ethnic diversity?

References

Anderson, J. (1981). *Social work methods and processes*. Belmont, CA: Wadsworth.

Anderson, J. D. (1991). Group work with families: A multicultural perspective. *Social work with groups*, *14*, 17–30.

Anderson, J. D. (1982). Generic and generalist practice and the BSW curriculum. *Journal of Education for Social Work*, *18*, 37–45.

Chestang, L. (1980). Competencies and knowledge in clinical social work: A dual perspective. In P. A. Ewalt (Ed.), *Toward a definition of clinical social work*. Washington, D.C.: National Association of Social Workers, 13–27.

Cox, C. B., & Ephross, P. H. (1998). *Ethnicity and social work practice*. New York: Oxford.

deAndra, D. (1997). *Controversial issues in multiculturalism*. Boston: Allyn & Bacon.

Gordon, M. M. (1973). *Human nature, class, and ethnicity*. New York: Oxford.

Gutierrez, L. (1990). Working with women of color: An empowerment approach. *Social Work*, *14*, 16–32.

Gutierrez, L., Fredrickson, K., & Soffer, S. (1999). Perspectives of social work faculty on diversity and social oppression content. Results from a national study. *Journal of Social Work Education*, *35*, 409–420.

Gutierrez, L., Yeakley, A., & Ortega, R. (2000). Educating social workers for practice with Latinos: Issues for a new millennium. *Journal of Social Work Education*, *36*, 541–560.

Harper, K. V., & Lantz, J. (1996). *Cross-cultural practice: Theory and skills*. Pacific Grove, CA: Brooks/Cole.

Ho, M. K. (1987). *Family therapy with ethnic minorities*. Newburg Park, CA: Sage.

Longres, J. (1991). Toward a status model of ethnic sensitive practice. *Journal of Multicultural Social Work*, *1*, 41–53.

Lum, D. (1992). *Social work practice and people of color* (2nd ed.). Monterey, CA: Brooks/Cole.

McAdoo, H. P. (Ed.). (1993). *Family ethnicity: Strength in diversity*. Newburg Park, CA: Sage.

McGoldrick, M., Giordano, J., and Pearce, J. K. (Eds.). (1996). *Ethnicity and family therapy* (2nd ed.). New York: Guilford.

McGoldrick, M., Pearce, J. K., and Giordano, J. (Eds.). (1982). *Ethnicity and family therapy*. New York: Guilford.

Norton, D. G. (1978). *The dual perspective*. New York: Council on Social Work Education.

Oates-Cannon, E. W. (1995). Religiosity and successful single mother headed African American families. *Black Caucus Journal of National Association of Social Workers*, *2*, 1–12.

Schiele, J. (1999). *Afrocentric human services*. Newburg Park, CA: Sage.

Wood, C. G., & Middleman, R. R. (1989). *The structural approach in direct practice in social work*. New York: Columbia University Press.

5

Value Orientation/ Worldview Framework

Wynne DuBray
Adelle Sanders

This chapter discusses some of the basic attributes of cultural values and how differences among them contribute to misunderstandings in the delivery of social services to minority populations. Guidelines for social workers to use in alleviation of these misunderstandings in generalist practice are included. The lack of understanding for cultural values of minority populations has contributed to much of the ongoing psychological, social, and economic problems faced by these groups today.

Cultural conflict arises primarily when a dominant culture has a set of values that conflicts with the values held by the minority culture (DuBray & Sanders, 1999). In the United States, the European worldview of materialism and a capitalistic/consumeristic value system are in conflict with the values of many minority populations. The incongruence between the competing value systems poses problems in both understanding the minority cultural group and with communication between the dominant and minority cultural groups. In addition, a growing body of evidence indicates "that deep-rooted changes in worldviews are taking place" (Inglehart, 2000, p. 215) and that these changes are reshaping economic, political, and social life in societies around the world. Recent research, in fact, reflects a shift from modern to postmodern values, which is taking place throughout the world in advanced industrialized societies (Inglehart, 2000). These changes will only further complicate the conflict that arises between the divergent value systems. Of course, this necessitates that even more care be taken by human services professionals in respecting their clients' value systems and in getting in touch with their own value systems. This chapter will offer strategies for assessing value differences and steps that social workers can take to assure an understanding of these value differences.

Defining Values

Values form the foundation of not only the culture, but the society, the community, the family, the group, the individual, and the profession of social work. John Rawls (1993) argues that values underlay what is defined as justice and even public reason. Consequently, values are broadly defined by a number of theorists. Values have been defined as "what is wanted, what is best, what is preferable and/or what ought to be done" (Scheibe, 1970, p. 42). John Rohr (1978) defines values as the "beliefs, passions, and principles that have been held for several generations by the overwhelming majority" (p. 59) of a group of people. Rohr further argues for a more specific concept, *regime values*, which means that the prevailing values are those held by the ones with the most power. Lynch, Omdal, and Cruise (1997) go even further than Rohr to define values as the beliefs, passions, and principles held by the overwhelming majority of mankind over recorded history; therefore, they redefine values to be much more than regime values associated with a given time and place, but suggest that values should be inclusive and reflect the accumulated spiritual wisdom of humankind.

In addition to the above, values represent deeply held or widely shared standards that guide individuals or groups in making choices (Kluckhohn & Strodtbeck, 1961). Stein (1985) states that "people not only use values to help them decide among choices but also to help them constantly define who they are, whom they belong to, and who and what are to be regarded as [the] outside" (p. 36).

Values are learned from the family of origin and the community/society in which the individual lives. Values furthermore become the foundation for the frames of reference that people use in making judgements about others and about life in general (Miley, O'Melia, & DuBois, 2000). Simmons and Dvorin (1977) argue that values (or frames of reference) influence policy decisions and the delivery of social services, as well as how these social services are managed. Berne (1995) agrees with this when he states that "there is no such thing as value free work in public service" (p. 82). Furthermore, Larue (1998) articulates the fact that values can undergo change over time. From what all theorists argue, it becomes clear that value pluralism does in fact exist, which means that different persons and groups hold different values, and these values must not be disregarded by social workers in service delivery (Dzur, 1998; Galston, 1999).

Defining Worldview

The worldview of a society is a shared perception of the world, usually shaped by the values of that society. The worldview is the picture created of the way the world is, and it includes the concept of nature, of self, of society and a comprehensive view of order, as well as people's "ethos—the tone, character, and quality of life, [and] its moral and aesthetic style and mood; it is the underlying attitude toward themselves and their world that life reflects" (Gertz as cited in Hutchinson, 1999, p. 279). Worldviews, like cultural values, change continuously according to societal pressures, people's needs, and the function of the worldview. Some values are lost as pressures from the dominant society impose other values leading to an alteration of the worldview.

Worldviews are also linked to the economic system of the culture. In the United States, where capitalism reigns, productivity is emphasized, and those who cannot produce, therefore, are seen as being of less value (i.e., the mentally ill, the disabled, the homeless, and the elderly). These groups have been discriminated against and seen as a drain on the economy and a burden to able-bodied taxpayers. The intrinsic worth of the individual is lost in the race to compete and to make more money.

Values and Culture

Values are greatly influenced by culture. Parents have the greatest influence upon children in their early years, and parents impart their values with modeling and positive reinforcement. Once children are exposed to the larger society, they then begin to question the values of the family, and by the teenage years, children begin to embrace the values of the larger society. This creates major divisions in families who have immigrated to the United States from countries with very different value systems. The parents and grandparents live by the values of their country of origin, while their children are socialized by American educational and social systems to hold values of the larger society. When language differences become an element in this process, parents who do not speak English feel threatened by the society that is taking their children away and teaching them values that differ from their own.

Most people are not conscious of their values; when asked to list their values, many are at a loss to identify them. The most reliable method of identifying one's values are by looking at behavior. Kluckhohn and Strodtbeck (1961) state that there are many possible solutions to human problems in all societies at all times, but these solutions are differentially preferred. Every society has a dominant profile of value orientation.

Theoretical Framework: Value Orientation

Kluckhohn and Strodtbeck's theory of value orientation, tested with consistent results over forty-nine years, has been selected as the most comprehensive and appropriate model. Theoretical predictions, based on anthropological data collected over seven years, were corroborated by the data. In only a very few instances was there a marked discrepancy between the prediction ventured and the result observed. No two cultures surveyed chose exactly the same pattern of preference on any of the orientations. In addition, the degree of similarity and difference proved to be, on the whole, the expected one.

An instrument called the **Value Schedule** measured value orientations reflecting patterns of family organization, economic activity, intellectual interests, religious beliefs and rituals, political behavior, attitudes toward education, and numerous other interests. This instrument was devised to test this theory cross-culturally with two European-American groups, one Spanish-American group, and two American Indian tribal groups.

The theory assumes that a limited number of common human problems exist for which all people at all times must find a solution. It also assumes that, while all problems have a variety of solutions, the solutions are neither limitless nor random, but are within a defined range of possibilities. The third assumption, the one that provides the key to the analysis of value orientation, is that all alternatives for solutions are present in all societies at all times, but are differentially preferred. Every society has a dominant profile of value orientation.

Four problems have been identified as commonly crucial to all human groups. Each problem is presented below as a question and a corresponding value orientation category:

Questions	*Categories of Value Orientation*
What is the modality of human activity?	Activity orientation
What is the modality of man's relationship to others?	Relationship orientation
What is the temporary focus of human life?	Time orientation
What is the relationship of man to nature?	Man–nature orientation

Philosophers have based differences in **activity orientation** on the distinction between **Being** and **Doing**. The **activity orientation** centers on a person's mode of self-expression in activity. **Being** mode prefers spontaneous expression of what is inherent in the human personality. It is a non-developmental conception of activity. **Doing** mode demands activity that results in accomplishments that are measurable by standards external to the individual.

The **relational orientation** refers to a person's relationship with others and consists of subdivisions: the **Lineal**, the **Collateral**, and the **Individualistic**. When the **Lineal** mode dominates, the goal most important to a group is the continuity of the group through time and positional succession. A dominant **Collateral** orientation calls for the goals and welfare of laterally extended groups to be primary. When the **Individualistic** principle dominates, individual goals have primacy over the goals of the collateral or lineal group.

Every society must deal with time problems; all have their conceptions of the past, the present, and the future. **Future-oriented** cultures stress the importance of planning and saving. **Present-focused** cultures stress the importance of the here and now. **Past-oriented** cultures cling to a traditional manner of doing things.

The **man–nature orientation** is established in the works of historians and philosophers. Those who believe that little or nothing can be done to protect themselves from acts of nature are considered subjugated by nature. The concept of being in **Harmony with Nature** indicates no separation of man, nature, and supernatural; each is an extension of the other, and wholeness derives from their unity. The mode of having **Mastery over Nature** believes that natural forces are to be overcome and emphasizes the use of technology (e.g., rivers spanned with bridges).

Definitions of these possible solutions are presented in **Table 5.1** (See page 53), which defines possible solutions to four life problems identified by Kluckhohn and Strodtbeck (1961). To use **Table 1** as an assessment tool in social work practice, the social worker would observe and discuss with the client their thoughts and ideas about values. The social worker would also study the client's culture of origin. The first column lists four problems: Man–Nature; Time; Activity; and Relationship. The second column lists corresponding solutions. Each problem has three possible solutions. The third column defines and explains each solution.

On a recent trip to Korea, Sanders used this model to understand the Korean culture, which enriched her cultural experience and her understanding of the wonderful people there. The chart illuminated the collision of Korea's traditional and modern value systems that manifests itself in Seoul and the towns that surround it. Beautiful sky scrapers and a modern subway system in Seoul proper clash with the traditional architecture in the little towns around Seoul. A characteristic of Korea's traditional architecture is irregular steps; for example, one step might be six inches high and twelve inches deep, while the next step might be twelve inches high and six inches deep. The steps may or may not be level. The brick sidewalks are laid the traditional way with nothing underneath to prevent them from sinking irregularly in the sand. In the midst of the traditional, long-standing buildings with Korean signs are a smattering of American-style businesses (e.g., Burger King, Pizza Hut, and Kodak), but most businesses in the little towns and districts around Seoul are traditional Korean businesses. Aside from the most modern city of Seoul, the Korean landscape does not reflect humanity's desire to dominate nature. In fact, buildings are built on natural hills, accommodating to the hillsides. Markets are built deeply underground so it seems that one can go farther and farther underground and find markets forever.

The time orientation common among Koreans is **present-focused**, although the people also tend to be **past-focused** in some activities (e.g., Koreans have clung to a tradition of bowing when greeting and departing). Their **present focus** is evident in how long it takes to complete tasks (not to mean that Koreans are slow, but rather that their sense of time is different than the American sense of time). For example, a tailor might say that some work would be done tomorrow, but when tomorrow came, the work would not be done. The tailor would say again that the work would be finished the next day, but still it would not be. Americans often lose patience with traditional Koreans because their time orientation is different. Waiters and waitresses serve meals with a present focus; for example, they might serve coffee for one person at a table of two and then come back and serve coffee to the second person later. And, while there is a lot of wealth in Korea, the banks are so broke that the government needs to bail them out; bank executives spend money as if it were unlimited, with no orientation toward saving for the future.

The **activity orientation** of the Korean culture is in the **Being**. This is most apparent when one hails a cab. Cab drivers will pull up to a fare, and if the fare wants to go somewhere that the cab driver does not want to go, the cab driver pulls away without the fare, even if it would have generated a significant amount of money. It is more important for cab drivers **to be** than **to do** the business part of driving the cab—making money. In a restaurant one day, Sanders could not get the dish she wanted because the owner—the only person who could cook the dish—was not in. Businesses open and close depending on what else is going on that day—not on set business hours. Some days people open their stores early, and other days, they might not open at all because something else is going on in their life that takes precedence.

The Korean culture also is **Linear** in **Relationship** Orientation. Family lines are important to Koreans, and marriage to secure the family lineage is expected. Multiple generations operate businesses and live together. The extended family is important, and that children and elders both hold value in Korea is evident throughout the culture.

Using the Kluckhohn–Strodtbeck chart as a cultural value assessment tool can produce information important to understanding a client. It is imperative that social workers build cultural competence, and this involves understanding and respecting value differences.

Guidelines for Social Work Practice

The following are guidelines for applying the theoretical model presented in this chapter:

- Social workers should be aware of the client's activity orientation.
- Social workers should be aware of the client's relationship orientation.
- Social workers should be aware of the client's time orientation.
- Social workers should be aware of the client's man–nature orientation.
- Social workers should be aware of the client's communication patterns.
- Social workers should be aware of how the culture treats its elders.
- Social workers must critically think about their own value orientation and where their values originated.
- Social workers must understand their own frames of reference through which they view the world.
- Social workers must assess the congruence between their own values and those of the social work profession and must adhere to the values presented in the NASW Code of Ethics.
- Social workers must own their own biases and work toward resolving them.

Discussion and Analysis

Activity Orientation

In the United States, mainstream culture values a **Doing orientation**, because it is in harmony with a capitalist economic system. Individuals are judged upon their education and skill level by a criterion that is external to the individual, such as college degrees, credentials, and licenses. The **Being orientation**, on the other hand, is usually valued only in religious institutions and church activities. Very little emphasis is placed upon intrinsic worth in a capitalist society.

Relationship Orientation

In the United States, the mainstream culture values an **Individualistic orientation**, because this also contributes to the capitalist economic system. Individuals are, therefore, encouraged to strike out on their own with little emphasis on the group of origin (Collateral) or of goals for continuity through time (Lineal).

Time Orientation

The mainstream time orientation in the United States is **Future orientation**, with an emphasis on becoming educated to prepare for a life of wealth and comfort; obtaining a job that offers a good retirement program for future comfort and enjoyment; and saving money for old age, just in case the retirement program does not materialize. This emphasis on the future sometimes robs individuals of enjoying the present, valuing lessons learned in the past, or valuing elders who are receptacles of history and education from a different era.

TABLE 5.1 *Definitions of Possible Solutions to Four Life Problems Identified by Kluckhohn & Strodtbeck*

Problem	Solution	Definition
Man–Nature	Subjugation by Nature	Little or nothing can be done about the future; simply accept the inevitable.
	Harmony with Nature	No real separation of man, nature, and supernature; one is simply an extension of the other; a concept of wholeness derives from their unity.
	Mastery over Nature	Natural forces of all kinds are to be overcome and put to use by human beings.
Time	Present	Pay little attention to what has happened in the past and regard the future as both vague and unpredictable.
	Past	Nothing new ever happened in the present or would happen in the future; it has all happened before in the far distant past.
	Future	Emphasis is placed on the future; it will be bigger and better; considers the past to be old fashioned and is not content with the present.
Activity	Being	Preference is for activity that is a spontaneous expression of what is conceived to be "given" in the human personality; non-developmental conception.
	Doing	Demand for activity that results in accomplishments measurable by standards conceived to be external to the acting individual.
Relationship	Individualistic	Individual goals have primacy over the goals of collateral or lineal groups.
	Collateral	Goals and welfare of the laterally extended groups have primacy.
	Lineal	Group goals have primacy; one of the most important goals is continuity through time.

Time orientation is one of the most powerful influences on human behavior. It influences the jobs people seek, the risks they take, the grades they get in school, and the addictions they develop. It also affects whether people take care of their health, whether they floss their teeth, whether they exercise, and much, much more. Furthermore, like other values, people's time orientation influences their activities almost at a subconscious level, and most people are not aware of it.

Choosing balance in time orientation, shifting according to the situation and the tasks at hand, can free people from a restricted time frame. This requires that people examine their biases toward a specific time orientation of a past, present, or future focus, which is usually inherent in their cultural orientation.

Man–Nature Orientation

The mainstream **Man–Nature orientation** in the United States is **Mastery over Nature**. Natural forces of all kinds are overcome and put to the use of human beings; rivers are rerouted by levees, the water used to create electrical energy; buildings and freeways are made earthquake proof, and so forth.

Communication Patterns

Communication patterns vary from culture to culture and may vary within some cultures based upon the educational levels and degrees of acculturation into the dominant society. For example, the communication pattern for Native Americans is indirect, while the communication pattern for African Americans is direct. Some cultures view a quiet, soft-spoken style as showing strength and diplomacy, while others interpret it as showing weakness. Some cultures are uncomfortable with intrusive questioning and become uncooperative in an interview, while **personalismo**, a sharing of one's personal life, is important with the Latino and Native American cultures as an introduction to more in-depth conversation. Communication patterns are based on value systems.

Treatment of Elders

Some cultures place great importance on respecting and listening to the advice of elders. In these cultures, elders are seen as a valuable resource for spiritual connection, guidance, and significant wisdom. Elders find comfort in being part of a great cycle of life, leaving their imprint on children and grandchildren, and they see human relationships as too important to sacrifice to "success." Elders have a more holistic perspective on life unfolding; experience has helped them sort out true value from fool's gold.

The mainstream culture of the United States does not appear to have much respect for elders. Elders are looked upon as unproductive burdens to society and are cast aside to make room for youth. Retirement can, therefore, be a crisis for people in American society because self-esteem for many elders is defined in terms of "being productive."

For many Americans, the aging population is seen as a drain on resources that will bankrupt Social Security and burden the Medicare program. In 1900, the average life span was forty-seven years, and there were three million United States citizens older than sixty-five. In the year 2001, people could expect to live to age seventy-six, and thirty-three million citizens were older than sixty-five. The centenarian population (people over one hundred years of age) is growing, and as the baby boomers age, this population will continue to grow in the coming decades.

The United States' culture has worked with models of aging that limit society and individuals. Aging gracefully has meant surviving disease or staying ceaselessly active—an extension of middle age; or it has meant sitting back and enjoying retirement, but with little meaningful contribution to society. These models are based on ideas of success or youth, and they can make aging feel anticlimactic.

America's focus is on materialism, sex, the latest technology, the latest toys, and the stock market. Instead, society's elders could look for a spiritual model of aging, working creatively through the aging process, taking a journey inward. Retirement can translate to more time for spiritual development, family time, and volunteer service to the community. Life can be about caring, wisdom, spiritual connection, and inner peace. This will take a shift in thinking and values as society ages in the coming decades.

Case Example

James is an American Indian and an active member of his tribe. He has a Native American wife and two sons; the oldest born with Down Syndrome. James comes from a culture where the activity orientation is that of **Being** (DuBray, l985). He values the intrinsic worth of his oldest son and is not concerned that the boy will not be able to achieve in activities that are evaluated externally. He prefers activity that is a spontaneous expression of what is conceived to be **"given"** in the human personality, a non-developmental conception. Had James come from a **Doing** culture, his retarded son might be a great disappointment because he would not be able to achieve academically.

James comes from a culture that values a **Collateral orientation**, placing the welfare of the group first. When making decisions, James consults with family members and the tribe's elders. He does not value individualism, but rather is concerned that his extended family approve of his activities.

James comes from a culture that values a **Present time orientation** (DuBray, 2000). He does not spend much time planning for his retirement; he enjoys the present to the fullest. He pays little attention to what has happened in the past and regards the future as both vague and unpredictable. He does not focus on saving money for the future; he is more concerned about enjoying the present.

James comes from a culture that values **Harmony with Nature** in the **man–nature orientation**. He knows the importance of harmony with family, community, and environment. He places great importance on the conservation of nature's resources. James feels no separation between himself and nature, even supernature; each is simply an extension of the others; therefore, wholeness derives from their unity. James would not build his home or a levee on a river bank; the river bed belongs to the river, and he would not infringe on it by changing the river's path (DuBray, 2000).

Summary

Although people are similar in many ways, they are also different in their value systems, worldviews, and communication patterns. Cultures also define the roles of their members differently, especially their elders. This chapter has discussed value and other cultural differences as they pertain to delivery of social services. As societal diversity increases, it is imperative that social workers come to understand these differences as important elements of human beings, and how they impinge upon and play out in the context of the lives of clients that social workers will be asked to serve. Social workers must also gain an understanding for their own values and worldviews, since they might collide with those of the clients and can affect social work practice with clients. It is only through continued self analysis that social workers will understand their own values and frames of reference. Furthermore, it is only through using social work practice tools, such as the one that is presented in this chapter, that social workers can gain an understanding for their clients' values and frames of reference. To foster growth and understanding for oneself and one's clients is part of social work.

Endnotes

1. For additional information see Kluckhohn, F. R. & Strodtbeck, F. L. (1961). *Variation in value orientation.*

2. For additional information see DuBray, W. (2000), *Mental health interventions with people of color* and DuBray and Sanders (1999), *Interactions between American Indian ethnicity and health care.*

3. For an explanation of acculturation see Lum, D. (1999). *Culturally Competent Practice: A Framework for Growth and Action*, p. 100, and for additional information on assessing acculturation levels see Paniaqua (1994), *Assessing and Treating Culturally Diverse Clients: A Practical Guide.*

4. See DuBray and Leigh, J. (1998). *Communicating for Cultural Competence.*

5. ibid.

6. For additional information see Weaver, H. N. (1999). Indigenous People and the Social Work Profession: Defining Culturally Competent Services, *Social Work, 44*(3), 217–225.

Questions for Critical Thinking

1. How can social workers prepare themselves to work with people who hold different values than theirs?[1]

2. How does cultural competence involve honoring the values of the client?[2]

3. What are the factors involved in the acculturation process?[3]

4. What can social workers do to assist new immigrants in adjusting to U.S. culture?[4]

5. Can social workers be effective working with clients from cultures that are very different from their own?[5]

6. How can social workers engage in ongoing self assessment of their own cultural orientations?[6]

References

Berne, R. (1995). Public administration in the twenty-first century: Beyond the prescriptive buzzwords. *Proceedings of NASPAA*. Austin, TX: NASPAA.

DuBray, W. (1985). American Indian values: Critical factor in casework. *Social Casework, 66*(1), 30–37.

DuBray, W. (1998). *Human services and American Indians* (2nd ed.). Pacific Grove, CA: Brooks/Cole.

DuBray, W. (2000). *Mental health interventions with people of color* (2nd ed.). Cincinnati: Thomson Learning.

DuBray, W., & Sanders, A. (1999). Interactions between American Indian ethnicity and health care. *Journal of Health & Social Policy, 10*(4), 67–84.

Dzur, A. W. (1998, Fall). Values pluralism versus political liberalism. *Social Theory and Practice, 24*(3), 375–376.

Galston, W. A. (1999, December). Value pluralism and liberal political theory. *American Political Science Review, 93*(4), 769–787.

Gibbs, L., & Gambrill, E. (1996). *Critical thinking for social workers*. Thousand Oaks, CA: Pine Forge Press.

Hutchinson, E. D. (1999). *Dimensions of human behavior: Person and environment*. Thousand Oaks, CA: Pine Forge Press.

Inglehart, R. (2000, Winter). Globalization and postmodern values. *The Washington Quarterly, 23*(1), 215–223.

Kluckhohn, F. R., & Strodtbeck, F. L. (1961). *Variation in value orientation*. Evanston, IL: Row, Peterson.

Larue, G. A. (1998, November). On developing human values. *The Humanist*, 38–41.

Leigh, J. W. (1998). *Communicating for cultural competence*. Boston: Allyn & Bacon.

Lum, D. (1999). *Culturally competent practice: A framework for growth and action*. Pacific Grove, CA: Brooks/Cole.

Lynch, T. D., Omdal, R., & Cruise, P. L. (1997, July). Secularization of public administration. *Journal of Public Administration Research and Theory, 7*(3), 473–488.

Miley, K. K., O'Melia, M., & DuBois, B. (2000). *Generalist social work practice: An empowering approach*. Boston: Allyn & Bacon.

Paniaqua, F. A. (1994). *Assessing and treating culturally diverse clients: A practical guide*. Thousand Oaks, CA: Sage Publications.

Rawls, J. (1993). *Political liberalism*. New York: Columbia University Press.

Rohr, J. A. (1978). *Ethics for bureaucrats: An essay on law and values*. New York: Marcel Dekker.

Scheibe, K. E. (1970). *Beliefs and values*. New York: Holt, Rinehart, and Winston.

Simmons, R. H., & Dvorin, E. P. (1977). *Public administration values, policy, and change*. New York: Alfred.

Stein, H. F. (1985). Therapist and family values in a cultural context. *Counseling and Values, 30*(1), 35–46.

Sterba, J. P. (1999, Spring). Reconciling public reason and religious values. *Social Theory and Practice, 25*(1), 1–21.

Weaver, H. N. (1999, May). Indigenous people and the social work profession: Defining culturally competent services. *Social Work, 44*(3), 217–225.

Part III

Ethnocultural/Oppression Perspectives

6

People-of-Color (Ethnic Minority) Framework

Doman Lum

The framework for social work practice with people of color originated in 1986 when this author formulated a process-stage approach for multicultural social work practice (Lum, 1986). This generalist framework for direct practice was designed to orient social work educators, students, and practitioners to working with people of color. It was a conceptual effort to unify similarities among Native, African, Latino, and Asian Americans in order to build an inclusive way of working with these groups. It affirms the similarities yet acknowledges the differences among and between the four major ethnically diverse groups in the United States.

The framework sets an operational perimeter and identifies certain procedural principles for social workers to follow as they work with ethnically diverse clients. It provides the social worker with a degree of flexibility within guidelines and emphasizes specific multicultural subthemes unique to working with people of color.

Generalist social work practice has taught several principles that are incorporated into this framework. First, the people-of-color framework conceptualizes a systematic process-stage approach, following the classic formula of beginning, middle, and end. Second, it offers generalist practice principles universal to people of color and supports them with examples from each of the key ethnic groups. Third, it uses a representative sample of case material from the ethnic clinical literature and develops direct-practice continuity by following a single family case study, the Hernandez family, through the various process stages of contact, problem identification, assessment, intervention, and termination (Lum, 2000).

Core Concepts

The framework for culturally diverse social work practice is based on the conceptual notion that common themes pertain to working with people of color. At the same time we recognize that each of the largest minority groups (Latino American, African American, Asian

American, and Native American) has its own unique cultural history, socioeconomic problems, and treatment approaches. The concepts of cultural commonality and cultural specificity reflect these emphases.

The question is: Can we articulate, from a social work perspective, a framework for culturally diverse practice that applies to people of color in general and yet recognizes particular subgroups? Part of the answer to this question is in the conceptual understanding of etic and emic goals.

Etic Versus Emic Goals

The term *etic* comes from the linguistic study of sounds and refers to the categorization of all the sounds in a particular language. The term *emic* refers to all the meaningful sounds in a particular language. From the cross-cultural perspective of social work practice, these two concepts are used to describe cultural behavior. The etic goal documents principles valid in all cultures and establishes theoretical bases for comparing human behavior. The emic goal documents behavioral principles within a culture and focuses on what the people themselves value as important, unique, and familiar to them (Brislin, 1981).

It is important, from this author's perspective, to maintain both emphases in social work practice; that is, to focus on culture-common characteristics of people of color and to identify and affirm them as well as on culture-specific traits of particular ethnic groups and to note them as distinguishing features.

In the helping situation, whether to focus on the distinctiveness of people or on their generally human universal experience is the choice of the worker. Moreover, it is important to distinguish between what is different and what is maladaptive within the client's culture. The continual shift between discovering what is humanly universal and what is particular to the client's culture makes cross-cultural social work a challenging field of study.

Sundberg (1981) furthered the discussion about universal/etic and culture-specific/emic aspects of counseling that are useful in social work practice. Important characteristics for the counselor to exhibit across cultures and clients are tolerance for anxiety in the client, positive flexibility in responding to the client, confidence in the imparting of helping information and a belief system, and an interest in the client as a person. Culture-specific counseling considers the unique background and personal resources of the individual, particularly his or her unique history, resources, strengths, and ability to use available cultural resources.

The people-of-color framework advocates that the social worker should use both etic and emic perspectives. The worker should discover the etic and emic characteristics of the client and cultural background during contact and relationship building. In a real sense, the worker communicates the message that the client is a human being with basic needs and aspirations (etic perspective) but is also a part of a particular cultural and ethnic group (emic perspective). Moving between these two points of reference is a challenging and creative experience for both worker and client.

Practice Categories

There are four categories within the framework for culturally diverse social work practice: practice process stages, worker-system practice issues, client-system practice issues, and worker–client tasks. Five process stages are used as major divisions of the framework. Practice process stages focus on the logical step-by-step sequence of client and worker movement in the helping process. Social work process has traditionally been characterized in terms of beginning, middle, and end. In this culturally diverse direct-practice framework, the beginning process stages are contact and problem identification; the middle stages include assessment and intervention; and the ending stage is termination.

The terms *client system* and *worker system* refer to those substructures (systems) of the framework that pertain to the individuals within the direct-practice relationship: the worker and the client and their interaction. Awareness of the client- and worker-system practice issues is essential to guiding both parties through the various stages. Many of these practice issues such as problem area detailing, assessment evaluation, and joint goals and agreement are common to most or all encounters between the social worker and the client. Some practice areas such as service delivery, professional self-disclosure, problem orientation, and socioenvironmental impacts must be emphasized and investigated when the client is a person of color.

As a person in the midst of a growth experience, the client must deal with the client-system issues in collaboration with the worker. The worker-system issues are the crucial functions the worker must undertake to move the client through the process stages. Worker–client tasks entail the obligations of the social worker to nurture, understand, learn, and focus. Throughout the middle and ending states, however, the client increasingly interacts, evaluates, creates, changes, and achieves, and in the process, resolves.

Core Principles for Practice

Principle l: Contact

Contact—the establishment of a relationship between social worker and client—consists of such client-system practice issues as *resistance*, *personal and family background*, and *acculturation*; worker-system practice issues as *service delivery*, *relationship protocol*, and *communication style*; and worker–client tasks as *nurturing* and *understanding*.

Contact as a Practice Process Stage.   Establishing a relationship between social worker and client is basic to the contact phase. Relationship is the primary requisite for retaining the client. The client and worker engage each other in the effort to develop a mutually trusting relationship. The client may be hesitant to disclose to the worker due to ethnic and cultural differences. Guadalupe (2000) discusses diversity in terms of a "theory of me" where people must understand their own personal and social identities, especially their identity formation and maintenance. These affect their cultural influence and cultural choice, meanings of identity and its effects, ways that people are similar and different from others, and their bio-psychosocial-cultural means for maintenance or attainment of health and individual well-being. As the client and the worker take the risk to reveal who they are to each other, a "theory of me" becomes a "reality of we."

The worker responds to the client with warmth, empathy, and genuineness (the "we" responses) and demonstrates listening and understanding, respect and concern for the client as a human being, and openness and spontaneity in the situation.

Client-System Practice Issues.   There is a natural *resistance* on the part of clients who are entering the formal helping system. Reasons may be due to institutional racism where the white majority have dominated and represent oppression in the bureaucratic structures. Suspicion and mistrust based on previous institutional contact, anxiety about the unknown, and shame about admitting the need for assistance are natural feelings of clients in general and people-of-color clients in particular. These feelings are exacerbated by racism and discrimination. The client often tests the worker to determine whether he or she has racist values and biases. Social workers should examine themselves for traces of racism and prejudice and evaluate their attitudes toward particular groups. Guadalupe (2000) teaches social work students to own their expressions of bigotry. He recommends, "In other words, rather than attribute a negative characteristic to a social group or to a member of that group, students begin with, 'this is how I have been taught to believe,' or 'I don't like to admit it but I do have the belief that . . .' " (p. 4). Sensitizing social workers at the beginning of their education to racism, sexism, and homophobia are important steps.

Personal and family background plays a major role in the contact stage. It is a natural way of beginning. Asking about ethnic family background may be an important signal to a client that his or her ethnicity is valuable information for the social work practitioner. The worker might ask, Tell me about your family? Where did your father and mother come from? How do you identify yourself? These areas for preliminary conversation may be relevant, depending on the client's responses, and may open up natural topics.

It is important to determine the client's *acculturation* to society. Acculturation is the process of adapting and adjusting to the dominant society as a member of a particular culture of origin. Although previous ethnic generations coming to America have abandoned their cultures of origin to become of the American melting pot, there has been a renaissance of the history and culture of ethnic groups. The revival of cultural awareness has led many third and fourth generations of culturally diverse people to rediscover their past cultural heritage and learn the history and language of their forebears. These later generations have embraced cultural pride and identity, adopting an ethnic life pattern. Some new immigrants are moving toward partial assimilation of American lifestyle and behavior patterns, which conflict with traditional cultural values. Parents tend to preserve authoritarian family roles and traditional values and are thus at odds with their children, who are exposed to the independent and individualistic lifestyles of their school and neighborhood peers. These parents often must deal with their experience of displacement and with economic and social uncertainty in their new homeland. Unable to find a comparable job or speak English fluently there is a role reversal where parents are dependent on their children who are able to make adjustments and negotiate with social institutions.

Fellin (2000) advocates four principles of multiculturalism and human diversity:

1. A multicultural perspective should be inclusive of all subcultural groups, viewed as distinct groups that are interdependent with mainstream U. S. culture.

2. A multicultural perspective should recognize that all people in U. S. society identify with "multiple cultures," with varying degrees of affiliation and social involvement.

3. A multicultural perspective should recognize that all members of U. S. society engage in various types of relationships within their various cultures, and in relation to a mainstream U. S. culture. Biculturalism, acculturation, amalgamation, and assimilation, as forms of attachment and social relationships with these cultures, are proposed as options for members of U. S. society.

4. A multicultural perspective would recognize the changing nature of U. S. society, as it is continually influenced by all of its subcultures, and by national demographic, social, and institutional trends (pp. 271–272).

Another important variable is the client's sense of ethnic community identity or the degree to which a person readily participates in the life and activity of his or her ethnic enclave. A continuum of ethnic community participation ranges from no or minimal contact to full involvement. Helping a client or family sort out their cultural conflicts in the acculturation adjustment process (e.g., traditional cultural values and traditions and family beliefs and practices vs. dominant societal mores and behavior) is a starting point for contact in practice with many people-of-color groups who are recent arrivals. For clients who have grown up in the United States and are in the process of becoming aware of their cultural identity issues, social work may focus on the rediscovery of past cultural values and tradition and the meaning of their ethnicity.

Worker-System Practice Issues.   To establish contact with ethnic communities and people-of-color clients, it is crucial for the social service agency to set up a responsive system of *service delivery* to meet multicultural client needs. Bilingual/bicultural workers, community education and prevention outreach programs, accessible facility location, and minimal fees can increase the use of services by people of color. To shape service delivery appropriately, social service agency administrators must understand the ethnic community. They should meet with ethnic community leaders and groups in their catchment area (mandated service region) to ascertain social needs, determine staff composition, and plan relevant programs. Social service staff should be oriented to the various ethnic client communities and their socioeconomic needs, lifestyle, and other key elements. Out of this data analysis should flow relevant treatment programs and intervention strategies. This groundwork must be performed before actual contact with clients.

When engaging an ethnic client, the social worker must observe certain *relationship protocols*, such as addressing the client by his or her surname, making formal introductions, acknowledging the elder or head of household as the authority, and conveying respect through other means. Rather than focusing immediately on the problem, the social worker should practice professional self-disclosure, whereby a point of interest common to the client and the worker becomes a means of forming a relationship. The worker should also structure the initial session to reduce anxiety by explaining the functions and procedures of the agency, the purpose of the sessions, and the range of problems encountered among a broad spectrum of clients. The social worker's *communication style* should convey friendliness, interest, and empathetic understanding; it is important to make the client feel at ease.

By modeling a relaxed and open personal attitude, the worker evokes a similar response from the client.

During the contact phase, the social worker gains a preliminary perspective on the client's psychosocial functioning. This perspective is based on the information that flows from the reciprocal interaction of the client and the environment. The emphasis is on obtaining a sense of adequate functioning or dysfunctioning as the person in the situation emerges.

Worker–Client Tasks.   *Nurturing* is crucial to the contact stage. The worker must communicate a willingness to engage in positive mutual involvement. Offering food and drink at the beginning of a session communicates the idea that nurturing is important. Translating this symbolic act into emotional nurturing involves healthy doses of empathy, warmth, and genuineness, which develop into rapport, openness, and trust. A client may reciprocate by inviting the worker to his or her home for a social activity or by bringing fruit, candy, or a token of appreciation to the session. If the worker is able to recognize and accept the meaning of this act, it can shape a mutually giving process.

Understanding is an important worker–client task. The worker should use open-ended reflection, recognizing the primacy of the client's feelings and thoughts. Understanding develops through careful listening and paraphrasing of the client's expressed thoughts and feelings to clarify or acknowledge the message communicated. These responses at the contact stage open up the client, releasing pent-up emotions and thought remnants that require later follow-up.

Principle 2: Problem Identification

Problem identification—delineating unsatisfied wants and unfulfilled needs—covers such client-system practice issues as *problem information*, *problem disclosure*, **and** *problem definition*; **worker-system practice issues such as** *problem orientation*, *problem levels and themes*, **and** *problem detailing*; **and worker–client tasks of** *learning* **and** *focusing*.

Problem Identification as a Practice Process Stage.   After contact has been established, a problem or a problem cluster set (a group of related problems) invariably emerges in the course of worker–client dialogue. Some clients continually face basic problems of survival such as unemployment, poor health, and substandard housing. Other clients are beset by situational, transitional, and life-stage problems due to circumstances and age crises. Problems have a chronological beginning and a progression toward a crisis climax. Tracing the history of a problem gives the worker a notion of what has happened to the client.

Client-System Practice Issues in Problem Identification.   When the client first conveys *problem information* to the worker, the client might need time to develop trust and overcome shame. Once the client can be assured that information about the problem will not be used against him or her, he or she will become more open with *problem disclosure*. Laird (1998) recommends taking an "informed not-knowing" stance, without appearing to be the expert, right, or in possession of the truth. Rather Laird (1998) explains: ". . . I believe that only if we become as informed as possible—about ourselves and those whom we perceive as different—will we be able to listen in a way that has the potential for surfacing our own cultural biases and recognizing the cultural narratives of the other" (p. 23). In a sense sharing a problem is revealing a narrative experience of one person to another. The worker and the client have the opportunity to understand a problem from two different perspectives. Furthermore, detailing a problem's chronological development helps the worker understand the person's historical journey and allows the worker to gain insight into the client and his or her ethnic or collective family and community.

Worker-System Practice Issues.   In the people-of-color framework, problems are regarded as unsatisfied wants or unfulfilled needs. This *problem orientation* contrasts with the pathological viewpoint, which is detrimental to people of color. Rather than trying to uncover the dysfunctional aspect of a problem, the worker interprets the problem as symptomatic of a positive striving that has been hindered by an obstacle in the client's life. This perspective casts a strengths dynamic on the identification of problems.

Various *problem levels and themes* are useful in categorizing the multifaceted problems of people of color. Recognition of micro (individual, family, and small group), meso (ethnic/local communities and organizations), and macro (complex organizations, geographic populations) levels intersect and layer the nature of problem identification. Parallel to problem levels may be a minority problem typology constituting the cognitive beliefs of racism, sexism, homophobia, the attitude of prejudice, and the resulting behavior of discrimination. Expressions of racism, sexism, and homophobia are seen in oppression, powerlessness, exploitation, acculturation, and stereotyping.

In problem identification, the psychosocial perspective focuses on the client's environment. *Problem detailing* entails matching the appropriate problem levels and themes. Ethnic clients tend to confront multiple problems. For example, African Americans and Latinos in urban industrial jobs have been laid off because of economic recession. Depression, loss of self-esteem, and family conflict have led to behavioral problems such as alcoholism, child abuse, and attempted suicide. Detailing these problems implies matching macro (state of the economy) and micro (unemployed worker and his or her family) levels with the problem theme of powerlessness.

Worker–Client Tasks.   Throughout problem identification, the tasks of the social worker and the client are learning and focusing. *Learning* consists of uncovering essential problem themes and then detailing them with facts. It is, above all, a mutual growth process, more so for the worker than the client in many respects. Laird (1998) reminds us, "For if we do not learn about our own cultural selves and the culture of the other, it will be difficult to move beyond our own cultural lenses and biases when we encounter practices that we do not understand or find distasteful; we will not be able to ask the questions that help surface subtle ethnic, gender, or sexuality meanings; and we may not see or hear such meanings when they are right there in front of us" (p. 22). *Focusing* is part of the learning process for the worker and the client. It occurs when the worker and client decide to settle on a particular problem that both parties consider primary. As the worker probes and the client responds, both learn about dimensions of the problem.

The worker describes the problem as a logical sequence of events on the basis of information supplied by the client. The client gains new insights into the problem. Which segment of the problem seems most manageable to the worker and client? What portion of the problem can most readily be detailed, studied, and analyzed? What is the sequence or pattern of problem events? Who are the actors involved? When does the problem occur? Where is the problem located? Problem identification moves from general learning about problem issues to focusing on a specific problem.

Principle 3: Assessment

Assessment—the interaction between person and environment—centers on such client-system practice issues as *socioenvironmental conditions* and *psycho-individual reactions*; worker-system practice issues as *cognitive, affective, and behavioral dimensions*; and worker–client tasks of *interaction* and *evaluation*.

Assessment as a Practice Process Stage.   In social work practice, assessment generally involves an in-depth study of a psychosocial problem affecting the client. Its purpose is to analyze the interaction of client and situation and to plan recommendations for intervention. How does the environmental problem affect the client? What resources are necessary to respond to the problem? With a person of color, it is useful to identify cultural strengths, significant others, and community support systems. Interactions of client and environment can change. It is important at each session for the client to brief the worker and for the worker to ask the client what has happened since the last session, because the focus of the problem may have changed, new factors may have been introduced, and strategies for change may need revision. Moreover, assessing entry points of change in the immediate client's environment is the heart of assessment.

Client-System Practice Issues.   Psychosocial assessment concerns the impact of the social environment on the individual client. *Socio-environmental conditions* affect and produce *psycho-individual reactions*. The influence of society is a strong force that shapes the reaction of people of color. Racially motivated hate crimes such as firebombing of churches and synagogues, murders of ethnic people of color and gays, and other related violence set the tone for how culturally diverse persons perceive the social disorder of the nation.

Positive social environment affects psycho-individual reactions in terms of self-esteem and ethnic strength. To what extent does a particular client value and maintain his or her culture? Extended family, kinship networks, church, respect for the elderly, art, music, and other cultural expressions are cultural assets that people of color use to fortify themselves.

Worker-System Practice Issues.   The psychosocial perspective on assessment focuses on the interaction of client and environment. On the *cognitive* level, the ethnic mind-set of the person of color affects thought patterns learned from parents, experiences, and formal and informal learning in his or her ethnic group. The individual incorporates a past, present, and future life script of his or her ethnic history. These learning situations form the basis of the individual's cognitive mind-set. In subsequent interactions with people, past experiences color a person's cognitive perception and response.

Assessment categories of cognition focus on intelligence, judgment, reality testing, coherence, flexibility, and self-concept. The worker must begin to assess the extent to which the client recognizes and analyzes the action of a racist society and still functions with ethnic-oriented ideas and beliefs about living. A person of color can cope by using a strong ethnic frame of reference, particularly cognitive thinking about who he or she is and about the reality of a racist society.

The client's *affect* involves the extent to which feeling states are expressed or masked to a range of persons: family, friends, acquaintances, people of color, and white persons. It is not unusual for people of color to change their affect responses according to their degree of familiarity with others present. Cultural limitations may restrict the expression of feelings. How affect is expressed in nonverbal communication is a crucial consideration in assessing ethnic clients.

Akin to the cognitive and affective states are the *behaviors* of the person that result from conscious decision making. An individual acts for a specific reason. In a threatening situation, a person of color may respond passively and stoically. A client may feel threatened in an unfamiliar setting or thoroughly at ease in a culturally familiar environment. The social worker can create an environment that puts clients at ease. The psychosocial perspective on the cognitive, affective, and behavioral dimensions of the ethnic client brings unique cultural knowledge to bear on clinical situations.

Worker–Client Tasks.   In the assessment stage, the worker-client tasks consist of interaction and evaluation. In the *interaction* process, the worker and client sort through multiple cultural environmental factors and settle on those that have an effect on the problem. In the process, the worker is the inquirer and learner, and the client teaches and clarifies. The philosophy is patterned after the ethnographic interviewing and learning. *Evaluation* identifies individual and environmental factors useful in designing an appropriate intervention strategy. It appraises the changes necessary to alter the client's situation. When detailed information has been assembled about the problem situation, the client's cultural resources, and the community support system, the evaluation process culminates in the establishment of intervention goals, a contract, and procedural strategies to implement changes. Attention focuses on present conditions, selected past events that influence the current problem, and the client's capabilities and motivation to work on the problem.

Principle 4: Intervention

Intervention—a strategy of change (coming in-between)—involves such client-system and worker-system practice issues as *joint participation in setting goals and a contract agreement*, *selection of an intervention strategy*, and *types of intervention*; and it involves worker–client tasks of *creating* and *changing*.

Intervention as a Practice Process Stage.   Social work intervention is based on a strategy for change that modifies and resolves the problem situation. Intervention occurs when the client's biopsychosocial needs are met through material and supportive resources in the individual, family, and community. The purpose of intervention is to effect change in the client and in the environment for mutual improvement.

Client-System and Worker-System Practice Issues.   The people-of-color framework joins the client and worker systems together, since intervention should be a collaborative and agreed-upon effort. The client and the worker *participate jointly in setting goals and a contract agreement.* Goals are terminal outcomes, while objectives are intermediate sub-goals that end with the accomplishment of goals.

Selection of an intervention strategy depends on the nature of the problem, the client's background, and the worker's professional judgment. It should be based on certain objective criteria:

1. Examine and resolve the problem.
2. Focus on immediate past and present time sequences related to the problem.
3. Alter the psychosocial dimensions of the problem.
4. Require tasks to mobilize the client in focused positive action.
5. Demonstrate in measurable terms that change has occurred in the problem area.

Types of intervention include the micro level involving task-centered problem-solving, crisis intervention, empowerment, existential, woman-centered perspective, family therapy, group work, and treating refugees and immigrants; the meso level involving the community, extended family, and the church; and the macro level centering on community networks, community organizing, and political impact. Ethnic intervention themes are liberation, empowerment, parity, maintenance of culture, and unique personhood.

Worker–Client Tasks.   The worker–client tasks of the intervention stage revolve around creating and changing. In formulating new ways to deal with existing problems, the worker and client are *creating.* Both facilitate movement and direction to implement the creative formulations devised in collaboration with each other. The interweaving of worker, client, community, and service in infinite variations means that each case involves a new creation.

The task of *changing* provides movement from one situation to another. Rather than talking to the client about the general idea of change, the worker provides specific courses of action that alter the situation. Clinical practice should emphasize change and measure its effect on the client and situation from point to point in a series of goal-oriented changes. The ethnic community must change unjust and exploitative social policies, regulatory laws, and institutional practices that are not in the best interest of people of color. In multicultural practice, intervention must encompass both clinical and community dimensions.

Principle 5: Termination

Termination—ending and closure—denote such client-system and worker-system practice issues as *destination* (arrival), *recital* (review), and *completion* (goal achievement); and it involves worker–client tasks of *achieving* and *resolving.*

Termination as a Practice Process Stage.   Termination denotes a closure of the relationship between client and worker. It may end the sessions that have focused on problems that have been identified and resolved. Termination can also mean major adjustment of goals and intervention approaches, resulting in a new series of sessions. This involves redefining the problem and negotiating new goals and intervention strategies. In some instances, termination results from counterproductive factors such as numerous client absences or a lack of significant movement on the problem. These factors may be due to unresolved client resistance, cultural and personal barriers, dissonance between the personalities of worker and client, or events beyond their control.

Client-System and Worker-System Practice Issues.   *Arrival* at a destination defines successful termination. Involvement or rejoining the client to his or her ethnic community is an example of an arrival point. That is, when an ethnic person is reunited and reconnected to his or her ethnic community, there is an arrival after a long journey away from one's roots. Measurable growth, insight, and change between contact and termination process stages is an accurate indicator of the progress made. *Recital* involves reviewing positive changes that have occurred in the helping process by taking a retrospective view and reflecting on what has happened at certain points in the client's life. *Completion* is the achievement of goals and resolution of issues, attended by a sense of accomplishment.

Follow-up strategies involve maintaining contact with the client after the conclusion of the practice sessions. Telephone calls and periodic follow-up meetings over several months help to evaluate the client's progress after completion of social services.

Worker–Client Tasks.   *Achieving* carries the connotation of accomplishing and attaining a certain goal. For the worker, it consists of helping the client through a problem. For the client, it means sustaining the effort to change a psycho-social situation related to the person and the problem. *Resolving* places closure on decision making and imparts a sense of finality.

Case Example

The Hernandez family case study is an integral part of the framework in *Social Work Practice and People of Color: A Process-Stage Approach* (Lum, 2000). Mr. Hernandez, age thirty-eight, is a Mexican American who works as a gardener. He and his family are making an inquiry at the Family Service Association (FSA) agency regarding a problem that one of his children is having in school. Ricardo has become disruptive in class, and his grades for the past six weeks have been poor. Mr. Hernandez has been under increasing pressure during the last few months to support his family and several in-laws who have moved to Los Angeles from Mexico. Because the unemployment rate for immigrants is high, his in-laws are having difficulty supporting themselves. Mr. Hernandez feels responsible for them and is working two jobs; as a result, he is unable to help Ricardo with his homework or play with him. Mrs. Hernandez, who works in a laundry part-time, cannot speak or read English. Mr. and Mrs. Hernandez have two other children besides Ricardo: Isabella, age eight, and Eduardo, age six. Mr. Hernandez is feeling extreme stress and taking it out on the children.

Contact

A White staff member, Mr. Platt, has been assigned the Hernandez case because the agency's Spanish-speaking worker has a full caseload. The Latino social worker will serve as a consultant and support base for multicultural issues that arise in the case.

Mr. Platt has worked with ethnically diverse clients in public welfare and in the FSA agency. He has traveled in Mexico and Central America and knows some Spanish phrases, but cannot carry on an extended conversation in Spanish. He begins by greeting the family and talking with Mr. Hernandez. He shares his travel experiences in Mexico: the various cities, people, and food. He asks about the Hernandez family and their upbringing in Mexico. He does not focus on the presenting problem; instead, he puts the family at ease by speaking Spanish. They laugh at his pronunciation of some Spanish words and phrases.

Mr. Platt talks about the agency's program and services. He explains the meaning of the helping process and gives them a brochure, written in English and Spanish, that explains the services and fee schedule. Mr. Platt notices that Mr. Hernandez speaks some English and can make himself understood, although he hesitates over a few words and concepts. Mrs. Hernandez speaks Spanish fluently but knows little English. The children speak English and assist in translation between the parents and the social worker. The parents speak to the children in Spanish throughout the session. Mr. Platt asks each family member how he or she feels about coming to Family Services and whether he or she is willing to continue the sessions. For Mr. Platt, the goal of the first session with the Hernandez family is to become acquainted with them. He puts the family at ease, acknowledges the authority of the father, and asks how the family feels about coming to the agency.

The second family session is a home visit where Mr. Hernandez tells the social worker about Ricardo's school problems: his poor grades, his truancy, and Ricardo's verbal abuse against his father's absence from home in the evenings. Mr. Platt listens and supports Mr. Hernandez. He reflects feelings, restates thoughts, summarizes major points, and clarifies certain areas.

Problem Identification

At the third session, Mr. Platt shares some of the conversation he has had with Ricardo's teacher. He mentions that the teacher, Mrs. Villa, is concerned about Mr. Hernandez's long hours. By relaying the teacher's expression of concern, Mr. Platt gives Mr. Hernandez an opening to express his feelings about the past three months. Rather than confronting Mr. Hernandez, Mr. Platt allows him to disclose the problems he's having, and the social worker gives Mr. Hernandez support as he tells about his two jobs, long working hours, and economic burdens.

Mr. Hernandez feels a family obligation to support his in-laws until they can find steady employment. Since the two families of in-laws arrived from Mexico, the husbands have held part-time jobs washing dishes in Mexican restaurants and harvesting tomatoes. Moreover, Mr. Hernandez and his in-laws feel they must send money to Mexico to support their elderly parents who are retired and living on small pensions. Mrs. Hernandez states that her family in Mexico sent money to them when they came to the United States ten years ago, and now it is their turn to support her family's immigration. Mr. Hernandez, however, recognizes that the demands on his time due to this obligation will not allow him to spend more time with Ricardo and help him with his homework.

Assessment

The Hernandez family case is an example of socio-environmental impacts interacting with psycho-individual reactions. Social work family assessment reveals socioeconomic survival issues. The arrival of in-laws from Mexico as recent immigrants to an uncertain economy has shifted a great financial burden to Mr. Hernandez. He will soon be unable to cope with the demands of the extra work. His obligation is to ensure adequate support for the other two families until his brothers-in-law can find steady employment; however, Mr. Hernandez complains of fatigue and the long hours he spends working at two jobs.

The social worker's task is to not only assess the community's resources for job hunting, school tutoring, English classes, and newcomer services, but also to assess areas such as role identity and stress tolerance that are affecting the family.

The Hernandez family's strengths are emerging. Mr. Platt notes the husband's and wife's energy and determination to work overtime and provide for their extended family's needs. He assesses the strengths available from the Latino community's support network in the local ethnosystem. Rather than clinically assessing the relationship between the father and son, Mr. Platt evaluates how external ethnic services could be marshaled and implemented to realign the family and reduce their stress.

Intervention

Based on what they have learned through contact, problem identification, and assessment, the Hernandez family and Mr. Platt are ready to devise an intervention strategy to cope with the three families' job situation and the eldest child's academic performance. Goal outcomes, expected behavioral changes, and task objectives revolve around resettlement support and job hunting for the in-laws, tutoring for the son, English classes for the mother, and a lighter workload for the father.

Mr. Platt will manage the case to coordinate resources in the ethnic community toward implementing these goal outcomes. Each family member will be responsible for following through on appointments made for job hunting, tutoring assistance, classes in English as a second language (ESL), and newcomers' services. The family and Mr. Platt agree that, within the next two weeks, he will contact Catholic Social Services, located in the neighborhood Mexican American church, and he will follow up on the effects of the services they provide a few weeks afterward. A number of behavioral changes will be expected during those four weeks.

Having established an intervention strategy, Mr. Platt begins to implement the plan with community resources and family members. Indispensable to the success of the plan is Father Carlos, a Catholic priest who directs the local satellite center for Catholic Social Services. He commands the respect of the community both as a Latino clergyman and as a competent, warm administrator of ethnic social service programs. Over the years, Father Carlos has brought together job hunting, tutoring, child care, and newcomers' services under one roof and identified the church as a practical instrument for helping with the problems of the Latino community.

At the next session the Hernandez family reports that the brothers-in-law were interviewed by a Spanish-speaking social worker who knew of a number of job openings with a local contractor. Although they are not skilled trade workers, the brothers-in-law have a promise of steady employment with apprentice-class status. Mr. Hernandez is able to take a leave of absence from his second job to spend evenings with his family. Ricardo has been assigned a high school senior to tutor him in math, spelling, and social studies. Mrs. Hernandez is taking an ESL class through the school district's adult education program. A Mexican American woman volunteering at the newcomers' center has helped the wives of the in-law families with practical problems of adjusting to immigration. The intervention plan is in motion and appears to be running smoothly.

Termination

At the four-week session, Mr. Platt encourages review of the family's major progress, changes, and goal achievements. It is apparent that the intervention plan is taking hold with the Hernandez family and their in-laws. The brothers-in-law are working steadily for the Mexican American contractor, and their families seem to be adjusting to urban American life. Mrs. Hernandez is enjoying her ESL class. Several of her friends are classmates, and the family helps her practice English words and sentences. Mr. Hernandez is home nearly every night with his children, particularly helping Ricardo with his homework. The latest report from Ricardo's teacher says that he is doing his work at school and is more relaxed and happier than he was a month ago.

Mr. Platt, the social worker, is satisfied with the progress the families have made. They have become linked to resources within their ethnic community. The families have gained a sense of satisfaction and pride in the many positive changes occurring in the family, and a sense of hope in knowing that further assistance is available in the Latino community. Together, the church, school, and social services have forged a strategy to help these families in need.

At their termination session, Mr. Platt and the Hernandez family agree to taper off on meetings. Mr. Hernandez will call Mr. Platt weekly to brief him on the family's progress. They will meet in a month for a progress update, to assess the extent of growth and to evaluate the usefulness of the ethnic community's social service system. Mr. Hernandez feels the family has been strengthened and can now handle other adversities should they arise, because they know how to use social services available in the local Latino community.

Mr. Platt recommends final termination if the family is still functioning adequately at home and school after another month, but welcomes the family to contact him at the Family Service Association if necessary in the future.

Contributions and Limitations

Lum's process-stage framework for people of color social practice has gained a steady stream of recognition in the social work field. Lum's framework has moderately influenced social work practice and multicultural social work during the last two decades. Devore and Schlesinger (1999) summarized Lum's process-stage approach in their pioneer and landmark text *Ethnic-sensitive social work practice*: "Lum (1992) aimed to break new ground by focusing on key differences between the emphases in current social work practice and minority characteristics, beliefs, and behaviors. He believes that social workers' professional orientation must be reexamined from the viewpoint of ethnic minorities, and he presented a framework for ethnic minority practice by proceeding from the assumption that minorities share a similar predicament as well as values and beliefs and that practice protocols applicable to these minorities can be developed" (p. 133). They, however, raise issues related to minority values that unify all people-of-color groups and want to include other issues and groups such as recency of migration, generational distinctions, and inclusion of European American groups such as Jewish and Italian people under an ethnic-sensitive perspective.

Hepworth, Rooney, and Larsen (1997) have strengthened their emphasis on cultural consideration in social work practice as a result of the people-of-color framework. They observe, "As Lum (1992) has indicated, minority persons may feel uncomfortable with non-minorities but mask their emotions as a protective measure. Moreover, in the presence of nonminority practitioners, minority persons may control painful emotions according to culturally prescribed behavior. An Asian American, for example, may react with politeness, quietness, and friendliness in the face of an overwhelming and threatening situation" (p. 251). Hepworth, Rooney, and Larsen have also acknowledged the importance of considering cultural norms and values and organizing ethnic client groups, both concepts from the people-of-color framework. At the same time Hepworth, Rooney, and Larsen lack a central focus on cultural diversity in their direct social work practice text, which is widely used by social work educators and students.

Recently, in a summary of the state of multiculturalism in social work, Fellin (2000) deals with the term *people of color* and interacts with the following points from the people-of-color framework: the construction of the term that encompasses the cultures of African Americans, Asian Americans, Hispanic/Latino Americans, and Native Americans; the use of the term to distinguish these groups from white populations, especially in relation to cultural diversity and discrimination and oppression in U. S. society; the primary focus of culturally diverse social work practice; and the limited coverage of people of color and their cultures in professional literature.

Sources for Further Study

Lum, Doman. *Social Work Practice and People of Color: A Process-Stage Approach*, 4th ed., Belmont, CA: Wadsworth/Thomson Learning, 2000. This text embodies the people of color framework. It starts with background chapters covering culturally diverse social work practice, people of color, culturally diverse values, and social work knowledge theory. The framework for social work practice with people of color is explained in depth with a chapter for each of the five process stages: contact, problem identification, assessment, intervention, and termination.

Lum, Doman. *Culturally Competent Practice: A Framework for Growth and Action*, Pacific Grove, CA: Brooks/Cole, 1999. This book is a companion volume to *Social Work Practice and People of Color*. It introduces cultural competence as the latest multicultural theme and its implications for multicultural social work practice. A framework for cultural competency is set forth with subsequent chapters on cultural awareness, knowledge acquisition, skill development, and inductive learning. The skill-development chapter summarizes the essence of the five process stages, which are arranged into process, conceptualization, and personalization skill clusters, and culturally diverse service delivery.

Questions for Critical Thinking

1. What social work practice conceptual framework encompassing all people-of-color groups might you design from your perspective?

2. What are your etic (universal) and emic (specific) cultural concerns for all people of color and for a particular people-of-color group that you could explain and differentiate?

3. What are the beginning, middle, and ending stages of social work practice with people of color that you consider are important to articulate in your practice perspective?

4. What cultural diversity and people-of-color social work practice issues concern you at this time?

5. Where does culturally diverse and culturally competent social work practice need to go in the next three years from a conceptual theory and practical skill basis?

References

Brislin, R. W. (1981). *Cross-cultural encounters: Face-to-face interaction.* New York: Pergamon.

Devore, W., & Schlesinger, E. G. (1999). *Ethnic-sensitive social work practice.* Boston: Allyn & Bacon.

Fellin, P. (2000). Revisiting multiculturalism in social work. *Journal of Social Work Education, 36,* 261–278.

Guadalupe, J. L. (2000). SW 202 (model syllabus) Social work and diverse populations: Theory and practice. California State University, Sacramento. Division of Social Work.

Hepworth, D. H., Rooney, R. H., & Larsen, J. (1997). *Direct social work practice: Theory and skills.* Pacific Grove, CA: Brooks/Cole.

Laird, J. (1998). Theorizing culture: Narrative ideas and practice principles. In M. McGoldrick (Ed.), *Re-visioning family therapy: Race, culture, and gender in clinical practice* (pp. 20–30). New York: Guilford.

Lum, D. (1986). *Social work practice and people of color: A process-stage approach.* Monterey, CA: Brooks/Cole.

Lum, D. (2000). *Social work practice and people of color: A process-stage approach.* Belmont, CA: Wadsworth/Thomson Learning.

Sundberg, N. D. (1981). Research and research hypotheses about effectiveness in intercultural counseling. In P. B. Pedersen, J. G. Draguns, W. J. Lonner, & J. E. Trimble (Eds.), *Counseling across cultures* (pp. 304–342). Honolulu: University of Hawaii Press.

7

Dual Perspective Framework

Arline W. Prigoff

Rarely is a conceptual framework developed with the degree of conscious planning and team effort that went into the formulation of the dual perspective. The task of conceptualizing a framework to facilitate the application of ethnic minority perspectives in social work practice was undertaken by a project under the auspices of the Council on Social Work Education (CSWE) in the 1970s.

Major Precursors and Developers

Dolores G. Norton was author and editor of a CSWE publication in 1978 on the concepts produced by the project, including topics on ethnic community issues authored by Edwin Garth Brown, Kenji Murase, E. Aracelis Francis, Ramon Valle, and Eddie Frank Brown.

> The concept of the dual perspective grew out of the work of a group of social work educators struggling to develop specific content and models for incorporating content on minorities into the social work curriculum. A series of meetings sponsored by the Council on Social Work Education in which educators discussed the problems and issues involved and shared materials began to yield a common theme: to prepare social workers to meet the needs of their total client system in a pluralistic society, social work education must produce graduates who are capable of understanding and intervening from a dual perspective. . . .
> The work of Leon Chestang of the University of Chicago, Edwin Garth Brown of the University of Utah, and E. Aracelis Francis of Adelphi University, who served as workshop leaders in many of the seminars and contributed their notes and suggestions, was crucial to the development of the concept. (Norton, 1978, p. v)

Prior to the date of that publication, Aracelis Francis had served as CSWE staffer for a Black Task Force and as editor of the *Black Task Force Report: Suggested Guides for the Integration of Black Content into the Social Work Curriculum,* published by CSWE in 1973. Several faculty members participated in the work of the Black Task Force, and published papers in 1972 that were circulated at Black Task Force meetings. The ideas presented in those papers were influential in shaping the perspectives presented in the *Black Task Force Report,* and the papers were listed in its bibliography. *The Black Task Force Report* notes this suggestion:

> . . . to utilize a conceptual framework of colonialism as a way of reviewing past and present relationships between whites and minorities in America, especially Blacks, and to speculate about the merits of a compensatory justice approach in the field of social welfare and the profession of social work. (Francis, 1978, p. 13)

A paper on "Neocolonialism and Compensatory Justice" by James A. Bush of the Ohio State University School of Social Work is then quoted,

> James A. Bush points out that the analogy of Blacks in America to classic colonialism is an imperfect one, but many factors are apparent that make the term "domestic colonialism" or "neocolonialism" applicable. Ghettos of America can be considered colonies or communities where ethnic minorities are exploited by white American realtors, landlords, civil servants, small businessmen, large corporations, and politicians. "For White Americans neocolonialism provides the advantage of *profit, privilege* and *power—*the three P's of colonialism." (Bush, 1972, as cited in Francis, 1973, p. 13)

Leon W. Chestang's paper on "Character Development in a Hostile Society," published in 1972, is mentioned in the *Black Task Force Report* as a " fairly clear formulation of the concept" that maturational processes are likely to be adversely affected by conflicts between behavioral norms and expectations of the self and those of society. Issues introduced in that paper were further developed in Chestang's chapter on "Environmental Influences on Social Functioning: The Black Experience," in *The Diverse Society: Implications for Social Policy,* published by NASW in 1976.

> Three conditions, socially determined and institutionally supported, characterize the black experience: social injustice, societal inconsistency, and personal impotence. The failure of many majority-group Americans to appreciate the psychic impact of these conditions can be attributed to the absence of what Warren calls an "institutional thought structure" supporting any but an individual-deficit model for understanding social problems. (Chestang, 1976, p. 61)

The CSWE publication, *The Dual Perspective: Inclusion of Ethnic Minority Content in the Social Work Curriculum,* also included chapters that were based on the work of other members of the CSWE ethnic minority task forces. Kenji Murase, author of the chapter on "Social Welfare Policy and Services: Asian Americans," wrote,

> . . . this source book represents an acknowledgement that commitment to the concept of ethnic pluralism requires that we look to the minority communities to define the Asian-American experience, the Black experience, the Latino experience, and the American Indian experience, each from their own perspective. This means that for social work education to be authentic and applicable to the needs of minority communities, the conceptual definitions and program implementation must involve the participation of the minority communities

concerned. This means that we must look to Asian-American communities for their definition of the Asian experience in America from their own perspective, for their articulation of the survival needs of their communities, and for their perceptions of the posture, strategy, and actions necessary for their own liberation and enhancement. . . .

The dual perspective, when applied to the history of Asians in America, can provide a basis for assessment and understanding of the profound impact of historical antecedents upon the current status and role of Asians in American society. By illuminating the incongruence and points of conflict between the dominant society's perception and treatment of Asians, and the Asians' struggles and contributions to the economic development of the West, the dual perspective serves to sharpen awareness of the historical sources of inequity for minority groups. . . . On the one hand, the hostile character of the dominant society is operationalized through its institutions, including those that provide social services. This institutionalized hostility is manifested in the delivery of social services that are essentially (1) remedial in character, that is, based on assumptions that consumers of services are deviant or pathological and must, therefore be "rehabilitated" or made to conform to norms of behavior as defined by dominant, white, middle-class values, (2) residual in scope and therefore insufficient in both quantity and quality, and (3) intended to perform a social control function aimed at the regulation of behavior, as well as a socialization function aimed at inducing behavior in conformity to the white, middle-class model. On the other hand, the dual perspective also should provide students with an appreciation and understanding of the Asian-American response to the institutionalized hostility of the dominant society . . . Asian Americans have continued to preserve their own indigenous support systems for mutual aid and comfort or have created their own alternative system of bilingual-bicultural social services. (Murase, 1978, pp. 34–35)

Eddie Frank Brown, author of the chapter on "American Indians in Modern Society: Implications for Social Policy and Services," corroborated the bitterness of past historic events experienced by minority ethnic groups in the United States.

Attempts have been made in the past to "civilize" and assimilate American Indians through systematic destruction of their major institutions, and in the process the Indian family has been severely attacked. One profession contributing to this has been social work. Because of their ignorance of Indian culture and traditional family structures, social workers—in their attempts to "do good"—have been used by bureaus and agencies to further weaken the Indian Family. This is evident in the policies, programs, and methodologies of treatment used in the areas of Indian child welfare, social welfare, aging and alcoholism.

The challenge for social work practitioners is to develop alternative delivery systems and treatment modalities that will promote the survival and strengthening of Indian tribes, communities, and families rather than to continue using modalities that have proven ineffective.

The Indian and the Euro-American concept of economic development has differed considerably. What was described by early European explorers as a "vast wilderness yet to be developed by man," was actually the home of the Indian where he had lived for hundreds of years. It was this ecological use of the land versus the early industrial development that caused the Euro-American to view Indians' use of the land as wasteful and unproductive . . .

Presently under policies related to Indian self-determination, tribal governments have been thrust into areas of community and program planning and development. Included in this development is contracting for the planning and delivery of social services by tribal governments. Social workers who reflect an American Indian perspective, are knowledgeable about Indian policy, and are skilled in program planning and development are being sought out by various tribes and community groups. (Brown, 1978, pp. 70–72)

Ramon Valle, author of the chapter on "The Development of a Polycultural Social Policy Curriculum from the Latino Perspective," highlights related issues.

> . . . when it comes to the presentation of the ethnic minority historical perspective it is apparent that Anglo/Northern European interpretive sets predominate within the overall treatment of the material . . . one would be hard-pressed not to find continual references to the Charity Society of 1869 and the Settlement House movement of 1884 as forerunners of the social work profession . . . At the same time the social policy literature has almost completely ignored the origins of counterpart Latino social institutions equally active and developing within the above historical time periods . . .
>
> An equally serious deficiency within social policy curricula is the neglect of the history of the social development of those native civilizations of the New World that predated the Ibero *conquistadores*. . . . These civilizations, along with other cultural groupings in the New World, established indigenous value structures providing for the common good that have endured among Latinos to the present. (Valle, 1978, p. 63)

Core Concepts

The framework of the dual perspective was defined in the original pamphlet, published by the Council on Social Work Education in 1978. The publication was intended to be a source book for practitioners as well as for social work educators. Central goals were (1) the integration of "content and methodology necessary for understanding and working with minority groups," and (2) the modification of social work curriculum "based on the conviction that integration of ethnic minority content in basic courses will significantly improve the curriculum" (Norton, 1978, p. 1).

> The dual perspective is the conscious and systematic process of perceiving, understanding, and comparing simultaneously the values, attitudes, and behaviors of the larger societal system with those of the client's immediate family and community system. It is the conscious awareness on the cognitive and attitudinal levels of the similarities and differences in the two systems. It requires substantive knowledge and empathic appreciation of both the majority societal system and the minority client system, as well as a conscious awareness of the social worker's own attitudes and values. Thus the dual perspective allows one to experience each system from the point of view of the other. . . .
>
> The dual perspective is an essential entity that exists whether or not a social worker recognizes and uses it. **The degree of incongruence** between the societal system and the client's system is a critical consideration. In a society that rejects the immediate environmental system of racial minorities, the achievement of **congruence** for the minority client is severely limited, if not impossible. It is this fact that makes the dual perspective uniquely suited for working with ethnic minority groups. . . . It increases the awareness of possible and actual points of conflict between the minority client's perspective and that of the dominant society. It enhances awareness of the structural-institutional sources that contribute to inequality of opportunity for minority groups. . . .

Chestang wrote of the duality of the Black experience. He called the larger and more dominant system of individual experience the "sustaining system." It houses the instrumental needs of man, the goods and services, the political power, and the economic resources, all of which factors confer status and power. Embedded in the larger system is the more immediate system, the physical and social environment of family and close community. A person's basic sense of identity grows out of this. Chestang referred to this as the "nurturing environment." The nurturing environment can be compared to Erikson's "significant others," those closest and most involved in the determination of an individual's sense of identity. . . . (Norton, 1978, pp. 3–4)

Norton identifies *Mind, Self and Society* by George H. Mead as the source of a principle within dual perspective theory that addresses processes of socialization through which individuals adopt as their own the values, attitudes and behavioral norms of the systems in which they reside.

Mead's concept of the "generalized other" also can be used to understand the dual perspective. He defined the generalized other as taking on the attitude of the wider society in regard to oneself. In this way one learns to become an object to oneself, to have an identity, to know oneself through role taking and from the reflections of others. In acting out the roles of others, children discover that the roles belong to their own nature and begin to know themselves.

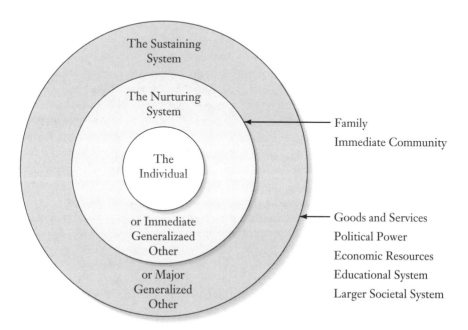

FIGURE 7.1 *The Dual System of all Individuals*

> From the many roles assumed, there gradually arises a generalized other. This attitude of the generalized other or organized community gives unity of self to individuals as they incorporate society's responses and react accordingly. (Norton, 1978, p. 4)

Norton acknowledged that Mead's concept of a "generalized other" was based on an assumption that socialization by significant others generally reflects a set of values, attitudes and behaviors consistent with normative standards in an individual's sociocultural environment. The CSWE study noted fallacies in assuming that normative standards provide positive guidelines for all.

> Mead spoke of only one generalized other. However, **minority persons who assume the attitude of the generalized other of the wider society have a strong possibility of seeing themselves devalued. The more they incorporate a negative image into their identity, the more they will be devalued in their own image**. Yet we know minority persons do attain a good sense of self. It is our assumption that **there is an alternative generalized other (a dual generalized other, if you wish) that balances or compensates for the potential destruction of self-worth coming from the wider society**.
>
> The alternative generalized other is the attitude of the family and immediate community environment, the nurturing environment of Chestang, the significant others of Erikson. If minority children receive love and care from their families, this can instill a positive sense of self. Since many minority children are reasonably isolated from the white community physically and socially, the attitude of the more immediate generalized other can develop, restore or help them maintain self-esteem. They can use it as a buffer against the effects of the attitude of the generalized other from the larger society as they experience the wider community. This cannot be accomplished totally though, for they are very aware of the attitude of the dominant generalized other. If the mechanisms of socialization in the nurturing environment or the more immediate generalized other are positive, it helps people **balance the destructive image coming from the larger community**. (Norton, 1978, pp. 4–5).

The concepts of the dual perspective are particularly relevant for social work practice with persons and populations different from the dominant culture and the status standards of the society in regard to a wide range of physical and cultural variables. As viewed through the dual perspective, high degrees of incongruence between the systems often result in exclusion of individuals or groups from opportunities for employment, access to resources and to decision-making power within the "Sustaining" System. Members of stigmatized groups are at risk for impaired self concept and lower self-esteem, as noted above, unless the Nurturing System provides dependable support. In behalf of health, exclusionary practices in the dominant culture must be confronted and changed.

Norton considers that the dual perspective is relevant in practice not only with persons of low social status or ethnic or racial minorities.

> The dual perspective then is not a concept to be applied solely to minority people and groups. It enhances our understanding of all people, but is particularly vital to the assessment and understanding of those whose immediate generalized other might differ or be in conflict with the major generalized other. And those are more likely to be minority people. (Norton, 1978, p. 6).

This view of the relevance of the dual perspective as a generalist framework for application to all populations, as subsystems of a macrosystem that needs to be monitored and often challenged and changed, is reiterated in the conclusions of the CSWE publication.

> The dual perspective should not be interpreted as being a concept for use only with minorities; it can be applied to all people. It should direct attention to the "common human needs of people" and the degree to which they are met within the nurturing society and within the major society. . . .
>
> Finally, the dual perspective represents the relationship between theory and problem solving that social welfare must turn to as our society becomes more complex. This concept developed out of the application of social science and personality theory to the problem of understanding diverse client systems. Use of social science theory in relation to the social and physical environment provides the theoretical concept of the dual perspective, which should give direction to the social welfare professional's search to understand the diverse kinds of client life-situations and their implications for practice. (Norton, 1978, p. 80)

In the application of the dual perspective, it is essential to recognize that valid assessments of nurturing and sustaining systems are based on general systems analysis. Dimensions for study and assessment include examination of their history, structure, functions, processes and the outcomes of those social systems, as measured by their impact on the development and health of individuals, families, and communities whose lives are supported or constricted by those social environments.

Core Principles for Practice

Guidelines for effective application of the dual perspective in social work practice are also guidelines for the development of social work leadership in campaigns for social and economic justice and for social change. For effective application of the dual perspective in social work practice, the practitioner engages the client system in the activities of social work's tried-and-tested problem-solving process, informed by

- **data** that clarifies the history of the client system, and the history of social and property relations that tend to define the distribution of economic and political power in the nurturing and sustaining systems that constitute its social environment;
- **data** that clarifies the historic and current resources and means of production of goods and services in the client system, as well as in the nurturing and sustaining systems; patterns of participation in production and distribution of material and/or natural resources, goods, and services that also influence the distribution of economic and political power;
- **information** on historic and current language usage and on cultural patterns of thought and behavior, worldviews and belief systems, attitudinal and value norms, the structure of social roles and decision-making authority, normative institutions, traditional and current behavioral codes in each of these systems;

- **assessment** of group cohesiveness and/or intra-group conflict and/or incongruence within the client system, and within and between the nurturing and sustaining systems;
- **assessment** of the extent to which relations of dominance and subordination in social and economic structures are resulting in psychological and physical damage to vulnerable groups and individuals in the client system, and within nurturing and sustaining systems;
- **summary assessment** of the strengths and needs of the client system, and of the nurturing and sustaining systems that constitute its social environment, based on observations, data collection through interviews, collateral testimony, literature, statistical findings on social indicators, etc.;
- **planning of interventions**, in partnership with the client system and related circles of nurturance and support, aims to modify the structure and/or functioning of any of these systems, on behalf of greater human health and development. Broader distribution of economic and material resources, and of decision-making power, are consistently associated with advancement in human health and development;
- **identification of priorities**, in regard to planned interventions. The most pressing issues, and/or the actions that, realistically, are most likely to produce positive results with less expenditure of time and effort, tend to be productive places to start. The achievement of some visible change builds commitment to long-term partnerships that can address, and can sometimes achieve, more fundamental shifts in structures of power. Small, visible changes make it evident that, "¡Si se puede! / Yes, it can be done!"
- **decisions on strategies and tasks** require culturally competent practice skills. While all communication between social workers, clients and client systems require the practitioner's ethnic sensitivity, decisions on strategies of intervention and on the assignment of related tasks require the fullest expression of client self-determination. The practitioner is also responsible to help the client assess potential consequences, both positive and negative, of available options, by sharing information and knowledge gained through careful preparation, judgment based on information and thoughtful reflection, and by honest feedback.
- **implementation of interventions** is the action phase of the problem-solving process, when the client system and allies in the nurturing and sustaining systems carry out strategies that have been planned to effect changes. The experience of collaborative work toward shared goals is a healing process for traumatized persons and other victims of abuse.
- **evaluation of planned interventions** is an important step in human growth and development. The ability to reflect on the consequences of decisions and actions is a cornerstone in the development of maturity and is linked to responsible exercise of power.
- **revision of assessments and plans, based on evaluation findings.** Reality tends to bring surprises; life is a great teacher if human beings learn from errors in judgment and from the consequences of unproductive behavior. The planning process is revisited to set in place new goals, priorities, and interventions.

The central goals of social work's problem-solving processes and interventions, which apply social work ethics, values and methods in order to produce social change, aim to increase the degree to which institutions and environments nurture and sustain healthy human growth and development. Health is the desired outcome.

Case Example

In assessing the strengths and needs of a client system and in planning problem-solving interventions with clients, careful observations and factual data in regard to environmental systems are likely to produce far more effective results. In his article on "The San Antonio Model: A Culture-Oriented Approach," Ernesto Gomez presents the San Antonio Model (SAM). This model features a Cultural Assessment Grid that illustrates the value of culturally sensitive practice that includes the assessment of environmental systems.

The Cultural Assessment Grid has helped SAM clients and practitioners, as partners, to identify those features of the client system and environmental systems that are resources for solving the client's problems, Types 1 and 2, and to differentiate them from features of those systems that may contribute to client problems, Types 3 and 4.

Using of the dual perspective framework can clarify and reinforce the effectiveness of the Cultural Assessment Grid because it differentiates distinct dimensions of "the environment." The culture of the dominant sustaining system, the macro-level environment, is competitive and often hostile to cultural diversity; its cultural features are more likely to fit within the category of Type 4 on the Cultural Assessment Grid. Social workers need to rec-

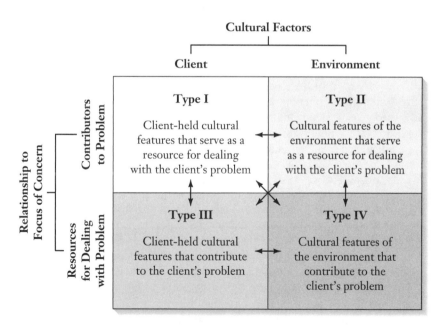

FIGURE 7.2   *Cultural Assessment Grid*

ognize that cultural features of nurturing systems of ethnic minority individuals, families, and communities are more likely to fit the category of Type 2 on the grid. According to principles of cultural sensitivity in practice, which hold client self-determination to be paramount, features of both the nurturing and sustaining social environments that are barriers to growth and development may be identified and addressed by the clients of the San Antonio Model, while members of a socially stigmatized ethnic community may be supported and empowered by features of community-based nurturing systems, in alliance with culturally competent social workers.

Contributions and Limitations

For students in field practicum, the use of the dual perspective teaches students to observe in a more focused manner the community in which they are placed. Norton suggests,

> A part of the students' orientation process in a minority community should include exploration of their fears, concerns for their safety, and their need for acceptance in the community as well as any hostile feelings in regard to the minority community. The motivations of non-minority students who aggressively seek out practice with minority groups should be explored. If they are meeting some personal need of their own, they should be aware of it. Minority students should have the experience of working with a group, person, or community of a different minority than themselves. This is particularly helpful in developing the dual perspective, since they may become aware of the stereotypes they hold of other minority groups despite being a member of a minority group themselves. Non-white students also should have some white clients. (Norton, 1978, p. 20)

In the course of my career as a social work educator, I have introduced many students to the theoretical concepts of the dual perspective in courses on cultural diversity, human behavior in the social environment, and in practice courses. I consider that several key benefits are derived from applying the dual perspective in practice. Cultural awareness and sensitivity are much enhanced by study and application of the framework. For generalist, advanced generalist, and multi-level assessment and intervention approaches to practice, I consider that the dual perspective framework is the framework of choice, for reasons that were articulated in the original publication.

> The dual perspective can lead to a process of assessment that systematically includes examination of the dominant environmental and institutional factors as well as any factors associated with client stress that are within the nurturing environment. This can lead to larger systems as targets for change. (Norton, 1978, p. 22)

In the early years of the new millennium, it is evident that there are national, even global systems and institutions that need to be confronted and changed, if the growing gap between rich and poor is to be reversed. Social workers who apply the dual perspective framework in their practice with culturally diverse populations will be prepared to provide leadership in community-based coalitions working for social justice and a better future for humanity.

A basic reality that limits the impact of the dual perspective framework is the fact that this framework is not well known by social work students and practitioners. Many outstanding social work educators who are providing leadership on the subject of ethnic and cultural diversity may be more focused on the documentation of racist discrimination that demonstrates attitudinal racism than on efforts to change structural inequities, which may be defined as forms of institutional racism. Racism in all its forms is brutally destructive. Some cultural diversity programs have focused principally on cultural and ethnic differences, an approach that sometimes results in stereotyping cultures. Study of historical events, property relations, social institutions, and cultures that affect people's lives teaches us that human history is about how groups achieve survival and change.

Conclusions

The conceptual framework of the dual perspective is particularly productive for social workers who use multi-level assessment and intervention and/or generalist and advanced-generalist approaches in their practice. The planning and implementation of multi-level interventions are facilitated by this framework, which recognizes that economic, political, cultural, social, and natural environments are potential sources of problems, as well as sources of strength and empowerment.

Because historical and current intergroup conflicts, power relationships and other structural and institutional features of stratified macrosystems are factors included in assessments guided by the dual perspective framework, those social assessments tend to include underlying issues that reflect fundamental conflicts in economic and political interests. Those assessments are, therefore, more realistic and are likely to lead to the planning of more productive interventions. Social workers grounded in dual perspective theory are taught to facilitate the empowerment and exercise of self-determination by ethnic communities.

When factors of outside controlling interests are not addressed, issues focused on cultural diversity may serve to divide and conquer ethnic populations. Ethnic-group conflicts may be surface manifestations of underlying contests for power that have more to do with conflicting economic and political interests than with cultural norms. Conflicts between ethnic communities often serve outside interest groups that promote policies divisive to neighboring communities. In that way military and political decision-making can be maintained by outside controlling interests in regions inhabited by ethnic people whose cultures are less aggressive and competitive. The history of the colonial and neocolonial eras is replete with examples. The dynamics of dominance continue to be evident in Africa, Latin America, Asia, and in the cities and rural regions of the United States.

Social workers, their professional organizations, and other non-governmental community organizations applaud the image transformation of U.S. society from a "White America" to a "Multi-Cultural America," which it truly is. The reality is that the Western Hemisphere, comprising the continental areas of North, Central, and South America, has been multi-cultural from the time of the European invasion and conquest—perhaps even before. As authors and participants in community forums, social workers can participate in and promote that kind of revisioning of U. S. society.

Fortunately, the dual perspectives framework provides conceptual tools that are powerful aids in analysis and opposition to economic and political interests that seek to prevent change and positive social transformation. Social workers—as researchers uncovering past and present truths, as activists marching in multi-racial, multi-ethnic unity, and as allies to people of all ages and other categories—can take action to deconstruct destructive social institutions.

A notable example of this kind of social action was the national Poor People's Economic Human Rights Campaign in fall 2000, initiated by the Kensington Welfare Rights Organization, assisted by social workers and faculty members at Temple University School of Social Work. The campaign called for the implementation of the Universal Declaration of Human Rights, which was adopted by the United Nations in 1948 but never ratified by the United States Senate. The articles of this United Nations document proclaim the rights of all people to share in specifically designated public services plus economic and material resources that support healthy human development.

In connection with the national campaign, a Freedom Bus Tour traveled through Northern California in fall 2000, mobilized by the Women's Economic Agenda Project, a social justice advocacy group based in Oakland, California. Mothers on welfare and other community activists traveled on the bus and spoke with community groups. A social work student who attended a Freedom Bus Tour Forum at California State University, Sacramento reported on its goals and views

- to eliminate poverty,
- to eliminate hunger,
- to eliminate homelessness, and
- to promote a universal national health care system.

> We are in peril as a nation and it is not by the people's hands at the bottom of this hierarchical society. The top 1 percent that controls 80 percent of the wealth are the ones who define and enact laws that prevent us from seeing the truth. The truth is that people are starving and the government has abolished the only entitlement program that provided Americans with a safety net in troubled times. We are only as good as the people we produce. Currently, TANF has replaced AFDC and is pushing single women with children off the roles in favor of minimum wage jobs with no future.

Questions for Critical Thinking

Classroom responses from social work students have provided an indication for the kinds of questions that are likely to produce critical thinking concerning the application of this framework:

1. What are some significant events in U.S. history that profoundly altered social and property relations among ethnic populations in the United States?

2. What are the current institutional and cultural practices that maintain and even increase ethnic stratification in the United States?

3. Is there a link between the social status of ethnic populations (reflected in their comparative

economic and political power) and the quality of health, education, housing, and/or occupational status and income enjoyed by members of those populations?

4. What are some notable strengths of specific ethnic populations and cultures? How have those qualities supported the survival and health of the members of their communities, in spite of hostile actions by an aggressive and competitive dominant culture?

5. How can social workers who are not members of a specific ethnic community provide services to that community that contribute to problem solving?

Sources for Further Study

References listed at the end of this chapter are readings that expand understanding of ethnic community systems operating within the dominant-culture environment of the United States. While listed texts examine social structures that may be defined as nurturing systems or sustaining systems, annotated sources provide not only dynamic interpretations of historic events that determined the status of ethnic communities, but also insights on structural inequalities and incongruences between the nation's dominant culture and the ethnic cultures of nurturing communities. Conclusions are consistent with the application of a dual perspective framework.

Burkey, Richard M. *Ethnic & Racial Groups: The Dynamics of Dominance.* Menlo Park, CA: Benjamin/Cummings, 1978. Burkey's observations and research focus on "four major ways in which ethnic groups from different societies become members of the same society in a system of dominant–subordinate relationships." According to Burkey, historic events that led to these results occurred at the point of encounter: "(1) Conquest. The military forces of one society invade and occupy another society. The ethnic groups within the conquered society then become subordinate to the invaders . . . (2) Voluntary Immigration. Members of ethnic groups from other societies voluntarily emigrate to a new society in the hopes of improving their condition. If they enter a society that has a dominant ethnic group, the immigrants become subordinate . . . (3) Annexation. When the government of one society annexes other societies or segments thereof, by purchase, plebiscite, petition, or by establishing a protectorate, the ethnic groups residing within the annexed territory become subordinate . . . (4) Enslavement. Members of ethnic groups in other societies who are taken into captivity by force become subordinate within the society of their masters" (p. 78).

Cafferty, Pastora San Juan, and Leon Chestang, eds. *The Diverse Society: Implications for Social Policy.* Washington, D.C.: NASW, 1976. This collection of articles addresses three principal themes: "Ethnicity in America," "Ethnic Identity," and "Ethnicity Issues for Social Policy." The articles focus on features of urban and rural life in the nation at that time. Alarms are sounded about social conditions and societal relations that the authors recognize will have major long-term consequences for human development. Articles include "New York Segregation: Implications for Social Policy" by Nathan Kantrowitz; "Environmental Influences on Social Functioning: The Black Experience" by Leon Chestang; "Residential Environment and Black Self-Image" by Dolores Norton; "Immigration, Work Expectations, and Labor Market Structure" by Michael J. Piore; "American Indian Tribal Support Systems and Economic Development" by Leonard D. Borman; and "Bilingualism in America" by Pastora San Juan Cafferty. This book was an early, authoritative source for integration of content on race and ethnicity in social work education.

Churchill, Ward. *Struggle for the Land: Indigenous Resistance to Genocide, Ecocide and Expropriation in Contemporary North America.* Monroe, ME: Common Courage Press, 1993. This text contrasts the values, ethics, and behavioral norms of the nation that was built through the conquest and capture of

Indian land in North America with the values and ethics of the indigenous Indian nations. The introduction's subtitle reveals principal conclusions of the study: "Introduction: Land Theft and the Mechanisms of Genocide and Ecocide." "Not only the people of the land are being destroyed, but, more and more, the land itself." Chapters focus on efforts by various Indian nations to preserve sovereignty and to protect the earth. Chapter titles include "Perversion of Justice: Examining the Doctrine of U.S. Rights to Occupancy in North America," "The Black Hills Are Not for Sale: The Lakota Struggle for the 1868 Treaty Territory," "Radioactive Colonization: Hidden Holocaust in Native North America," and "The Water Plot: Hydrological Rape in Northern Canada."

Gibbs, Jewell Taylor, ed. *Young, Black and Male in America: An Endangered Species.* Westport, CT: Auburn House, 1988. Jewell Taylor Gibbs has assembled data on critical life conditions and declining life options that confront young Black males in the United States who "have been miseducated by the educational system, mishandled by the criminal justice system, mislabeled by the mental health system, and mistreated by the social welfare system." As editor, Gibbs has brought together articles in chapters that address issues in education, employment, unemployment, delinquency, crime, substance abuse, unwed teenage pregnancy, homicide, and suicide. Findings indicate that "delinquency among black youth is deeply connected with the variety of stressors affecting them, their families, and their community. Failure to respond creatively to these problems is as inhumane as it is socially destructive."

Gibson, Guadalupe, ed. *Our Kingdom Stands on Brittle Glass.* Silver Springs, MD: NASW Press, 1983. The purpose and focus of this fruitful collection of essays addresses "the state of the art in social work practice and education in relation to Chicanos." Federico Souflée, Jr., author of the article on which the title of the book is based, concludes that "whatever models we do develop will be multi-dimensional, eclectic ones," and by practice responsive to cultural diversity. Practice-based wisdom about effective mental health practice with Chicanos is presented by gifted educators and practitioners. In addition to Guadalupe Gibson, contributors include Tomás Atencio, Ismael Dieppa, Norma Benavides, Joseph Gallegos, Eunice García, Ernest Gomez, Javier Sanchez, Juliette Silva and Albert Vasquez. Gibson reminds her colleagues "¡Podemos seguir adelante; hemos visto que sí se puede!"

Lum, Doman. *Culturally Competent Practice: A Framework for Growth and Action.* Pacific Grove, CA: Brooks/Cole, 1999. This text presents principles and methods for the development of skills and approaches in social work practice that enhance cultural sensitivity and awareness of cultural diversity among clients and self. The power of listening as a stimulus to self reflection is highlighted. Ethnographic approaches to interviewing are promoted, including the use of life-story narratives. Inductive methods are used in data gathering and theory building, for deeper and fuller understanding. The strengths perspective, also, is seen as responsive to cultural variables in the nation of origin, the past history of the ethnic community, and the family and personal life history. In culturally competent practice, assessment and intervention aim to promote growth, empowerment, and advocacy in partnership with the client.

Solomon, Barbara B. *Black Empowerment: Social Work in Oppressed Communities.* New York: Columbia University Press, 1976. This classic work convinced the social work profession that the sources of many problems of individual psychosocial dysfunction "lie in the racist operations of major social institutions," and "that change strategies be directed at these institutions and not at the victims." The book honors the strengths of Black Americans, as survivors of brutal slavery, exploitation, and gross discrimination. Solomon declared that the power represented by Black survival in America merits recognition and challenged the profession to acknowledge and respect that power. The work led to the development of empowerment as a principle in social work practice.

Takaki, Ronald. *A Different Mirror: A History of Multicultural America.* Boston: Little, Brown, and Company, 1993. Ronald Takaki recounts the history of the five hundred years following the European conquest of the Western Hemisphere in this text. The historic documentation and analysis address issues of power and property relations, of mass migrations and, at times, mass movements. Takaki clarifies the fact that America was always multi-cultural and multi-ethnic, and never merely "White America." European American tendency to distort reality, and to create mythologies that justified systematic extermination, exploitation, and discrimination directed at people of color is a central aspect of Takaki's work.

References

Acuna, R. (1972). *Occupied America: The Chicano's struggle toward liberation.* San Francisco: Canfield Press.

Barrera, M. (1979). *Race and class in the Southwest.* Notre Dame, IN: University of Notre Dame Press.

Berlowitz, M. J., & Edari, R. S. (Eds.). (1984). *Racism and the denial of human rights: Beyond ethnicity.* Minneapolis, Minnesota: MEP Publications.

Billingsley, A. (1968). *Black families in White America.* Englewood Cliffs, NJ: Prentice-Hall.

Billingsley, A., & Giovannoni, J. M. (1972). *Children of the storm: Black children and American child welfare.* New York: Harcourt Brace Jovanovich.

Brown, D. (1971). *Bury my heart at Wounded Knee.* New York: Holt, Rinehart & Winston.

Brown, E. F. (1978). American Indians in modern society: Implications for social policy and services. In D. Norton (Ed.), *The dual perspective.* New York: CSWE.

Brown, E. G. (1978). Minority content in the first-year practice course. In D. Norton (Ed.), *The dual perspective.* New York: CSWE.

Burkey, R. M. (1978). *Ethnic & racial groups: The dynamics of dominance.* Menlo Park, CA: Benjamin/Cummings.

Bush, James A. Neocolonialism and compensatory justice. An occasional paper of the Consortium of Texas Schools of Social Work, April 1972.

Cafferty, P. S. J., & Chestang, L. W. (Eds.). (1976). *The diverse society: Implications for social policy.* Washington, D.C.: NASW Press.

Chestang, L. W. (1976). Environmental influences on social functioning: The Black experience. In P. Cafferty & L. W. Chestang (Eds.), *The diverse society: Implications for social policy.* Washington, D.C.: NASW Press.

Churchill, W. (1993). *Struggle for the land: Indigenous resistance to genocide, ecocide and expropriation in contemporary North America.* Monroe, ME: Common Courage Press.

Clark, K. B. (1955). *Prejudice and your child.* Boston: Beacon Press.

Dubois, W. E. B. (1969). *Black reconstruction in America, 1860–1880.* New York: Atheneum Press.

DuBray, W. (2000). *Mental health interventions with people of color.* Cincinnati, OH: Thompson Learning.

Erikson, E. H. (1968). *Identity: Youth and crisis.* New York: W. W. Norton.

Fanon, F. (1967). *Black skin, white masks.* New York: Grove Press.

Francis, E. A. (Ed.). (1973). *Black task force report: Suggested guides for the integration of Black content into the social work curriculum.* New York: CSWE.

Francis, E. A. (1978). Integrating Black minority content into social welfare policy and services. In D. Norton, (Ed.), *The Dual Perspective.* New York: CSWE.

Gibbs, J. T. (Ed.). (1988). *Young, Black and male in America: An endangered species.* Westport, CT: Auburn House.

Gibson, G. (Ed.). (1983). *Our kingdom stands on brittle glass.* Silver Springs, MD: NASW.

Knowles, L. L., & Prewitt, K. (Eds.). (1969). *Institutional racism in America.* Englewood Cliffs, NJ: Prentice-Hall.

Lerner, G. (Ed.). (1972). *Black women in White America: A documentary history.* New York: Vintage Books.

Lum, D. (1999). *Culturally competent practice: A framework for growth and action.* Pacific Grove, CA: Brooks/Cole.

Mead, G. H. (1934). *Mind, self and society.* Chicago: University of Chicago Press.

Murase, K. (1978). Social welfare policy and services: Asian Americans. In D. Norton (Ed.), *The dual perspective.* New York: CSWE.

Norton, D. (Ed.). (1978). *The dual perspective: Inclusion of ethnic minority content in the social work curriculum.* New York: Council on Social Work Education.

Shibutani, T., & Kwan, K. M. (1965). *Ethnic stratification: A comparative approach.* London: The Macmillan Company.

Solomon, B. B. (1976). *Black empowerment: Social work in oppressed communities.* New York: Columbia University Press.

Takaki, R. (1993). *A different mirror: A history of multicultural America.* Boston: Little, Brown and Company.

Valle, R. (1978). The development of a polycultural social policy curriculum from the Latino perspective. In D. Norton (Ed.), *The dual perspective.* New York: CSWE.

Part IV

Oppression Perspective

8

Ethnic-Centered (Afrocentric) Framework

Robin Wiggins Carter

An underdeveloped concept for the study of diversity in social work is the idea of ethnic centeredness or *centricity*. As defined by Harris (1999), "centricity refers to a perspective that involves locating oneself within the context of one's own cultural perspective" (p. 1). Underlying the idea of centrality is the belief that many groups' contribution to the construction of knowledge and therefore the development of ideas about human behavior in this society have been historically excluded. Centrist perspectives emphasize the need to include the cultural values and worldviews of marginalized groups as the theoretical base to develop new models of human behavior.

Anderson and Collins (2001) call for a "shifting of the center" from paradigms developed from an ideological position that does not accurately reflect the history and experiences of marginalized people. They state:

> Who has been excluded from what is known, and how might we see the world differently if we were to acknowledge and value the experiences and thoughts of those who have been excluded? Many groups whose experiences have been vital in the formation of American society and culture have been silenced in the construction of knowledge about this society. The result is that what we know—about the experiences of both these silenced groups and the dominant culture—is distorted and incomplete. (p. 13)

Core Concepts

Why a Culturally Based Perspective

Proponents of culturally-centered perspectives argue the need for development of new theoretical models drawn from the unique perspective of the group for which it is used. Centrist perspectives believe that aggregate groups tend to have their own cultural attributes, values, worldviews, and experiences because of their unique histories. For this reason, merely adapting theoretical models developed by and for majority groups do not effectively take these differences into account. According to Everett (1991),

> Much of the work on integrating knowledge about people of color into practice has been relatively superficial. In educational institutions and training programs three general patterns or trends have emerged: the occasional inclusion of various, but limited, cultural illustrations as teaching tools; assessments of the dissonance between theory and the existing culture, and modifications in theoretical constructs to respond to cultural differences. (p. 10)

Some of the dominant approaches for working with diverse populations in the field of social work encourage the adaptation of existing frameworks for more effective use with diverse groups. These approaches have contributed greatly to social work practice by introducing models for "culturally sensitive" practice that acknowledge the effects of racial oppression in the lives of racial and cultural minorities (Turner, 1991). The ethnic-centered frameworks differ in that they offer an alternative model, developed through the cultural lens of the group for which it is intended.

Social Work and Theory Development

In social work, the importance of the theoretical model in the organization and delivery of services cannot be overlooked. Intervention is based on assessment, and biased assessments lead to inappropriate and ineffective intervention. Programs are developed and policies formulated on the basis of what we know about human behavior. Traditional Western theories, many of which are rooted in mainstream American ideology, may not be adequate to address the service delivery needs of a diverse society.

According to Appleby (2001), three principles of traditional American culture combine to make up the prevailing national ideology. The first principle is *Eurocentricity*, the assumption that the European rooted values and traditions are inherently superior to all others. The Eurocentric worldview with all of its accompanying assumptions about human behavior is the current and most dominant center from which many theories currently used in social work have derived. This domination leads to inappropriate and ineffective assessment, planning, and intervention in social work practice as practitioners attempt to apply the worldview universally. This domination leads as well to the devaluing of and pathologizing of the unique cultural attributes of diverse groups (Everett et al., 1991; McLaren, J., 1998; McPheil, M., 1998). According to Schiele (1998), "to the degree that European Americans constitute the dominant group in the United States, it can be argued that their particular cultural truths and worldviews are imposed on all who live in America" (p. 170).

The second principle—one that has come under serious attack from the feminist movement—is *patriarchy*. Women scholars have long noted that the socialization of the family is rooted in this patriarchal system of "hierarchical control and coercive authority." This system defines acceptable gender-prescribed roles based on a male-dominated worldview that holds males in the authoritarian role and other family members as subordinates. This dominance can be so pervasive that it seeks to label as deviant behaviors those that do not fit neatly into this paradigm.

Capitalism is the third principle, "the economic system that emphasizes private ownership of property and free enterprise, with its accompanying importance on profits and competition, inequitable distribution of resources (income and wealth), economic recessions and depressions, and poverty" (Schiele, p. 44). This system requires an emphasis on individualism and personal responsibility as precursors to "success."

Many of the traditional models used to explain human behavior have these ideological positions as their underlying assumptions. This perspective highlights the obvious contradiction between the nation's rapidly changing demographics and multicultural origins and its dominant identity as White and European. Many of these deeply ingrained ideological positions form the basis of our analyses of human behavior. Those who do not accept and adhere to these beliefs are seen as deviants or outsiders. This way of thinking marginalizes many people of color, women, the differently abled, the aged, gays and lesbians whose worldviews may be in sharp contrast to the mainstream ideologies (Lawson, E., et al., 1997). As Appleby (2001) concludes,

> These ideological principles have left us a heritage of divisiveness and inequity. These tenets have been used to rationalize prejudice, negative attitudes about certain groups, and to justify discrimination, actions that flow from those prejudices. (p. 44)

Cultural Feminism and Centering

An example of a centrist model discussed in social work literature is "cultural feminism." Cultural feminist scholars have long challenged the use of male-focused and male-developed models of human behavior in their application to women. With particular criticism of traditional Freudian psychology and its view of gender differences, feminist scholars have also challenged the assertions in other developmental models as well. According to Miller (1991),

> . . . the self has often been separated from its surrounding environment and studied as a separate entity. It is seen as developing through a complex series of processes leading to a sense of psychological separation from others. From this, there follows a quest for power over others and power over natural forces, including one's own body. (p. 25)

Similarly traditional Western psychological development theories emphasize the idea that mature "self" is highly differentiated, independent and autonomous (Worden, 2001). These models have implications for how women are viewed, as their tendency is to view feminine gender development as inferior to male gender development.

In response to this, feminist scholars have attempted to isolate features that define a woman's way of being. Labeled "cultural feminism," this model seeks to revalue what have come to be regarded as women's qualities from a "woman-centered" as opposed to a "male-centered" woldview. As Braun-Williams (1999) stresses, "these models, whether race or gender based, by offering antidotes to racism and sexism, enable women to recognize the powerful effect of negative cultural evaluations and begin to undo the damage to self-esteem wrought by the internalization of racist and sexist representations" (p. 3).

The Afrocentric Perspective

This chapter focuses on the Afrocentric perspective. The origins of this concept and its usefulness in the development of social work theory will be examined.

The earliest articulation of Afrocentric thought came from scholars in the field of Black Psychology beginning in the mid 1960s. This perspective, similarly referred to as the Africentric or African-centered perspective, rose in response to the critical examination by African American scholars of what were the prevailing social science paradigms as they relate to African Americans and other marginalized people. This period marked the introduction of revisionist scholarly activity on the Black family and Black community. Andrew Billingsley's (1968) work on the "strengths of black families" made a significant contribution to the efforts of African American scholars to solidify what came to be considered the "core attributes" of African American families.

The main proponents of the Afrocentric intellectual school of thought are Asante, Keto, Diop, and Karenga. Afrocentricity is derived in part from earlier intellectual centrist movements, specifically "Negritude" and "Pan Africanism," which emphasized the cultural achievements of Africans in historical context. Afrocentricity views the dominance of Eurocentric ideals as the central major threat to African Americans.

Afrocentric thought maintains that African Americans have, to a great degree, retained some of the original aspects of African culture. For that reason culture is an important consideration in the understanding of African American families. "The African American family is not simply a functional adaptation to new social conditions, but a product of history and culture that has been conducive to the survival of the African American family" (McDaniel, 1990, p. 7).

The Afrocentric perspective is a culturally based perspective, which presents a model of resistance, self-esteem, and skills to resist negative cultural images. Afrocentrism claims validation in that it elevates a particular position of centrism, therefore presenting a new system of ideology that advances the community interests. The Afrocentric view posits that no group can claim to be a center to the exclusion of others. Each group has a center of its own, but the holistic nature of Afrocentrism sees these "polycenters" as a part of the whole and emphasizes the importance of "self-centering."

Afrocentrists do not argue that their views should replace or dominate other views, but that "the acceptance and due recognition of all perspectives is far more likely to lead to genuine human knowledge and intercultural understanding than reliance on one absolute worldview" (Asante, 1992). Afrocentricity is one of those perspectives. "Afrocentricity seeks to strengthen cultural awareness and unity among blacks in the United States, and also infuse in them knowledge and appreciation of their historical identity and heritage as a distinct group" (Harris, 1999, p. 11).

According to Turner (1991),

> All theories, models, and paradigms of human behavior are inherently culturally biased or ethnocentric; they are bound by the culture, historical time, life experience, and knowledge base of their proponents. The construction of models from an Africentric perspective attempts to portray African Americans, the people of the African Diaspora in the Western hemisphere, in ways that are free of European ethnocentrism and androcentrism. The Africentric perspective implicitly contends that differences in culture, world view, and historical

experiences exist between African Americans and European Americans, as there are differences between Asians and Europeans, and between the indigenous populations of the Americas, the Americans, and Europeans. The Afrocentric perspective delineates and explicates some of these differences, many of which have implications for the construction of paradigms of human behavior. (p. 36)

The use of Afrocentric principles for African American families counters enduring models that view the African American family from a dominant Eurocentric framework, resulting in the crystallization of a range of negative beliefs about African American families. These beliefs, adopted and advanced by practitioners and scholars alike, have been detrimental to the effective intervention with African American families (Crosbie-Burnett & Lewis, 1993; McDaniel, 1990).

Descriptions of the African American family in the past focused on its disintegration. Frazier (1966) and Moynihan (1965), for example, argued that the African Americans did not retain much of their original culture—that most, if not all, of it was destroyed during slavery. These writings resulted in less emphasis on culture and more emphasis on structure and other "socially generated" phenomena to view African Americans.

Many of these studies accepted the assimilationist view that there was a single homogenous American culture. Much of this research, therefore, focused on the differences between white American families and African American families with the underlying belief that they should be alike. These studies gave further fuel to the tendency to view African Americans from a deficit model.

The perceived "dysfunction" of the African American family became a focus of study for a dearth of scholars during the decades preceding the Moynihan report. Using a deficit model, most looked at pathology associated with African American life. Family structure was studied as it related to the "problem" associated with single-parent households (Mosely-Howard & Evans, 2000; Auslander et al., 2000).

According to Crosbie-Burnett and Lewis (1993),

. . . ideal and adaptive family structure and functioning have been developed from the world-view of the dominant European American culture. These ideas or theories have then been used to assess the functional status of families of color, thus resulting in distortion and incomplete views of African American family life. (p. 8)

Major Tenets of Afrocentricity.   According to Covin (1990), the five measures of Afrocentricity are

1. People of African descent share a common experience, struggle and origin.
2. Present in African culture is a nonmaterial element of resistance to the assault upon traditional values caused by the intrusion of European legal procedures, medicines, political processes, and religions into African culture.
3. African culture takes the view that an Afrocentric modernization process would be based upon three traditional values: harmony with nature, humanness, and rhythm.
4. Afrocentricity involves the development of a theory of an African way of knowing and interpreting the world.

5. Some form of communalism or socialism is an important component for the way wealth is produced, owned, and distributed. (p. 2)

Similarly, Schiele (1990, p. 2) draws his list of the tenets of the Afrocentric paradigm from the works of several scholars:

1. Human beings are conceived collectively.
2. Human beings are spiritual.
3. Human beings are good.
4. The affective approach to knowledge is epistemologically valid.
5. Much of human behavior is nonrational.
6. The axiology or highest value lies in interpersonal relations.

Collective Identity.   From an African-centered view individual identity is not conceived as separate from collective identity. The individual cannot be understood separate from his or her social world. "Because of this, Afrocentrism gives preeminence to the group: The welfare of the group takes precedence over the welfare of the individual" (Schiele, 1990). This also involves the notion of shared responsibility, producing an interdependent relationship between people of African descent and their community. "Sharing a collective identity suggests that the praise, blame, or shame of an individual is assumed by the group" (Turner, 1991, p. 4). African Americans are said to place a high value on interpersonal relations. The maintenance of interpersonal relationships is considered more important than the acquisition of material objects (Schiele, 1990).

The notion of collectivity is also illuminated in the way African American families are structured. The term "twinlineal" was coined to define African family lineages that come from the mother and father rather than only the mother or father, as in matrilineal and patrilineal family systems. These family systems include members who are not biologically related, an extensive network of cousins, including distant cousins and half- and step-siblings (Graham, 1999). Other common patterns in families of African descent also illustrate collective identity, including shared child-rearing arrangements (family members assist or take over the care and nurturing of a child whose parents are unable to do so), and flexible gender roles (traditionally more so than in Euro-American families) (Turner, 1991).

Spirituality.   Spirituality has been defined as that invisible substance that connects all human beings to one another and to a creator (Schiele, 1994). This is also evidenced in the belief that the interconnectedness of all things sees no separation between the material and the spiritual. Human beings are perceived as an integral part of nature, and living in harmony with the environment helps them to become at one with all reality. The concept of oneness relates to those not yet born and those who have died; all human beings are linked spiritually across time and space.

The Afrocentric model recognizes the spiritual or nonmaterial aspect of human beings. The spiritual essence of human beings requires a shift in thinking toward valuing human beings above the social and economic status that has been assigned to them.

African Epistemology.   In the Afrocentric model, emphasis is placed on an affective epistemology. Several scholars (Asante, 1988; Akbar, 1984; Schiele, 1997) have discussed the importance of affect as a valid way of knowing for African Americans.

The Afrocentric perspective uses African epistemology—about African Americans, formulated based on African American experiences, and exhibited through the use of symbolic imagery and rhythm. This focus on affect in Afrocentric thought does not preclude recognition and use of rationality. Instead, affect, as a means of knowing, is viewed as offsetting the use of rationality (Akbar, 1984).

According to proponents of the Afrocentric perspective, these tenets are viewed negatively: spirituality as superstition and voodoo, communalism as dependence, rhythmic orientation as hyperactivity, expressive individualism as showiness, and an affective orientation as immature and irrational (Harris, 1999).

Although the cultural patterns described above are rooted in the African experience, not all African Americans adhere to these values or ascribe to these principles. According to English (1991), "these variations occur based on a range of complex factors, including social mobility, urban experiences, the impact of racism and discrimination on life experiences, and childhood socialization" (p. 23).

For this reason, proponents of the Afrocentric view do not attempt to generalize this view as the universal reality as it relates to African Americans. Everett et al. (1991) and Mosely-Howard and Evans (2000) believe that determining the degree to which the Afrocentric cultural values exist in an individual, family, or group is essential to the effective use of the Afrocentric view.

Core Principles for Practice

Although an Afrocentric framework has yet to be systematically applied to social work intervention on a wide scale, some efforts of its application have appeared in social work literature. The concept of Afrocentricity was not developed solely as a social work theory—its richness is in multidisciplinary roots. It is useful in social work practice because it offers conceptual and analytical tools for working with African Americans. For this reason, Afrocentricity requires the deliberate, conscious effort of social workers and others committed to its promulgation. A number of social work scholars and practitioners have incorporated Afrocentric practice into principles in their scholarly work and in their practice in the areas of chemical dependence, child abuse, relationships, child rearing, and youth crime. Some of these applications will be described here.

Buffer Against Oppression

The widest application of the Afrocentric perspective has been in Eastern cities with large African American populations. Elementary school educators have used the principles to boost the self-esteem and a sense of pride in African American children. Similarly, many predominately African American schools have used Afrocentric principles in an effort to socialize the children to resist racism and to combat internalized oppression.

Proponents of the Afrocentric worldview purport that those who embrace it are more likely to be self-accepting, even in the face of negative societal messages to which they are repeatedly exposed. In this view, Afrocentricity is seen as a boost to African American self-identity and self-acceptance. For instance, Hatter and Owens (1998) found that African American students who more closely identified with an Afrocentric worldview reported a higher level of self-assessed adaptation in a predominantly white university. This study has implications for the education of social work students as well as others in a university setting. Schools of social work, especially those who have difficulty retaining African American students, might consider promoting and enhancing the development of the Afrocentric perspective in its curriculum. This may mean educators' examining policies and practices that devalue the African-centered perspective as well as including Afrocentricity in the curriculum.

Harris-Johnson (1999) developed and implemented an Afrocentric mentoring program for university students involving a "developmental process of empowerment in which each stage promotes skill development, self-confidence, and eventually the acumen to mentor others" (p. 1). The goals of the program are to use the paradigm to promote individual, academic, and social success.

Clinical Treatment

Todisco and Salomone (1991) provide useful tools for incorporating an Afrocentric perspective in cross-cultural counseling, specifically when the counselor is white and the client is African American. In a discussion about cultural bias they enumerate common assumptions made in cross-cultural encounters: "(a) all people share a common measure of what constitutes 'normal' behavior, (b) there is a dependence on linear 'cause and effect' thinking, (c) people of all cultures understand the intended meanings of abstract words frequently used in Western culture, and (d) counselors are already aware of their own assumptions" (p. 4). They support and encourage the need for non-African American counselors to develop a deepening awareness of their inherent biases and how those will affect their work with African American clients. They also encourage white practitioners to gain an understanding for the Afrocentric worldview to prevent bias and the tendency to pathologize normative behaviors.

Informing Research on African American Families

Scholars (Crosbie-Burnett & Lewis, 1993; McDaniel, 1990; Mosely-Howard & Evans, 2000; Auslander et al., 2000) believe that the African American family maintains vestiges of the African culture and, therefore, promote using Afrocentric models in social work with African American families. Crosbie-Burnett and Lewis (1993) propose that strategies and coping mechanisms used by functional African American families can assist the growing number of European American families living in "nontraditional" family structures due to divorce. African American families have traditionally maintained many structure variations that are quite functional when viewed from an African-centered paradigm.

The research method used by Crosbie-Burnett & Lewis (1993)—most aptly labeled "resiliency research"—"seek[s] to identify the factors or mechanisms that enhance the resilience of disadvantaged groups over various stages of their life development" (p. 244). Focusing on the strengths of African American families is not a new concept; other scholars have conducted similar research in the past decade, yet little has been done to advance the idea that new approaches to family practice can and should be developed using observed and documented strengths.

Assessment, Planning, and Program Development in Child Welfare

In an attempt to address concerns about the disproportionate numbers of African American children who enter and remain in the child welfare system, several scholars have promoted the usefulness of the Afrocentric paradigm. Everett et al. (1991) maintain that services and practices for child welfare have historically been designed using models that pathologize and devalue the unique cultural attributes of African Americans. Their book entitled *Child Welfare: An Africentric Perspective* provides useful guidelines for incorporating this model into the assessment, planning, and delivery of services to African American children and their families. They believe that a "one size fits all" approach to child welfare policies and practices is inherently oppressive, since it is based on Eurocentric models of human behavior, which have resulted in "minority children receiving insufficient, inadequate, and often inappropriate and damaging child welfare services" (p. 59). The book offers a "culturally based perspective—the Africentric perspective . . . used to describe the social context, value base, attitudes, and behaviors that shape the belief systems, coping strategies, defensive styles, help-seeking behaviors, and treatment responses of African American families and children" (p. 11). Some of the guidelines include using existing mediating structures in the community such as churches; recognizing family-structure variations in the African American community and thus considering a wider range of options for the placement of children removed from their homes; and using "cultural amplifiers," people who have their finger on the pulse of the community and "who can articulate certain perspectives and points of view that are unavailable from the worker" (Everett et al., 1991, p. 72). Recent developments in child welfare have seen some infusion of the importance of viewing African American families from their unique perspective and some change in child welfare organizational practices nationwide based on that. African American and other children of color represent a growing majority of cases in the child-welfare system, suggesting a growing need for social workers in this field to adopt an Afrocentric perspective and to encourage its acceptance.

Everett et al. (1991) suggest some principles for enhancing the quality of child welfare practice to children of color:

> . . . (1) utilizing conceptual frameworks that provide sound foundations for understanding the cultural contexts of various families and communities; (2) incorporating specific knowledge about the organization, structure, and functioning of culturally and racially different families, including values, beliefs, attitudes, and behaviors, into practice; and (3) designing responsive service-delivery systems based on this knowledge. (p. 10)

Designing Substance-Abuse Programs

An example of Afrocentric perspective applied in the treatment of substance abuse is "Iwo San," a residential treatment program for African American women and their children. The principles applied include encouraging a sense of community among residents in the program; involving the external community in some aspects of treatment, including allowing children to live with their recovering mothers; incorporating "rites of passage" to expose participants to Afrocentric thought; affirming respect for tradition through establishing a council of elders selected by the participants "based on the degree of esteem and perceived wisdom in which the Elders were held by fellow residents, staff and community" (Jackson, 1995, p. 8).

The Cultural-Alignment Framework for Violent Crimes Among Youth

Jerome Schiele (1998) offers a framework to explain African American male youth violence and offer solutions. The "cultural-alignment framework," as it is entitled, seeks to combine a "political economic perspective with the concepts of cultural oppression and cultural alienation" (p. 168). According to Schiele (1998), "Cultural oppression is the imposition of the dominant group's culture on oppressed and powerless groups, wherein the culture of the oppressed is considered marginal, illegitimate, or nonexistent" (p. 168). To do this, the culturally dominant group gains control over the interpretations of history, knowledge validation, and social reality by dominating and controlling society's socializing institutions. Cultural alienation occurs when the culturally oppressed are disconnected from their own cultural history and cultural traditions as a result of their having internalized the negative messages received from the dominant group about themselves and others like them.

Schiele (1998) further contends that the internalization of these messages leads to negative self-images and the adoption of cultural standards that are contrary to the African-centered worldview. He concludes that the very values that are "endemic to the European American worldview (i.e., individualism, materialism, and rugged competition) represent the very basis for political and economic oppression in the United States" (p. 172).

Cultural-alignment solutions seek to align the client—in this case African American male youth—with Afrocentric values. This approach seeks to foster a more culturally centered male who is capable of resisting violence and other forms of self-destructive behavior and thus capable of contributing to the community and the society. Specific approaches include developing "manhood training" and "rites of passage" programs. Manhood training programs proliferated during the 1990s, their emphasis being to "help African American male youths to reconstruct and internalize a definition of manhood that stems from the sociocultural and philosophical traditions of African Americans" (p. 174). Rites of passage programs mark a youth's change in status in the developmental process, signifying the successful movement toward adulthood.

The cultural-alignment framework recognizes that for Afrocentric socialization to be successful, the youth needs to be immersed in the Afrocentric concepts and those same concepts must be reinforced through other aspects of the community, such as the church, the schools, and recreational organizations.

Contributions and Limitations

There is no dearth of literature on African American cultural beliefs produced by African American scholars. What has yet to be determined is the extent to which the published ideas and theories can affect the prevailing paradigms and practice in social work. "At the heart is the question, Whose vision of the role of African Americans, other people of color, and the disenfranchised will prevail?" (Gordon, 1990, p. 1).

The Afrocentric perspective has received very little attention in the major social work journals, this despite its persistence as a major theme in the scholarly work and practice of African American social workers. Furthermore what does appear in mainstream journals is not yet accepted into the mainstream practice, though it has received widespread attention in collegiate intellectual circles and appears to have a strong audience among African Americans. The concept has not yet been applied systematically to social work, although some efforts to change this appear in recent literature. This author will examine some of the challenges and present considerations for developing the approach for use in mainstream social work practice.

For the Afrocentric perspective to emerge as a more widespread alternative paradigm for social work, more conceptual work needs to be done to address two areas of conceptual weakness. The first involves centrality of race versus the centrality of other defining features, such as gender, age, sexual orientation, or socioeconomic status, in the development of identity or worldview. Although the Afrocentric perspective acknowledges the presence of other centers and the multidimensionality of each individual in this perspective, it does not adequately address the intersection and interrelatedness of other centers or sources of identity. In elevating race and ethnicity above other sources of identity, the Afrocentric perspective as currently described does not confirm the multidimensionality of individuals, but rather assumes that one dimension—race or ethnicity—provides an adequate view of the individual. More needs to be done to recognize and attempt to deal with these dualistic categories in the Afrocentric perspective.

The second conceptual problem relates to how to address the differences in adherence to the acceptance of the Afrocentric worldview within the African American community. The pervasive assertion in many of the published works on the Afrocentric paradigm is that African Americans share certain cultural attributes. The Afrocentric perspective may assume commonalties in the African American experience that do not actually exist. Proponents of the Afrocentric worldview acknowledge that people of African descent vary in the degree to which they have internalized an Afrocentric worldview, but most argue that even if African Americans do not possess all of the attributes most commonly associated with an Afrocentric worldview, the common bond of oppression, felt and manifested in various ways, still exists. English (1991) makes a useful attempt to address this concern by developing a typology of worldviews to measure the participation and commitment of African Americans to their own culture versus participation and commitment to mainstream or another culture. This work needs to be continued and built upon to address obvious and recurring concerns about the perspective.

Case Example

Her attending physician referred Staci and her family to the Hospice program of a large university hospital. She was the mother of a twelve-year-old girl, Tia, who was in the terminal stages of bone cancer. Staci was a single thirty-three-year-old African American mother of Tia and three-year-old James. The family lived in a government subsidized home in a socioeconomically depressed section of the city. Staci had not worked since James's birth and was receiving welfare for her children.

The Hospice team accepted the referral with some hesitation as the hospital had reported that Staci was uncooperative during her daughter's hospitalizations and had not always complied with the medical team's advice regarding her daughter's care. She was deemed "unstable" because of her frequent emotional outbursts and "dependent" because she seemed to need her family's involvement in every aspect of her life. She often allowed family to move into her home, which caused her small home to be overcrowded and hectic. Some team members suspected she might be running an unlicensed daycare—she often had several children besides her own in her care. Further evidence of her "instability" was that Staci, it was noted, was never married to Tia's father, and he seemed to have little role in Tia's upbringing. James's father seemed to have a larger role in the care of the children, but he had fathered James while married to a woman with whom he continued to reside. It was also reported that Staci was from a large dysfunctional family, and many of the family were interfering in the child's care.

As a consultant to the hospice team, I was asked to assist the family's social worker, a recent MSW graduate, to develop a plan for intervention aimed at securing the family's cooperation in carrying out the work needed to prepare for the child's imminent death. Hospice's involvement had, it seemed, only intensified the problems reported by hospital staff. Members of the hospice team concluded that Staci's attitude toward them made it difficult for the family to receive the full benefits of hospice involvement.

During our initial contacts with Staci, she was admittedly very guarded. Each inquiry into her history or current situation was met with skepticism, which she said stemmed from her having "talked about my business too much in the beginning and now it is being used against me." Staci revealed that she was born to a single mother in Georgia but raised by her mother's sister and husband, a childless couple, since she was two years old. She had maintained a close relationship with her mother and siblings over the years; in fact, her mother had cared for Tia for almost a year after James was born. It was during this time that Tia began to complain of leg pain, but she was not diagnosed until months later when she returned to her mother's care. Staci reports that members of her medical team reminded her on numerous occasions that an earlier diagnosis may have resulted in a better outcome for her daughter. This, she concluded, meant she was being blamed for her daughter's impending death.

Staci referred frequently to family members who she felt had been very supportive to her: the aunt and uncle who raised her—she referred to them as "Momma and Daddy"—helped out financially; two cousins who help with child care; and an aunt—a nursing assistant who helped her to understand medical terms and procedures. I invited her family and anyone else Staci felt was important in her daughter's care to the next visit. They all attended, and James, her son's father, attended as well.

It was during this visit that members of the extended family revealed their ongoing concerns about Tia. This was the first time they had an opportunity to voice their concerns, and they expressed anger, disappointment, and confusion that they had often been ignored and pushed aside by Staci's health care team as if their input did not matter. They expressed the desire to be part of any plans for the child's further treatment and ongoing care.

At a subsequent visit, Staci reported that Tia's father, Joe, had been over earlier to visit. He did not come often because he found it unbearable to visit. She then revealed that she and Joe, high school sweethearts, had lived together for three years before Tia's birth and had a loving, stable relationship. She had become pregnant with his child in her senior year, and they decided to move in together after graduation to raise their son, Terrence. He secured a job with the post office and she worked as a bank teller. Two years later, when she was in her eighth month of pregnancy with Tia, they were driving home from a family outing when a drunken driver crossed the divider and hit their vehicle. Joe suffered a head injury that left him unable to work. Staci escaped with a broken leg and fractured wrist. Their son, Terrence, was killed instantly. Joe moved in with his mother, fell into a deep depression, and the relationship deteriorated. This would be the first time she revealed this to anyone other than her family since her daughter's diagnosis.

Intervention with this family began with helping the social worker as well as the rest of the hospice team "shift the center" of their thinking about this client to an African-centered perspective. Much of what had been labeled as dysfunctional or problematic had to be reframed in a way that would allow members of the team to appreciate the many strengths of this family. Members of her hospice and medical team were encouraged to view Staci from these perspectives:

1. Staci's strong ties to her family provided her with not only emotional but material support, critical to her survival as a single parent. She and her extended family were part of a mutual aid network; they often ate at each other's houses, traded childcare, and shared material resources. They also had to understand that the shared child-rearing arrangements described in her history were not part of a dysfunctional pattern, that children born to one set of parents may well be raised in another family's household as part of a normal, functional arrangement made in the best interest of the child. When the advice of her medical team was in conflict with that of her family, she would side with her family because she had been taught to observe their rules and to respect them—especially the older members of her family. This worker included the family in the overall treatment plan and ongoing care and support for Staci and Tia.

2. Much attention was focused on the "nontraditional" structure of Staci's family. Even though Staci had revealed little about her past relationships, members of the team had assumed she was "dependent" and "irresponsible" to have had three children out of

wedlock and "multiple" unsuccessful relationships. This social worker revealed a more accurate picture of Staci, which was evident in her maintaining stable relationships with the fathers of her children, caring for and nurturing her children, and maintaining strong and mutually supportive relationships with family and friends. The use of shared child-rearing arrangements should not, therefore, be seen as "dysfunctional."

3. Staci was seen by the team as a victim needing to be rescued—a "poor" African American single parent who needed some sort of intervention. Her resistance to accept the services as rendered was seen as proof of her dysfunction. Staci did not see herself as poor. She lived in a clean, well-kept neighborhood, had adequate material resources to meet her family's needs, and had enough to share with others that were in greater need. She chose to live in this neighborhood to be near her family and friends. She refused volunteer services that she felt she did not need, and in many ways she saw the hospice team as intruders in her home. This social worker encouraged members of the team to individualize Staci's plan, allowing her to define her own problems and actively participate in her treatment plan—rather than imposing the "standard services" on her. Information about the normative help-seeking behaviors of African Americans was also introduced, helping the team to understand that Staci was more likely to use and be comfortable with natural helping resources such as her friends, family, and church members, than with established institutional care.

4. Staci's relationship with the medical/hospice team had been complicated, in part, by experiences she and her family had had with other institutions that had assaulted her cultural views and value systems by seeking conformity. Staci and her family thus came into the medical system with a defensive stance, feeling that they needed to keep control. This worker sought to help members of the team understand that any reactions to Staci that measured her by white, middle-class standards and that did not affirm her strengths could be likened to "cultural oppression." For instance, Staci spoke non-standard English, which led some to draw early conclusions that she was not smart enough to understand what was needed for her daughter's care. Medical staff tended to make decisions "in Tia's best interest" without Staci's input and then imposed those decisions on her after the fact. The staff complained that she either did not read or she disregarded written material given to her that would help her understand her daughter's disease and how best to care for her. Staci reports that she did read the material, but she did not rely on it as her sole source of information. She felt that she knew her daughter better than anyone, and she relied as much on her intuition and Tia's responses as she did the written information she was given. This worker sought to affirm Staci's "way of knowing" that—while it may not appear to be rational from the rest of the team's point of view—was an important cultural attribute that had been very useful to her in the past.

The Afrocentric perspective was a useful tool for assessing and developing a culturally appropriate treatment plan for Staci and her family. The team was encouraged to take a non-judgmental stance with this client, to validate her efforts to be effective as a parent and responsive to her family, and to support her use of natural helping resources and her family's involvement in carrying out what they believed to be the best available care and treatment for Tia.

Questions for Critical Thinking

1. What, if any, theories used in social work embrace "centrist" perspectives such as those presented by cultural feminists and the Afrocentric perspective?

2. What is the meaning of self-identify in the context of diversity, and how is one's identity developed?

3. How could the basic underlying premise of the Afrocentric perspective, which is centrism, be used to assist other marginalized groups?

4. What parallels exist between Afrocentricity and cultural feminism?

5. How could non-African American social workers use the Afrocentric paradigm?

Sources for Further Study

Asante, Molefi K. *Afrocentricity*. (3rd ed.). Trenton, NJ: Africa World Press, 1992. Asante argues for a redefinition of what it means to be an American—at least for African Americans. "Afrocentricity is pro-African and consistent in its beliefs that technology belongs to the world; Afrocentricity is African genius and African values created, reconstructed, and derived from our history and experiences in our best interests. If one understands properly African history, an assumption can never be made that Afrocentricity is a back to 'anything' movement. It is an uncovering of one's true self, it is the pinpointing of one's center, and it is the clarity and focus through which black people must see the world in order to escalate. . . . Afrocentricity is a concern for some, a possibility for others, and an imperative for the Africans of the world" (p. viii).

> Afrocentricity builds upon several intellectual foundations such as Garveyism, Kawaida, and Negritude. Yet, without the genius of those ways of viewing the African presence and reality, Afrocentricity could never have been. Quite correctly, there is not another truth more necessary for the intellectual political, economic, and cultural advancement of the world than African people immersing themselves in the waters of a cultural rebirth. This is the hard truth of history, and the only real lesson we need to learn for the total liberation of ourselves and our children. (p. 104)

Asante, Molefi K. *The Afrocentric Idea*. Revised and Expanded ed. Philadelphia: Temple University Press, 1998. In his book's new edition, Asante seeks to achieve three basic intellectual aims: first, to provide an expansive portrait of the Afrocentric idea; second, to address a new group of critics who have emerged in response to the expansive thrust of the movement he initiated; and third, to pose some concepts and categories for fruitful development of the discourse within the discipline of Black studies.

> Asante reaches across disciplines to equip himself with a solid armature of evidence in his ongoing battle against deconstructionists, racists, integrationists, Marxists, liberals, cultural chauvinists, and a host of other Eurocentric claimants to single truths, universality, objectivity, and other problematic pretensions. His method is to outline and identify critical weaknesses in cherished Eurocentric conceptions, dismiss them, and then introduce alternative pathways to pursue in an ongoing engagement with the products and processes of the Afrocentric project.

> Asante defines Afrocentricity as "literally placing African ideals at the center of any analysis that involves African culture and behavior." Necessary to the idea of centering is attention to location and stance. As in his other works (*Afrocentricity and Kemet, Afrocentricity and Knowledge*), he is rightly concerned with critical self-understanding in the context of one's own culture and the world. Asante suggests three fundamental themes for a transcendent Afrocentric discourse: relationships humans have with each other, relationships humans have with the supernatural, and relationships humans have with themselves; however, this discussion is not as extensive as other parts of the book. There is not the vast array of African literatures in which to frame his discussion, or pursue either the basis for such choice or its varied expressions.

Diop, Cheikh Anta. *The African Origin of Civilization: Myth or Reality*. (M. Cook, ed. & trans.). Westport, CT: Lawrence Hill, 1974. This is only one of Diop's many publications on African history that present exhaustive research backing the claim that ancient Egypt was a black civilization. Diop also believed that Africans could not remove the chains of colonialism from their psyche until they had a fully reconstructed history—in other words, until they had a usable past. Diop brought together three important elements in understanding the origins of Afrocentrism: first, the tradition of professional, politically motivated historical research that buttresses the claims of untrained, amateur historians; second, the explicit connection between knowledge of one's "proper" history and one's psychological and spiritual well-being; third, the connection between knowledge of one's proper history and the realization of a political mission and purpose.

Everett, Joyce, Sandra S. Chipungu, and Bogart R. Leashore, eds. *Child Welfare: An Africentric Perspective*. New Brunswick, NJ.: Rutgers University Press, 1991. The editors provide a careful and deliberate description of problems facing African American children in the child welfare system and thoughtful ideas for how to address them. The ongoing problem of African American children being overrepresented on child welfare caseloads and in foster placement nationwide was the impetus for this book. Using the Africentric perspective as a guiding framework, the authors develop an alternative approach for working with African American families and for reconceptualizing the way services are delivered to this population. This book represents the most well-developed application to date of the Africentric perspective in social work practice.

Williams, Chancellor. *The Destruction of Black Civilization: Great Issues of a Race from 4500 B.C. to 2000 A.D.* Chicago: Third World Press, 1987. This is an account of Williams' many research trips to Africa. He did a great deal to combat the view that Africa does not have a history. He researched records of institutions, traditions, political ideologies, and complex societies. He claimed that Eurocentric education was antithetical, both politically and intellectually, to African interests—a common refrain in Afrocentrist thought.

References

Abbary, A. S. (1990). Afrocentrcity. *Journal of Black Studies*, *21*(2) 123–126.

Akbar, N. (1984). Afrocentric social sciences for human liberation. *Journal of Black Studies*, *14*, 395–414.

Appleby, G. (2001). *Dynamics of oppression and discrimination, diversity, oppression, and social function: Person-in-environment assessment and intervention*. Eds. Appleby, G., Colon, E., & Hamilton, J., pp. 36–51.

Asante, M. K. (1987). *The Afrocentric idea*. Philadelphia: Temple University Press.

Asante, M. K. (1988). *Afrocentricity*. Trenton, NJ: Africa World.

Asante, M. K. (1998). *The Afrocentric idea* (Revised and Expanded Edition). Philadelphia: Temple University Press.

Auslander, W., Haire-Josher, D., and Williams, J. H. (2000). African American family structure. *Journal of Family Issues*, *21*(7), 838–858.

Billingsley, A. (1968). *Black families in white America*. Englewood Cliffs, NJ: Prentice–Hall.

Braun-Williams, C. (1999). African American women, Afrocentrism, and feminism: Implications for therapy. *Women and Therapy*, *22*(4).

Collins, P. H., & Anderson, M. L. (2001). *Race, class, and gender: An anthology* (4th ed.). Belmont, CA: Wadsworth Publishing Company.

Covin, D. (1990). Afrocentricity in O Movimento Negro Unificado. *Journal of Black Studies*, *21*(2), 126–145.

Crosbie-Burnett, M., & Lewis, E. (1993). Use of African-American family structures and functioning to address the challenges of European-American postdivorce families. *Family Relations*, *42*(3), 243–249.

Early, G. (1995). Understanding Afrocentrism. *Civilization, 2*(4), 31–40.

English, R. (1991). Diversity of world views among African American families. In Chipungu, S., Everett, J., & Leashore, B. (eds.), *Child welfare: An Afrocentric perspective.* New Brunswick, NJ: Rutgers University Press, pp. 19–35.

Everett, J. (1991). Introduction: Children in crisis. In Chipungu, S., Everett, J., & Leashore, B. (Eds.), *Child welfare: An Afrocentric perspective.* New Brunswick, NJ: Rutgers University Press, pp. 1–14.

Frazier, E. F. (1966). *The Negro family in the United States* (Rev. ed.). Chicago: University of Chicago Press.

Graham, Mekada J. (1999). The African-centered woldview: Toward a paradigm for social work. *Journal of Black Studies, 30*(1), 103–123.

Gordon, B. M. (1990). The necessity of African-American epistemology for educational theory and practice. *Journal of Education, 172*(3), 88–107.

Harris, F. (1999). Centricity and the mentoring experience in academia: An Africentric mentoring paradigm. *Western Journal of Black Studies, 23*(4), 229–236.

Hatter, D. Y., & Ottens, A. J. (1998). Afrocentric world view and black students' adjustment to a predominantly white university: Does worldview matter? *College Student Journal, 32*(3), 472–481.

Hoskins, L. A. (1992). Eurocentrism vs. Afrocentrism. *Journal of Black Studies, 23*(2), 247–258.

Jackson, M. S. (1995). Afrocentric treatment of African American women and their children in a residential chemical dependency program. *Journal of Black Studies, 26*(1), 17–31.

Keto, C. T. (1991). *The Africa-centered perspective of history: An introduction.* Laurel Springs, NJ: K. A. Publishers.

Landrine, H., & Klonoff, E. (1999). Acculturation and alcohol use among blacks: The benefits of remaining culturally traditional. *Western Journal of Black Studies, 23*(4).

Lawson, E., Gibbs, T., & Reed, W. E. (1997). Afrocentrism in the 21st century. *Western Journal Black Studies, 21*(3), 173–180.

Lowry, R. F. (1998). Development theory, globalism, and the new world order. *Journal of Black Studies, 28*(5), 594–616.

Lum, D. (2000). *Social work practice and people of color: A process stage approach* (4th ed.). Pacific Grove, CA: Brooks/Cole.

McDaniel, A. (1990). The power of culture: A review of the idea of Africa's influence on family structure in Antebellum America. *Journal of Family History, 15*(2), 225–239.

McLaren, J. (1998). Ngugi wa Thiong'os' moving the centre and its relevance to Afrocentricity. *Journal of Black Studies, 28*(3), 386–398.

McPhail, M. (1998). From complicity to coherence: Rereading the rhetoric of Afrocentricity. *Western Journal of Communication, 62*(2), 114–141.

Miller, J. B. (1991). The development of women's sense of self. In A. G. Caplan et al., *Women's growth in connection: Writings from the Stone Center.* New York: Guilford Press, pp. 23–51.

Mosely-Howard, G., & Evans, C. (2000). Relationships and contemporary experiences of the African American family. *Journal of Black Studies, 30*(3), 428–453.

Moynihan, D. P. (1965). *The Negro family: The case for national concern.* New York: Bantam.

Schiele, J. H. (1990). Organizational theory from an Afrocentric perspective. *Journal of Black Studies, 30*(2), 145–162.

Schiele, J. H. (1994). Afrocentricity: Implications for higher education. *Journal of Black Studies, 25*(2), 150–170.

Schiele, J. H. (1996). Afrocentrism: An emerging paradigm in social work practice. *Social Work, 41*(3), 284–295.

Schiele, J. H. (1997). The contour and meaning of Afrocentric social work. *Journal of Black Studies, 27*(6), 800–820.

Schiele, J. H. (1998). Cultural alignment, African American male youths and violent crime. In Lee, L., *Human behavior in the social environment from an African American perspective*. New York: The Haworth Press, pp. 165–181.

Todisco, M., & Salomone, P. R. (1991). Facilitating effective cross-cultural relationships: The white counselor and the black client. *Journal of Multicultural Counseling and Development, 19*(4), 146–158.

Turner, R. (1991). Affirming consciousness: The Afrocentric perspective in child welfare. In Chipungu, S., Everett, J., & Leashore, B. (Eds.) *Child welfare: An Afrocentric perspective*. New Brunswick, NJ: Rutgers University Press, pp. 36–57.

Verharen, C. (1995). Afrocentrism and acentrism. *Journal of Black Studies, 26*(1), 62–77.

Worden, B. (2001). Women and sexist oppression. In Appleby, G., Colon, E., & Hamilton, J. (Eds.), *Diversity, oppression, and social functioning: Person-in-environment assessment and intervention*, pp. 70–89.

9

Social Justice Framework

Arline W. Prigoff

The Social Justice Framework is an orientation in social work practice that is based on the profession's recognition that all human beings, in order to achieve healthy development and productive, rewarding lives, require (1) access to and utilization of life-supporting, life-enhancing resources; (2) opportunities to participate, within the cultural institutions of their societies, in decision-making on critically important issues in their lives; and (3) respect for self-expression and human rights, and protections that enable people to live in dignity and without fear of persecution on the basis of culture, religion, or other aspects of personal identity.

Within and among the world's nations, access to and utilization of life-supporting, life-enhancing resources, as well as opportunities to exercise political decision-making power and to live without fear, are extremely unequally distributed. Distribution of **economic power**, the control of and access to goods, services and productive resources; **political power**, participation in decision-making; and legally protected **human rights**, including freedom of expression, are associated with variables of race and ethnicity, gender, class, age, physical ability/disability, national origins, education, occupation, and other categories or classifications that are factors in social status. The gap between rich and poor continues to widen, as does the gap between small groups of elite, politically powerful individuals and powerless, vulnerable populations. In the political rhetoric of leaders around the world, respect for human rights is universally proclaimed; yet, the violation of human rights by powerful interest groups that aim to maintain power and control is extremely widespread (Brown, 2001; United Nations, 1948; United Nations Development Programme, 2001).

Major Precursors and Developers

From the start of social work as a profession, social workers have been vocal on issues of social justice. Violence against individuals, families, and communities, and abuses that violate human rights and human dignity are viewed with alarm. Oppression, the use of violence to exercise power, is by definition the institutionalized, systematic imposition of inequality. Its dimensions include inequality in access to resources, in decision-making power, in social roles and social status, based on group characteristics such as economic wealth, race or ethnicity, gender, age, occupational status and income, sexual orientation, physical ability, etc. Opposition to institutional racism and other structural forms of oppression have shaped the development and expression of a social justice framework in the field of social work. The energy of community groups acting for social justice truly is contagious. The social work profession also applies the social justice framework in social work practice through policy pronouncements and activity in national, international, and community-based local coalitions that oppose oppression.

Movements for the abolition of slavery and labor's right to organize inspired social workers to add community organizing, group work, program development, administration and social action to the repertoire of social caseworkers. The Settlement House Movement in social work arose in response to environmental conditions of living that were humiliating and degrading for immigrant families. Political protests in response to the Great Depression, mobilization of support for refugees from fascism, the Civil Rights Movement, and Poor People's campaigns for economic and social justice called for political mobilization, and social workers responded. They marched with Martin Luther King Jr. and with Cesar Chavez in mass protests against racial and ethnic injustice. These activists brought communications and group-process skills to organizations they joined, and they even provided leadership in the development of relevant public services. Jane Addams, Henry Hopkins of the New Deal era, Richard Cloward, Frances Piven, and George Wiley, who designed strategies of the Welfare Rights Movement; David Gil, Janet Woods Wetzel, and Diane Falk, who focused on human rights issues; Helen Graber of the CSWE Women's Commission who was instrumental in bringing feminist issues into course curricula; Dorothy Van Soest and the NASW Violence and Development Project that disseminated key concepts under her leadership all contributed to constructing of a social justice framework. Social work educators who added international dimensions to that framework include Jim Billups, Maria Julia, Martin Tracy, Yvonne Asamoah, Richard Estes, Vera Mehta, Terry Hokenstad, Saliwe Kawewe, Lena Dominelli, Jim Midgley, Rosemary Link, Chathapuram Ramanathan, Lynne Healy, Maureen Wilson, and many others. These people understood the legacy of colonialism, and their contact with social work programs in Africa, Latin America, Asia, and the Pacific Islands prepared them to apply a social justice framework in the field of international social work.

At the close of the historic colonial era, the five hundred years from 1492 to the latter part of the twentieth century, voices with integrity spoke out from oppressed nations and national minorities. Among the articulate activist authors who provided insights that enlightened a process of global social transformation were Albert Memmi, Frantz Fanon, Walter Rodney, Simone de Beauvoir, Paolo Freire, Nelson and Winnie Mandela, Manning Marable, and bell hooks. Their works, listed as references in the bibliography at the close of this chapter, are core source materials for understanding the social justice framework. These writers were familiar with the conceptual frameworks of Karl Marx, Frederick Engels, and Vladimir Ilyich Lenin and cited the works of these revolutionary thinkers in their own texts. Based on their studies and their experience with processes of social change, they knew that mental concepts are powerful tools for deconstructing and transforming social systems and human institutions. Studying and disseminating their writings and using their approaches to praxis (Freire's term) are empowering in behalf of the liberation of oppressed communities.

Core Concepts

The social justice framework is founded on social work values that recognize the worth and value of every member of the human family. Like the dual perspective framework (Chapter 7), the social justice framework recognizes that structural features of human societies and institutional systems, group norms, and cultural patterns may support and facilitate the actualization of healthy human development and productivity, or they may serve as barriers to growth and fulfillment in human populations. Deprivation—lack of essential resources and supports for the achievement of physical, social, and cognitive development—impedes the actualization of human potentiality in individuals, families, and communities. Application of a social justice framework promotes the analysis of the causes of inequality and maldistribution of resources. This framework calls for public resources to be invested in and distributed through programs, processes, and activities that will provide maximum benefit to the largest number of people—especially those who are vulnerable, powerless, and deprived of supports that are essential for growth and physical and mental health.

Carole R. Swenson (1998) states that "Social justice is increasingly being seen as the organizing value of social work" (pp. 527–537). In support of that thesis, Swenson credits the works of John Rawls, David Gil, Dorothy Van Soest, and the NASW Code of Ethics for social work's advocacy of social justice as a primary ethical value and principle. It was Rawls whose concept of distributive justice was especially relevant for the field of social work, in view of its social mission. "Rawls (1971) developed two principles: (1) Basic liberties must be equal, because citizens in a just society must have equal rights; (2) there should be equality of opportunity and of social resources for each person" (Swenson, 1998, p. 529).

J. C. Wakefield noted the relevance of Rawls's concept of distributive justice for social workers.

> I believe that a Rawlsian approach to distributive justice has the power to make sense of the social work profession and its disparate activities in ways not yet generally appreciated. Social work can be conceived as a profession engaged in alleviating deprivation in all its varieties, from economic to psychological; social workers identify people who fall below the social minimum in any justice related good and intervene in order to help them rise above that minimally acceptable level. (Wakefield, 1988, as cited in Swenson 1998, p. 529)

Dorothy Van Soest, in the *Encyclopedia of Social Work* (1995), defines three components of social justice: legal justice, concerning what a person owes to society; commutative justice, what people owe to each other; and distributive justice—following Rawls—"what society owes to a person" (p. 1811). Van Soest states that distributive justice, involving decisions about the allocation of resources, and supporting the other two dimensions in social justice, has the most profound impact on human health and on the physical, emotional, and cognitive development of human beings.

Swenson (1998) reviewed formal statements on the subject of social justice formulated by the CSWE's 1992 Curriculum Policy Statement and the NASW's 1996 Code of Ethics.

> In the curriculum policy statement, promotion of economic and social justice are mandated content areas, as are diversity, populations at risk, and ethics and values. All of these can be seen as different perspectives on the concept of social justice. Populations at risk are people from whom social resources have been unjustly withheld; diversity entails respecting the cultures of everyone, not just the privileged few; and social work ethics and values emphasize the dignity and worth of each person, respect for difference, promoting social change, and multicultural competence. All of these are elements of a just society. The newly revised *Code of Ethics* includes substantially more attention than the previous one to social justice as a responsibility of all social workers, including attention to diversity, oppression, and populations at risk. All social workers are expected to influence social policy, engage in social action, and advocate for disadvantaged groups. (p. 528)

The social justice framework promotes social action by professional groups, organizations, and individuals in alliance with community groups and social movements on behalf of social change. This transformational perspective empowers social workers as well as vulnerable, oppressed communities, and it has implications for both policy practice and clinical practice. This approach to practice is analytical and action-oriented. Community organizing skills are utilized to expose and eliminate institutional practices that are oppressive and to remove, or at least reduce, barriers that block the exercise of community and personal power.

The framework is very compatible with therapeutic approaches; in fact, it can itself be considered a therapeutic modality. In its application, knowledge about the challenge of life stages and tasks in the development of individuals and families is integrated with knowledge about the impact on human development of structural features of societies and their institutions. Judith Herman, M.D., author of *Trauma and Recovery* (1992), clarifies the link between interpersonal oppression and political oppression.

> Psychological trauma is an affliction of the powerless. At the moment of trauma, the victim is rendered helpless by overwhelming force. When the force is that of nature, we speak of disasters. When the force is that of other human beings, we speak of atrocities. Traumatic events overwhelm the ordinary systems of care that give people a sense of control, connection, and meaning.
>
> It was once believed that such events were uncommon. In 1980, when post-traumatic stress disorder was first included in the diagnostic manual, the American Psychiatric Association described traumatic events as "outside the range of usual human experience." Sadly, this definition has proved to be inaccurate. Rape, battery, and other forms of sexual and domestic violence are so common a part of women's lives that they can hardly be described as outside the range of ordinary experience. And in view of the number of people killed in war over the past century, military trauma, too, must be considered a common part of human experience; only the fortunate find it unusual.

Traumatic events are extraordinary, not because they occur rarely, but rather because they overwhelm the ordinary human adaptations to life. Unlike common misfortunes, traumatic events generally involve threats to life or bodily integrity, or a close personal encounter with violence and death. They confront human beings with the extremities of helplessness and terror, and evoke the responses of catastrophe. According to the *Comprehensive Textbook of Psychiatry,* the common denominator of psychological trauma is a feeling of "intense fear, helplessness, loss of control, and threat of annihilation.". . . (p. 33)

Herman notes that "traumatized people feel and act as though their nervous systems have been disconnected from the present" (ibid., p. 34). Like other experts on the long-term consequences of traumatic experience, Herman observes that the main symptoms of post-traumatic stress disorder fall into these three categories: (1) hyperarousal, a persistent expectation of danger; (2) "intrusion," also called "repetition compulsion," the memory of the traumatic experience repeatedly intruding into consciousness in response to a mental association that triggers instant recall; and (3) "constriction," a numbing response also termed "dissociation" or "depersonalization." Denial of feelings is also likely to become characterological over time if healing is not achieved through positive action and the reconstruction of social supports.

Members of oppressed communities are at high risk to be afflicted by post-traumatic stress disorders and by cycles of violence. During the colonial era in some African nations, as well as under neocolonial regimes in the '80s and '90s, repression by national military forces in collusion with outside financial and corporate interests was brutally effective in maintaining exploitative systems of power and control. A high incidence of post-traumatic stress disorder, violence, and trauma exists in oppressed African American neighborhoods in U.S. urban centers, and in neighborhoods populated by Central American refugees. Oppressed communities populated by racially stigmatized ethnic groups and by immigrant refugees, as well as families within those communities, are at risk to reenact scenes of brutality and victimization at an interpersonal level that were experienced or witnessed during earlier historic events.

Other writings by Dorothy Van Soest present concepts and perspectives that identify connections between systems of oppression, acts of violence, dynamics that produce cycles of violence and traumatization, and processes of healing and social action that can achieve empowerment and liberation. Her leadership of the NASW Violence and Development Project in the early '90s expanded the application of a social justice framework in social work practice.

Inequality, the aftermath of injustice, breeds further crime and social unrest. The likelihood of arrest and harsh sentencing in the criminal justice system are raised, Charles Hurst (2001) reminds us, by other facets of inequality that are pervasive within the criminal justice system itself,

We looked at the relationship between class, race, sex and crime rates, as well as the relationship between capitalism/inequality and crime rates in general, and found that in each case inequality is implicated in the generation of crime. Official statistics reveal a relationship between being Black and of low income and the probability of being arrested. The bulk of the studies on sentencing suggests a bias against groups of lower socioeconomic standing. This is especially borne out in cases of rape and homicide when the victim is White. A variety of data, then, raise questions about the fairness of the criminal justice system. (p. 265)

Hurst examines and summarizes the implications of health statistics in regard to the impact of inequality on personal qualities of life and life chances.

Most basically, social inequality affects the life chances of individuals . . . *personal* life chances: physical and mental health, personality, and relationships and abuse in the family . . . There is nothing more basic to life than physical health, and it is evident that individuals rate their own health status differently, depending on their race and income. Generally, Blacks and Hispanics are more likely than other groups to rate their own health as only fair or poor, and in all groups it is those with lower incomes who are most likely to assess their health as fair or poor . . . Interestingly, this self-assessment is a good predictor of a person's actual health, and indeed, individuals in lower-status categories are worse off on virtually all fundamental health measures. (National Center for Health Statistics 1998, as cited in Hurst, 2001, pp. 214–215)

These findings make it clear that health is related to *individual* socioeconomic status. But what is also interesting is that the health of individuals also appears to be related to the socioeconomic status of the *community* as a whole and to the degree of income inequality in a *society,* independent of the effect of one's *individual* status. Communities with lower average incomes and higher unemployment rates report higher rates of chronic conditions and societies with greater income inequality have poorer health status among individuals. (ibid., p. 216)

Life conditions for children are a matter of priority for social workers because of children's vulnerability and the long-term consequences of early deprivation, both material and emotional. In a 1998 book edited by Fred R. Harris and Lynn W. Curtis, *Locked in the Poorhouse: Cities, Race, and Poverty in the United States,* comparative data on urban poverty and child development were among the variables included in multivariate analysis of factors related to poverty.

In 1968, when the Koerner Report was published, one in eight (12.8 percent) residents of our nation's inner cities was poor. This count is based on a Census Bureau comparison of total family income with a poverty income threshold that varies by family size . . . The fraction of inner-city residents who are impoverished has generally increased over the past thirty years and has always been much higher than poverty rates for metropolitan residents who live outside of inner cities. By 1997, one in five (19 percent) inner-city residents was poor, half again more than thirty years earlier. Worse yet, the extent of poverty is twice as high for urban children as urban adults. In 1996, some 31 percent of children living in the inner cities of our nation's metropolitan areas were poor, as compared with 16 percent of adults living in inner cities.

A plethora of studies, books, and reports demonstrate correlations between child poverty and various methods of child achievement, health, and behavior. The strength and consistency of these associations is striking. For example, in terms of physical health, the risk to poor children relative to non-poor children is 1.7 times for a low-birthweight birth, 3.5 times for lead poisoning. 1.7 times for child mortality, and 2.0 times for a short-stay hospital episode. In terms of achievement, the risk to poor children relative to non-poor children is 2.0 times higher for grade repetition and high school dropout and 1.4 times for learning disability. For other conditions and outcomes, these risk ratios are 1.3 times for parent-reported emotional or behavior problems, 3.1 times for a teenage out-of-wedlock birth, 6.8 times for reported cases of child abuse and neglect, and 2.2 times for experiencing violent crime. (Duncan and Brooks-Gunn, as cited in Harris and Curtis, 1998, pp. 21–23)

The Harris and Curtis study (1998) identifies public programs that have worked to benefit children, families, and communities as well as those that have not been beneficial to the public. It concludes,

> We have the money to do what needs to be done. We must reorder the federal budget and its priorities—moving away from programs and policies that do not work and cutting down on unneeded military expenditures and corporate welfare. We must return to human investment—in programs that do work. We must raise the minimum wage and renew our affirmative-action and desegregation efforts.
>
> To accomplish this, we must, first, help Americans see that things are getting worse again for millions of Americans. Many do not know this. Second, we must communicate what works. Third, we must reduce the growing power of money in American politics, drastically reforming our system of campaign finance—so that our policy and budget priorities can be changed. Fourth, we must all realize our common self-interest in forming political coalitions across racial, ethnic, and class lines that can produce political action.
>
> We must begin to think of our inner cities, and wherever and among whomever else great poverty exists, as internally wastefully underdeveloped areas. It makes economic sense to provide our underskilled, undereducated, underemployed, and underutilized fellow Americans a real chance for success and productivity. It will cost less to do this than what we are doing now. That is fiscal sense. It will save a lot of tragically lost American lives and unrealized human potential. And it will ensure a more stable and secure America for all of us. (p. 153)

Core Principles for Practice

The application of the social justice framework requires clear and well-organized problem-solving in which there is united grassroots planning and action in support of this sort of agenda.

1. **Goals of assessment, planning and intervention** aim to achieve a multicultural society in which policies consider equally and benefit all citizens.
2. **Political decision-making and governance processes** in social institutions are conducted through inclusive participation of diverse members and groups in the population who work collaboratively toward sustainable human development and the broadest possible distribution of goods and services.
3. Genuine **campaign finance reform** is enacted to eliminate "soft money" and other forms of corruption in political campaigns.
4. **Passage of legislative policies of affirmative action and a living wage campaign.**
5. Promotion of **economic development focused on enhancing social well-being,** rather than corporate maximization of profit without concern for the impact of production on the environment, human health, jobs, and a sustainable economy.

6. Promotion of **economic development focused on local production** for local consumption, especially in food production, rather than maximum investment of resources for export trade by multinational corporations.

7. Promotion of **economic development by local cooperatives or worker-owned enterprises.**

8. **Deprivatization, reregulation of public utilities, public services, and public resources** (e.g., water, power, education, health, housing) to protect the public interest.

9. **Organization, maintenance and empowerment of multiracial, multicultural coalitions** dedicated to preserving community values and life-sustaining environmental resources to be shared by all and by future generations.

The voice of William Ryan (1976) was one that sharply warned social workers to guard against "blaming the victim" when assessing sources of social and health-related problems.

> Blaming the Victim is, of course, quite different from old-fashioned conservative ideologies. The latter simply dismissed victims as inferior, genetically defective, or morally unfit; the emphasis is on the intrinsic, even hereditary, defect. The former shifts its emphasis to the environmental causation. The old-fashioned conservative could hold firmly to the belief that the oppressed and the victimized were born that way—"that way" being defective or inadequate in character or ability. The new ideology attributes defect and inadequacy to the malignant nature of poverty, injustice, slum life and racial difficulties. The stigma that marks the victim and accounts for his victimization is an acquired stigma, a stigma of social, rather than genetic origin. But the stigma, the defect, the fatal difference—though derived in the past from environmental forces—is still located *within* the victim, inside his skin. With such an elegant formulation, the humanitarian can have it both ways. . . . It is a brilliant ideology for justifying a perverse form of social action designed to change, not society, as one might expect, but rather society's victim. (p. 7)

Ryan (1976) observed that another organizing framework for analyzing social problems was less prevalent but likely to be far more useful, productive, and relevant to the application of a social justice framework in social work practice:

> Adherents of this approach tended to search for defects in the community and the environment rather than in the individual; to emphasize predictability and usualness rather than random deviance; they tried to think about preventing rather than merely repairing or treating—to see social problems, in a word, as social. In the field of disease, this approach was termed public health, and its practitioners sought the cause of disease in such things as the water supply, the sewage system, the density and quality of housing conditions. They set out to prevent disease, not in individuals, but in the total population, through improved sanitation, inoculation against communicable diseases, and the policing of housing conditions. In the field of income maintenance, this secondary style of solving social problems focused on poverty as a predictable event, on the regularities of income deficiency. And it concentrated on the development of standard, generalized programs affecting total groups. (pp. 16–17)

Case Example

A notable example of the application of a social justice framework in social work action involves the participation of a small group of social workers affiliated with the California and Washington state chapters of the National Association of Social Workers (NASW). While the World Trade Organization held ministerial meetings from November 30 to December 3, 1999, in Seattle, Washington, the social workers held educational and protest events and forums in Seattle's Labor Temple and Methodist Church. Social work students, practitioners, and faculty members participated in an AFL-CIO rally at a ballpark stadium. The rally was followed by a march uniting trade union organizations, environmentalists, and a wide variety of non-governmental organizations in protest against policies of the World Bank, International Monetary Fund, and World Trade Organization that promote privatization of national natural resources, and deregulation of health, safety, and environmental standards. Those policies of economic globalization contribute to increasing control of world resources by multinational corporations and to more profound maldistribution of access to life-sustaining, life-enhancing resources essential for healthy human growth and development.

During those days in Seattle, social workers marched again to demonstrate in support of Jubilee 2000, an international movement calling for debt cancellation for most of the Highly Indebted Poor Nations (HIPN). Loans that had been made by international financial institutions to past governments of developing nations were arranged without responsible planning and accountability to their citizens. In many cases the loans funded projects that produced lucrative contracts for large construction firms and munitions and aircraft manufacturers. Some of the loans propped up military dictators who suppressed their own citizens when they attempted to organize internal political opposition. Many poor nations are now burdened with debt payments that consume a large percentage of their export earnings, leaving little if any funds for public education and other public services. This issue calls for social work action for social justice in alliance with other groups, such as worldwide religious communities, dedicated to social development. For more information on this movement, see http://www.j2000usa.org, or write: Jubilee 2000/USA Campaign, 222 East Capital Street, NE, Washington, D.C. 20003.

Contributions and Limitations

The social justice framework, well articulated by social workers, has effected positive changes in economic and political decision making, primarily at local levels. Social workers who have expressed aspects of the social justice framework in movements for civil, labor, or immigrant rights have had some effect on attitudinal and institutional changes. But principles of the social justice framework have only occasionally been institutionalized in national public policy, and those changes were accomplished by broad community movements for social change rather than by application of the framework in social work practice.

In later decades of the twentieth century the World Bank, International Monetary Fund, and the World Trade Organization, after its founding in 1994 at Punta del Este during the Uruguay Round of the General Agreement on Tariffs and Trade, established new international agreements that invalidated international, national, and even state laws for the protection of health and safety, jobs and the environment in behalf of the "deregulation of barriers to trade." When the agreements resulted in the penetration of multinational corporations and foreign capital investment into national and regional markets around the world, the implications of Gil's analysis became ever more visible. Economic globalization, achieved through policies that favor privatization of public resources; deregulation of health, safety, and environmental standards; and unrestricted entry for foreign investors and multi-national corporations into fragile local markets, is fueling the widening of the gap that now exists between rich and poor, within and among all nations. Disparities in levels of income and wealth, access to housing, education, health, and other public services, and in opportunities for cultural and political expression are sharper.

These changes in international trade policies are causing profound, historic structural changes in national and international economies. The impact of "neo-liberal" trade policies, promoted and implemented by those international financial institutions and multinational corporate interest groups, is recolonizing nations in Africa, Latin America, Asia, and Eastern Europe. Capture of vital resources of those nations by U.S. and European corporations in the past decade has been as rapid as was achieved in an earlier era through the use of military forces. Financial and corporate penetration of Global South nations should be added to Burkey's list of historic sources for the establishment of dominance and subordination among ethnic peoples (see Burkey's analytical framework, Chapter 7, p. 143 of this text). Social workers need to become aware of these structural changes in global economic and political power in order to consider realistic strategies for social work action to promote economic and social justice. Midgley (2000) reminds us that social development is a constructive application of the social justice framework:

> The social development perspective insists on the integration of economic and social policy and gives us two axioms: firstly, it requires that economic development should be inclusive, integrated and sustainable and bring benefits to all; and secondly, it proposes that social welfare should be investment oriented, seeking to enhance human capacities to participate in the productive economy. (Midgley, 1995; Midgley & Sherraden, 1999)
>
> The approach transcends the residualist-institutional debates that have characterized social policy thinking for decades and offers a new perspective that may facilitate a renewed basis for state intervention in social welfare.
>
> Social development ideas have the potential to support a reconceptualization of globalization that legitimates efforts to regulate the global economy. Used positively by progressive political leaders, committed officials at the international agencies, members of NGOs and local activists, a new rationale for economic globalization which will garner widespread electoral support may emerge.
>
> This rationale should recognize that properly regulated, international economic integration can enhance economic development and promote social welfare. It must be realistic about economic and social change, recognizing the realities of a postmodern, post-Fordist world and the fact that small scale production, self-employment, continuous reskilling and increased mobility will play a far greater role in economic life in the future. It should shape economic and social policies to fit these realities and be able to respond rapidly to change. (Midgley, 2000, p. 24)

These times of national and global uncertainty in decision making and direction are even more reason to apply a social justice framework in social work practice.

Issues for Further Study

1. Are factors in the client's social context and environment especially stressful at the present time?
2. Is this problem affecting other people in the area or in the community?
3. Is uncertainty about income and job security a stressful factor at this time? Is health jeopardized due to job-related uncertainty or fear related to changes in access to material and/or social supports that are important for well-being?
4. Is abuse or violation being imposed by a powerful person or institution? If so, what allies can help address this situation?
5. Is there a gap between a program or policy's stated goals and objectives and its products and outcomes? If the program's rhetoric states that its goal is to benefit the public, and if the public is not benefiting—then who is?

Conclusions

Application of the social justice framework is especially relevant for social workers at times and places in which power is being exercised by leaders without integrity, responsibility, or commitment to govern in the public interest. A system in which control of decision making resides with individuals who are not acting on behalf of the productivity and positive functioning of the whole system is likely to become dysfunctional. When leaders operate, not to benefit the vitality of the entire nation, state, or organization, but rather to exploit the resources under their control in order to maintain their own positions of power, oppression is the outcome.

The end of the twentieth century and the start of the new millennium appear to be an epoch of serious risk, in terms of the ecological sustainability of a livable planet. The vast powers of military and electronic technology, of media and psychologically astute commercial advertising, of healing and deadly pharmaceuticals, and of high-risk genetic experimentation, confront every individual, family, and community on earth with many challenges. Life and health require the ability to confront the challenges of daily living, and to face and address problems. The problem-solving approaches of the social work profession prepare social workers for leadership in these challenging times. The social justice framework provides the profession with concepts that are needed at times when those in power are corrupt, self serving, and ignorant of the extent to which they are destructive. Coalition building is needed to address the political realities of our times, and social workers have skills that are very useful on behalf of coalition building.

In the final analysis, when the negative consequences of malfunctioning social systems and institutions are not prevented through vigilance and effective problem solving, lessons must be learned the hard way, through painful and costly losses. National and international economic policies that support privatization of national natural resources; deregulation and unrestricted access to financial and commodity markets; and control by multi-national corporations and financial institutions of local markets and local services, including those in the fields of health, education, and public utilities. The ideology and policies of "free trade" promote business ethics that consider the maximization of profit to be the single legitimate goal and basis of decision making by company officers. When markets are controlled, profits are maximized, not through expanded production, but through higher prices and limited production to supply affluent consumers who can pay more. The amounts supplied and the prices of commodities and services, including education, health services, and public utilities, are set at levels that maximize revenues while limiting production costs. Rapidly rising costs of water and electricity, paired with restricted access to them places community health and well-being in jeopardy and therefore are key issues mobilizing protest movements from Cuchabamba, Bolivia, to northern California.

The future is full of challenges, as well as opportunities for further research. Resources and solutions exist, and so do greed, injustice, and oppression. Social movements of the past and present provide instruments for study, organization, and action on behalf of social justice. The social justice framework of this field is a gift that enhances the meaning of life for those who want to apply it.

Sources for Further Study

Social work students, faculty, and practitioners vary widely in their exposure to, and commitment to, the application of a social justice framework in social work practice. But it is clear that caring social workers and responsible professionals will respond with interest, reflection, and action if they are challenged to examine the relationship between a system's products and outcomes and its decision makers' interests. When the products and outcomes of a system serve the interests of those in power, rather than the interests of its constituencies (i.e., the workers and the general public, as consumers of the products and outcomes) those social workers may come to understand the fundamental issues that the social justice framework addresses. Critical thinking about prevention and issues of social justice then become priorities for social workers who aspire to be professional in practice and effective in problem solving.

Fanon, Frantz. *The Wretched of the Earth.* 15th printing. New York: Grove Press, 1968. Frantz Fanon was born on July 20, 1925, into a middle-class Black family on the island of Martinique, province of France. He was educated as a physician in France and specialized in psychiatry. His experience of racism in France led him to establish his practice in Algeria, then a French colony in Northern Africa. As a psychiatrist, his intimate knowledge of colonialism and its psychological consequences made him an advocate of social struggle and decolonization. He came to view the struggle for decolonization as a therapeutic, liberating activity, essential for the dignity and mental health of colonized peoples. Frantz Fanon become a partisan for Algerian independence and decolonization in Africa. This book documents his observations on the destructiveness of colonial systems.

Freire, Paolo. *Pedagogy of the Oppressed.* 11th printing. New York: Seabury Press, 1970. Paolo Freire dedicated this text "to the oppressed, and to those who suffer with them and fight at their side." An educator in Brazil, Freire developed community-based methodologies for the "conscientización," the awakening of critical consciousness and empowerment by the people of colonized nations.

> To surmount the situation of oppression, men must first critically recognize its causes, so that through transforming action they can create a new situation, one which makes possible the

pursuit of a fuller humanity. But the struggle to be more fully human has already begun in the struggle to transform the situation. Although the situation of oppression is a dehumanized and dehumanizing totality, affecting both the oppressors and those whom they oppress, it is the latter who must, from their stifled humanity, wage for both the struggle for a fuller humanity; the oppressor, who is himself dehumanized because he dehumanizes others, is unable to lead this struggle. (Freire, 1970, pp. 31–32).

Gil, David G., *Violence Against Children: Physical Child Abuse in the United States*. Cambridge, MA: Harvard University Press, 1970.

Unravelling Social Policy: Theory, Analysis, and Political Action Toward Social Equality. Cambridge, MA: Schenckman Publishing Company, 1973.

The Challenge of Social Equality: Essays on Social Policy, Social Development, and Social Process. Cambridge, MA: Schenckman Publishing Company, 1976.

Our study of the sources and dynamics of the poverty syndrome has led to the conclusion that this social problem is an inevitable, structural consequence of the economic, political, and ideological dynamics of capitalism. At the same time, we also realized that many other social problems, such as psychological alienation, are intrinsic to capitalism. Having identified these causal links, the requirements of an effective strategy for the elimination of the poverty syndrome seem now self-evident. Such a strategy must aim to replace an economic and political system of which poverty is an intrinsic aspect with an alternative system which is so constituted as to preclude poverty as a structural possibility. . . .

Revolutionary interpretation and reeducation as conceived here should, therefore, identify the "enemy" not in specific individuals and abstract groups, such as the "ruling class," but in the non-egalitarian, competitive, oppressive and exploitative value premises and organizing principles of the prevailing order, in the institutional arrangements and social policies derived from these values and principles, and in the destructive, interpersonal and intergroup relations and conflicts generated by these arrangements and policies. Such an interpretation should also reveal how we all, oppressed and oppressors alike, are trapped in, and act in accordance with, the same dehumanizing, irrational arrangements which humans have created and continue to maintain, and hence, how the liberation of every group depends on the liberation of all groups from the shackles of the existing order. (Gil, 1976, pp. 201–204)

Greider, William. (1997). *One World, Ready or Not: The Manic Logic of Global Capitalism*. New York: Simon and Schuster, 1997. Greider's challenge here is to clarify the structure and processes of the new world economic order, which he perceives to be hazardous.

If my analysis is right, the global system of finance and commerce is in a reckless footrace with history, plunging toward some sort of dreadful reckoning with its own contradictions, pulling everyone else along with it. . . . The first imperative is to impose some order on the global marketplace, to make both finance and commerce more accountable for the consequences of their actions and to give hostage societies more ability to determine their own futures . . . it will be impossible to redirect the global system's energies toward a pro-growth strategy without also establishing new standards for the behavior of commerce and finance. The first priority is to re-regulate finance capital. (Chap 14, "The Economic Question," pp. 316–317)

hooks, bell. *Talking Back: Thinking Feminist, Thinking Black*. Boston: South End, 1989. Bell hooks, author, was born Gloria Jean Watkins. She adopted the pen name of bell hooks—her great-grandmother on her mother's side, a woman who spoke her mind—as a form of protection against punishment for speaking out and telling the truth in print. The pen name

was connected with feelings about representations of the self, about identity . . . "It has been a political struggle for me to hold to the belief that there is much which we—black people— must speak about, much that is private that must be openly shared, if we are to heal our wounds (hurts caused by domination and exploitation and oppression), if we are to recover and realize ourselves." (pp. 1–3)

In bell hooks's writings, the eradication of attitudinal racism and sexism are goals linked to eradication of patriarchal domination and white supremacy as institutional systems.

> Feminist struggle to end patriarchal domination should be of primary importance to women and men globally not because it is the foundation of all other oppressive structures but because it is that form of domination we are most likely to encounter in an ongoing way in every day life. (p. 21)
>
> For our efforts to end white supremacy to be truly effective, individual struggle to change consciousness must be fundamentally linked to collective effort to transform those structures that reinforce and perpetuate white supremacy. (p. 119)

Lee, Judith. *The Empowerment Approach to Social Work Practice*. New York: Columbia University Press, 1994. A clear formulation of concrete and practical ways in which the social justice framework may be applied in social work practice is presented by Judith Lee in this text. The following are principles that she sees and shares through "the lenses through which we view social work practice with people who are poor and members of oppressed groups"

> 1. All oppression is destructive of life and should be challenged by social workers and clients. 2. The social worker should maintain holistic vision in situations of oppression. 3. People empower themselves; social workers should assist. 4. People who share common ground need each other to attain empowerment. 5. Social workers should establish an "I and I" relationship with clients. 6. Social workers should encourage the client to say her own word. 7. The social worker should maintain a focus on the person as victor, not victim. 8. Social workers should maintain a social change function. (p. 26)

Marable, Manning. *How Capitalism Underdeveloped Black America*. Boston: South End, 2000. This is an updated edition of a classic work originally published in 1983. Marable views underdevelopment not simply as the absence of development, but as the inevitable product of an oppressed population's integration into the world market economy and political system. The foundation of the underdevelopment of Black America was, undeniably, the slave system that provided rapid capital accumulation during the colonial era. As Marable explains, however, following the abolition of slavery, the super-exploitation and expropriation of surplus value produced by Black labor, first in agriculture and later in industry, continued and thus perpetuated underdevelopment. Marable also analyzes the role of Black poverty within a Black underclass of underpaid, super-exploited laborers, the super-exploitation of Black women and the racist character of a growing prison-industrial complex. The book links gender, race and class as interlocking factors in the underdevelopment of Black America and shows how struggles against racism and capitalism are inseparable from those against patriarchy and sexual oppression in both the dominant U.S. culture and the Black community.

Memmi, Albert. *The Colonizer and the Colonized*. Boston: Beacon Press, 1970. Albert Memmi, a Tunisian Jew, as a young student encountered levels of racism previously unknown to him when he enrolled in philosophy studies at the Sorbonne in France, the colonial power. In his preface to the "American" edition, he summarizes the findings of his research:

> The colonial relationship which I had tried to define chained the colonizer and the colonized into an implacable dependence, molded their respective characters and dictated their conduct. Just as there was an obvious logic in the reciprocal behavior of the two colonial partners, another mechanism, proceeding from the first, would lead, I believed, inexorably to the decomposition of this dependence. Events in Algeria confirmed my hypothesis; I have often verified it since then in the explosion of other colonial situations. . . . Privilege is at the heart of the colonial relationship—and that privilege is undoubtedly economic. . . . However, colonial privilege is not solely economic (Preface, pp. ix–xii).

Memmi recognized that, as non-Muslims, the Jewish population in Tunisia and Algiers identified as much with the colonizers as with the colonized, and sought to identify themselves with the French, as did members of other colonized groups, until they reached the point of revolt. Memmi joined the colonized, denouncing colonialism. The examination of his own ambivalence about identity and affiliation makes this text both personal and universal.

Rodney, Walter. *How Europe Underdeveloped Africa*. 5th printing. Washington, D.C.: Howard University Press, 1982. Early in this book Rodney summarized his own message:

> The question as to who, and what, is responsible for African underdevelopment can be answered at two levels. Firstly, the answer is that the operation of the imperialist system bears major responsibility for African economic retardation by draining African wealth and by making it impossible to develop more rapidly the resources of the continent. Secondly, one has to deal with those who manipulated the system and those who are either agents or unwitting accomplices of the said system. The capitalists of Western Europe were the ones who actively extended their exploitation from inside Europe to cover the whole of Africa. In recent times, they were joined, and to some extent replaced, by the capitalists from the United States; and for many years now even the workers of those metropolitan countries have benefited from the exploitation and underdevelopment of Africa. None of these remarks are intended to remove the ultimate responsibility for development from the shoulders of Africans. Not only are there African accomplices inside the imperial system, but every African has a responsibility to understand the system and work for its overthrow. (pp. 27–28)

References

Barnet, R. J., & Cavanaugh, J. (1994). *Global dreams: Imperial corporations and the new world order*. New York: Touchstone.

Beauvoir, S. (1949). *The second sex*. (H. M. Parshley, Trans. and Ed.) New York: Knopf.

Bradshaw, Y. W., & Wallace, M. (1996). *Global inequalities*. Thousand Oaks, CA: Pine Forge.

Brecher, J., & Costello, T. (1994). *Global village or global pillage: Economic restructuring from the bottom up*. Boston: South End Press.

Brown, L. R., Flavin, C., and French, H. (2001). *State of the world 2001: A Worldwatch Institute report on progress toward a sustainable society*. New York: W. W. Norton.

Bulhan, H. A. (1985). *Frantz Fanon and the psychology of oppression*. New York: Plenum.

Burkey, R. M. (1978). *Ethnic & racial groups: The dynamics of dominance*. Menlo Park, CA: Benjamin/Cummings.

Collins, C., & Yaskel, F. (2000). *Economic apartheid in America: A primer on economic inequality & insecurity*. New York: The New Press.

Daly, H. E., & Cobb, J. B., Jr. (1989). *For the common good: Redirecting the economy toward community, the environment, and a sustainable future*. Boston: Beacon.

Danaher, K. (1994). *50 years is enough: The case against the World Bank and the International Monetary Fund*. Boston: South End Press.

Dominelli, L. (1997). "International social development and social work," *Issues in International Social Work*, Hokenstad, M. C. and J. Midgley, eds. Washington, D.C.: NASW Press.

Engels, F. (1973). *The origin of the family, private property and the state*. New York: International Publishers.

Fanon, F. (1967). *Black skin, white masks: The experiences of a Black man in a White world*. New York: Grove Press.

Fanon, F. (1968). *The wretched of the earth*. New York: Grove Press.

Frank, A. G. (1978). *World accumulation, 1492–1789*. New York: Monthly Review.

Freire, P. (1970). *Pedagogy of the oppressed*, 11th printing. New York: Seabury Press.

Freire, P. (1973). *Education for critical consciousness*. New York: Seabury Press.

Galeano, E. (1973). *Open veins of Latin America: Five centuries of the pillage of a continent*. New York: Monthly Review Press.

Gil, D. (1970). *Violence against children: Physical child abuse in the United States.* Cambridge, MA: Harvard University Press.

Gil, D. (1976). *The challenge of social equality: Essays on social policy, social development and political practice.* Cambridge, MA: Schenkman.

Gil, D. G. (1990). *Unraveling social policy: Theory, analysis, and political action towards social equity* (rev. 4th ed.). Cambridge, MA: Schenkman.

Greider, W. (1997). *One world, ready or not: The manic logic of global capitalism.* New York: Simon and Schuster.

Harris, F. R., & Curtis, L. A. (Eds.). (1998). *Locked in the poor house: Cities, race and poverty in the United States.* Lanham, MD: Rowman & Littlefield.

Hearn, G. (Ed.). (1969). *The general systems approach: Contributions toward an holistic conception of social work.* New York: Council on Social Work Education.

Herman, E. S. (1982). *The real terror network: Terrorism in fact and propaganda.* Boston: South End Press.

Herman, J. L., M.D. (1992). *Trauma and recovery.* New York: Basic Books.

Hockenstad, M. C., and Midgley, J. (1997). *Issues in international social work: Global challenges for a new century.* Washington, D.C.: NASW Press.

hooks, b. (1984). *Feminist theory: From margin to center.* Boston: South End Press.

hooks, b. (1989). *Talking back: Thinking feminist, thinking black.* Boston: South End.

Hurst, C. E. (2001). *Social inequality: Forms, causes and consequences* (4th ed.). Boston: Allyn & Bacon.

Ife, J. (2000). "Local Needs and a globalized economy: Bridging the gap with social work practice," *Social Work and Globalization,* Special July 2000 Issue of the Journal of the Canadian Association of Social Workers (CASW).

Koning, H. (1993). *The conquest of America: How the Indian nations lost their continent.* New York: Monthly Review Press.

Korten, D. C. (1995). *When corporations rule the world.* West Hartford: Kumarian.

Lee, J. (1994). *The empowerment approach to social work practice.* New York: Columbia University Press.

Lerner, G. (1986). *The creation of patriarchy.* New York: Oxford University Press.

Marable, M. (2000). *How capitalism underdeveloped Black Africa.* Boston: South End Press.

Marx, K. (1967). *Capital: A critique of political economy.* New York: Modern Library.

Massey, D. S., & Denton, N. A. (1993). *American apartheid: Segregation and the making of the underclass.* Cambridge, MA: Harvard University Press.

Memmi, A. (1968). *Dominated man.* Boston: Beacon Press.

Memmi, A. (1970). *The colonizer and the colonized.* Boston: Beacon Press.

Midgley, J. (1995). *Social development: The developmental perspective in social welfare.* Thousand Oaks, CA: Sage.

Midgley, J. (2000). "Globalization, Capitalism and Social Welfare: A Social Development Perspective," *Social Work and Globalization,* 2000, Special Issue of the Journal of the Canadian Association of Social Workers (CASW).

Midgley, J., & Sherraden, M. (1999). The social development perspective in social policy. In J. Midgley, M. B. Tracy, and M. Livermore (Eds.), *The handbook of social policy* (pp. 435–447). Thousand Oaks, CA: Sage.

National Association of Social Workers. (1996). *Code of ethics.* Washington, D.C.: NASW.

Prigoff, A. (2000). *Economics for social workers: Social outcomes of economic globalization with strategies for community action.* Belmont, CA: Brooks/Cole.

Ramanathan, C. S., & Link, R. J. (1999). *All our futures: Principles and resources for social work practice in a global era.* Belmont, CA: Brooks/Cole-Wadsworth.

Rawls, J. (1971). *A theory of justice.* Cambridge, MA: Harvard University Press.

Rodney, W. (1982). *How Europe underdeveloped Africa* (5th ed.). Washington, D.C.: Howard University Press.

Ryan, W. (1976). *Blaming the victim* (2nd ed.). New York: Vintage Books.

Stoner, M. R. (1995). *The civil rights of homeless people: Law, social policy, and social work practice.* New York: Aldine de Gruyter.

Swenson, D. R. (1998). Clinical social work's contribution to a social justice perspective. *Social Work, 43*(6), 527–537.

United Nations. (1948). *Universal Declaration of Human Rights.* New York: United Nations Department of Public Information.

United Nations Development Programme. (2000). *Human development report 2000.* New York: Oxford University Press.

Van Soest, D. (1995). Peace and social justice. In R. L. Edwards (Ed.), *Encyclopedia of social work* (19th ed., Vol. 3, pp. 1810–1817). Washington, D.C.: NASW Press.

Van Soest, D. (1997). *The global crisis of violence: Universal causes, shared solutions.* Washington, D.C.: NASW Press.

Part V

Vulnerable Life Situations/ Ethnocultural Diversity Perspectives

10

The Ethnographic Perspective: A New Look

Andrew Bein

An ethnographic perspective is at the heart of culturally competent social work because it orients the social worker to tune into and understand the client's narrative. Social workers learn to put aside broad-stroke social constructs so they can intimately learn from their clients. Practitioners taught in this tradition learn that they cannot make assumptions about what it means for *this* woman to be a parent of an autistic child, nor can they assume they know about the particular struggles of *this* African American adolescent. Cornerstones of social work practice—respect, empowerment, presence, partnership, and committed action emanate from an ethnographic perspective.

This chapter presents the guiding principles of an ethnographic approach and discusses the implications of ethnographic practice. Recent work on the ethnographic perspective (Green, 1999; Bein & Lum, 1999) has been humanistic; practitioners can, thus, ascribe to ethnographic principles and learn to *tolerate* their clients and work with them from a cool distance. This chapter, however, will emphasize the personally transformative and spiritual nature this perspective can embody as well as the rich working partnerships that consequently emerge in client–worker relationships.

It should be noted that for the last six years, the ethnographic perspective has formed the foundation of the Undergraduate Practice sequence at California State University, Sacramento. Students experience, in their course and fieldwork, that they are best able to connect with clients and communities when they genuinely want to learn from them. People and communities are not placed in diagnostic or sociological boxes. Mutual exploration replaces the kind of expert-driven, deductive assessment (Bein & Allen, 1999) that too often occurs on the MSW level and out in the field.

Ethnographic Approach

James Green (1982) made, perhaps, the first extensive explorations regarding the potential applicability of ethnography—born from an anthropology tradition—to social work practice with multiethnic populations. Green, an African American scholar, strongly critiqued human service agencies as being unaware and unresponsive to the wide variety of help-seeking traditions and ways of framing problems that were found among people of color. He exhorted social workers to recognize their own biases (which were often White and middle class) and to assume a student role and allow clients to teach them about their reality. Green (1982) argued that the social worker's own constructs, use of language, and belief systems often blinded him or her from the unique meanings and the stories of people of color; he asserted that utilization of an ethnographic approach would enhance social worker efficacy and take workers and agencies beyond being "well meaning" with diverse clients and communities.

A social worker who uses the ethnographic perspective approaches the client in an open manner without the pitfalls of the expert–non-expert dichotomy. The worker sets aside universal categorizations of behavior, or an *etic* approach, in favor of a specific investigation of the client's meaning of events or behavior, an *emic* approach. Social work students enjoy hearing the story that follows, which illustrates the etic–emic difference and depicts my own cross-cultural failure.

Case Example

A young Filipino man (in his late 20s), Eduardo,* had been seeing me for counseling and had reported feeling less depressed by the fifth session. Our relationship seemed positive; he was enthusiastic to work and, perhaps because he was a "psych-tech," was familiar and accepting of the counseling session protocols. During one session, Eduardo reported how he was financially supporting other siblings and his parents in the Philippines. He believed that, as the oldest son, he had some responsibility to help the rest of his family; however, his finances were limited, and his ability to buy things for himself and to go places was becoming severely constrained.

I was immersed in training, consultation, self-help, and reading that emphasized the evils of codependence, so I quickly assessed Eduardo's situation and consequent suffering as a classic case of codependence. I operated as if codependence were an etic or universal construct and "enlightened" him regarding his dysfunctional behavior. Codependence, of course, is not a universal construct; in fact, what may appear as codependence to one is healthy interdependence and caring to another. Focusing on and prioritizing one's *own* financial well-being is a solution for one, but for another this approach is seen as cold-hearted and irresponsible. There is some chance that Eduardo believed that his concerns for his parents and siblings did not remotely resemble any sort of pathology, and that he sensed that I had had little appreciation about what it meant for him that his parents and family

---

*Not actual name

receive his financial assistance. I will never know Eduardo's actual thoughts because he never returned to counseling.

I did not understand the nature of giving and responsibility for Eduardo or how cultural threads were woven throughout his tapestry. Instead of having him teach me about giving money to his family (ethnographic perspective), and embracing the uniqueness and suspending categorization of his story (emic), I applied my own lenses to Eduardo's situation and assigned, without awareness and true understanding, a story line, "codependence" (etic).

Help-Seeking

The effective utilization of an ethnographic approach also demands that the social worker tune into the expectations and meanings of the client's help-seeking efforts (Green, 1999; McMiller & Weisz, 1996). Some clients expect concrete suggestions or assistance to relieve distress and would regard an emphasis on process or worker non-directedness as unhelpful or a waste of time. On the other hand, some clients may expect and wish that, more than anything, they would be heard. These individuals would experience concrete worker suggestions or assistance as overly intrusive or patronizing. Remaining true to the ethnographic perspective means that social workers cannot generalize about who will respond in which manner. In other words, whether our clients are African American, Asian, Caucasian, bi- or tricultural, Latino, gay, straight, or bisexual provides little predictability about how they will respond. Learning about these groups sensitizes the social worker to possibilities, but should not lead to deterministic thinking (i.e., because this client is X, you can expect Y).

There is a strong tradition in social work scholarship of mythologizing and stereotyping diverse groups—and in particular, people of color (Guadalupe, 2000). In the attempt to advance alternative (non-Caucasian) lenses of normative values and behavior, writers, including James Green himself, often have associated people of color with cultural underpinnings, characteristics, or "things to look out for." These discussions help social workers to embrace such arrangements as grandparents raising children or people seeking help through spiritual or religious channels. Unfortunately, discussions and reifications of group traits also compromise an ethnographic perspective. How many writers have commented on the inevitable role and importance of such factors as the Black Church, Latino distrust of social service providers and acceptance of healers, Asian shame, Native American harmony with nature, and Caucasian individualism. When social workers enter relationships with clients, they are prone to filtering the clients' individual stories through such overgeneralized constructs, and they miss the person who is sitting next to them. Upon hearing, for example, the story of a Latino client who left counseling early, a social worker may start to assume that she entered counseling already skeptical and perhaps had a vast Latino support network that made her early termination decision that much easier and likely. The social worker begins to construct his or her own story about this client's past counseling and help-seeking experience and about other elements in her life based upon the social worker's supposedly insider's view of cultural issues. Only when the worker *truly* listens to the woman's story and suspends all categories—including "ethnic sensitive" ones—can he or she learn that this Latina was quite isolated and unsupported, had a high regard and trust for the institution of counseling, and was essentially pushed out of counseling because of provider incompetence. (See Bein, Torres, & Kurilla, 2000, for a discussion of similar cases and assumptions about Latino clients.)

The true application of the ethnographic perspective regarding client help-seeking means that practitioners do the hard work of understanding what kind of help people are expecting, without making assumptions. They are open to the multitude of possibilities and are fully aware that client expectations will not remain static, are dynamically related to the service provider, and can even change as the relationship evolves. Therefore, they look to the client or client system to continue to define the helping relationship to the greatest extent possible. When social workers consider communities, families, and individuals as their *teachers*, they learn about their clients' ever-evolving thoughts and feelings. They also learn that *many* times people are not as spiritual or non-spiritual, extended family-oriented or nuclear family-oriented, collective oriented or individualistic, or suspicious or self-revealing as textbooks predict.

Thus, Green (1999) is correct in orienting social workers to tune into help-seeking traditions and expectations of clients; workers need to especially appreciate, however, the uniqueness and dynamism of client and community expectations. They become most effective in this endeavor when they co-construct the client's narrative concerning the helping experience. The following questions can assist social workers:

- What are you hoping to get from seeing me?
- How can we work together on this?
- What has been helpful for you in the past? What has not worked?
- Sometimes it's hard to tell social workers that what they are doing is not helping or that things they have said make you angry or upset. You can tell me about those things; I really want to be helpful, and talking with me about times that I have said things that you found unhelpful or bothered you is important. How do you feel about (what do you think about) what I said last week?

Thoughts and Feelings

Social workers may be most effective in understanding their clients if they focus on narrative description and client interpretations (thoughts) than if they attempt to elicit client feelings concerning particular events or interactions (Green, 1999). Reaching for feelings can be sticky business because some clients may not speak the language of feelings. Insisting that people attach feeling words to their narrative or that they in some manner or another show how they are feeling can be an error. People of all cultures and ethnic groups can experience this kind of worker expectation as overly intrusive and not necessarily helpful. Social workers and field students may be inclined to pursue feeling-content because of their own therapy experiences or because living in dominant society's therapy culture has inculcated them with the notion that the expression of feelings is the essence of a helping relationship. This elevated status of feelings can be summarized by a quote appearing on one social worker's wall: "You are what you feel."

Another potential pitfall in focusing on feelings in a cross-cultural context is that social workers can incorrectly assume that they and their clients have a mutual understanding of emotional language and expression.

> I would argue that where significant cultural boundaries exist, it is far more reasonable to work with the hypothesis that worker and client do *not* share an emotional universe, and that even where their language of emotional states derives from a common grammar and lexicon, that is not proof that they are expressing identical emotional states. As a rule of thumb, it makes much more sense to assume that the more remote the client's culture and experiences are from those of the social worker, the greater possibility for distortion and failed understanding of emotional signals, whether those signals are communicated through words, body language, or facial expressions. All the more reason that empathy should be recast as attention to communication and information, not displays of emotional congruence. (Green, 1999, p. 108)

Thus, worker empathy in a cross-cultural context is not about feeling or experiencing the client's feelings but in understanding the client's story and his or her concerns.

The focus on content over feelings can be powerfully instructive and can help workers avoid the etic pitfall of assuming (1) that the deepest and truest depiction of reality and personal narrative resides in the expression and articulation of feelings, and (2) that the foundation for a successful, empathic working relationship is the open and vulnerable expression of emotion. Social worker agendas and insensitivity regarding the expression of feelings can, in fact, be destructive to positive client outcomes, and the social worker's focus on feeling-content or so-called congruence can be tangential to the task at hand.

This knowledge—as well the discussion on help-seeking—can be applied in an overly generalized manner. One can start to assume that when working with people of color or, especially, when working with people who are culturally discrepant than the worker, the worker should avoid feeling-content. This kind of "do and don't" injects the notion that culture is static and cross-cultural work is not dynamic. Instead of encouraging an emic understanding of the client–worker relationship, Green (1999), in this case, is implicitly proposing an *etic* rule that governs cross-cultural relationships. However, some African Americans, Latinos, Asians, Caucasians, and biracial clients are emotionally expressive with social workers and some are not; some will project the message that they are grieving and that they want to trust the worker enough so that they can share their grief with the worker, and others let the worker know that they are grieving, but their agenda with the worker is to address an immediate, concrete problem not related to their grieving. Stereotypes and generalizations about the nature of empathy with different groups or of the nature of empathy with different client–worker combinations undercut the essence of the ethnographic perspective.

A Spiritual Ethnographic Perspective

The ethnographic perspective literature does not address the affective and spiritual nature of the committed partnership that develops when clients and workers make the journey to address and discuss traumas, needs, and vulnerabilities. A social worker can understand a client, yet see himself or herself as superior. A social worker can hear, validate, and piece together the client's narrative, but can take shortcuts, because of lacking commitment or compassion, that obviate against the client's becoming empowered or benefiting from positive outcomes. This section will discuss the implications of an ethnographic perspective infused with Eastern-influenced spiritual principles. These perspectives are compatible with non-Eastern spiritual and religious traditions, and social work practitioners and students are encouraged to explore how their values and beliefs interface with the ideas presented here. The pillars of understanding, love, and compassion will be explored and their natural interface with the ethnographic perspective revealed.

Understanding and the Ethnographic Perspective

The social worker's mentality and approach when applying the ethnographic perspective is "I will learn from you." This mentality means that the worker is free to pursue a respectful, collaborative relationship with the client. The social worker does not have the answers in his or her back pocket, nor is the social worker waiting to gather enough information to slot the client into a diagnostic category that comes with *its* own set of answers. MSW and BSW students particularly thrive on utilizing the ethnographic perspective because it removes them from the expert role; the client is the expert of his or her own story and the social worker's job is to understand the events, conditions, behaviors, and decisions that relate to the story. Problem solving or solution generation emerges from the client's narrative and—to the greatest extent possible—is a mutual process. The worker seeks client feedback regarding the worker's problem assessment; solutions are jointly arrived at; and worker advocacy efforts are offered that the client is free to accept or reject.

It is essential when cultivating ethnographic understanding to recognize and suspend assumptions about the client and his or her life. A worker with a female Hmong client may tend to assume that she is dealing with cultural conflicts, while a worker with an African American male at a predominantly non-African American high school may assume that he is struggling with ethnic or racial identity issues; however, these assumptions interfere with the ability to truly listen to the client, and the assumptions may either be inaccurate or their real-life manifestations may have forms that no one else can imagine.

In some Eastern traditions, knowledge is regarded as an obstacle to understanding (Nhat Hanh, 1988). Knowledge—rather than engagement in deep listening with a calm, receptive mind—can lead a worker to enter relationships with lenses that facilitate attaching meanings, categories, and labels to the worker's—rather than the client's—experience. As the client speaks, the worker's mind becomes an endless chatter of theoretical banter, craving for direction, assumption creation, and judgment.

Workers begin to experience a chasm between themselves, the practitioners, and the others, the clients. They listen but sometimes do not seem to care; they hear the stories but sometimes judge themselves as superior; they develop interventions with their clients but sometimes are impatient and wish their clients would stop being so needy.

A spiritual approach (Faiver, Ingersoll, O'Brien, & McNally, 2001) can be mobilized to address the problems of understanding and working with clients and bridging the gulf between practitioners and clients through practices that enhance a sense of oneness. Thich

Nhat Hanh (1998), a social worker from Vietnam who was nominated by Martin Luther King Jr. for the Nobel Peace Prize, cautioned against "get[ting] caught in our own knowledge . . . [because it] is not the highest truth" (p. 26). "If we were to cling to our knowledge, we would lose the opportunity to advance in our understanding" (p. 27). The process of entering helping relationships with the mind full of ideas and concepts about "the other" reinforces the separateness of the worker and the client. On a *relative* level, this separateness is considered healthy and provides boundaries. On an *absolute* or *ultimate* level this separateness, from a Buddhist perspective, is considered an illusion. This separateness/oneness dynamic can be seen in many aspects of life.

One may, for example, give a name—"wave"—to each ripple or curling and foaming pattern observed at the ocean; however, water represents the ultimate reality for the purposes of this metaphor. One wave is big, another is small; one wave lasts a relatively long time, another is around for a few seconds. What is most striking about the waves is their lack of ultimate separateness from one another, in other words, their interdependence. Similarly, while clients have stories, names, and ethnic backgrounds that may differ from a social worker's, their lives are inextricably connected and non-separate. The ultimate manifestation of this reality is that the client and the worker will both be forever transformed by each other's presence. The social worker maintains awareness of this reality in order to appreciate the divinity or cosmic dance occurring in the midst of the client–worker interaction. As workers bring a spiritual perspective to their work, they experience a common humanness with their clients, they are more likely to reach out with their hearts and their effort, and they become less inclined to judge and burn out. They view and experience their time with clients and communities as sacred encounters.

An ethnographic perspective devoid of this kind of view *can* lead to unhealthy and unnecessary dualities between social workers and clients. Unnecessary distance and, in fact, objectification can easily occur for African American practitioners working with Asian clients, Latino practitioners working with Caucasian clients, or Caucasian practitioners working with Latino clients. This kind of unhealthy objectification, perhaps tinged with bitter irony or anger, comes through when cultural competence scholars refer to White people as "people without color."

Case Example—Ethnography and Spirituality

Recent work with an adolescent boy has provided me with insight regarding the potential marriage between an ethnographic perspective and spirituality. Manuel is a sixteen-year-old Mexican American boy with a history of gang involvement, violent crime, and time spent in juvenile detention and on the streets. There is an extensive history of child abuse—his mother was once incarcerated for abuse—and Manuel is now in foster care (his third home), and Manuel's probation officer has questions about the follow-through of the agency providing the foster care. Manuel is reading at the third-grade level.

My approach with Manuel has been to not relate to him through the adjectives that could describe him: Latino, gang banger, violent, abused child, foster child, low academic achiever, poor, anxious. Instead, I have focused on learning about Manuel's story through Manuel and on forming a human-to-human connection that transcends the etic constructs.

Genuinely listening and forming a connection was a challenge because of some of the violence that he had engaged in as well as his apparently stylized behavior and his infatuation with violent and misogynous adolescent culture. Connecting with him meant that I needed to **honestly acknowledge** the violent "seeds" or potential for violence within myself and how I, under circumstances similar to Manuel's, may have done and embraced some of the same things. In other words, I am not as separate from Manuel as I initially appear, and no matter what his behavior, I am not superior. He, in fact, can teach me about the dignity that he has maintained in his life as well as his courage to persevere.

Part of understanding Manuel is tuning into his strengths and his passion. Manuel has a sweet, very lovable side, and he is highly appreciative when he is cared for and shown respect. He loves low-rider cars, he has a good sense of humor, and he can show remorse. He has had a girlfriend for four months and is respectful toward her. He wants to live an honorable, loving life.

Understanding Manuel through a spiritually oriented ethnographic perspective demanded a mind-set that involved three related elements:

- I will learn from you. I will hear your story and do the best I can to understand what you need and what you would like my role to be in your life. I will do the best I can to not make assumptions about who you are or what you need.
- You and I are connected. This connection is manifested in our being together and our interdependence. I may have done similar things under circumstances you found yourself in. I am not superior. It is a gift to be with you.
- I see your strengths.

Case Example—Cultural Issues and Understanding

Cultural lessons were important here; however, they were not the most salient issues for Manuel's progress (Sue & Zane, 1987).

On the first meeting with Manuel, I joked about how he had probably been excited all day about seeing me. This comment was designed to break down some of the perceived barriers between ourselves: teenager and man, Latino and Caucasian, youth offender and professional, poor and upper-middle class. I related to him with utmost respect and learned that he had a special distrust for White people; this distrust was supported and nurtured by his African American foster mother. Manuel appreciated a personalistic approach that may have roots in his Latino culture (though many adolescents are this way), so I consistently gave him a ride to the train to help him get home and treated him to a snack on the way. I understood the loss he felt about not being able to speak Spanish; I understood the shame and other issues children encounter regarding Spanish speaking. His biological family was severely stressed economically, and living quarters were tight. These conditions could have contributed to the family violence and eventual life on the streets that occurred. Manuel is proud of Cesar Chavez, and I used his story as an inspiration to Manuel's pursuing a path of non-violence. Manuel made the strong connection—through his foster mother—of Cesar Chavez to Martin Luther King Jr. Manuel and his foster mother were delighted that I attended an IEP meeting at Manuel's high school. My pushing for a more rigorous reading curriculum comes from my knowledge about the low expectations that sometimes exist for students of color in urban high schools, particularly special education students of color. Because I had Manuel bring his low-rider magazines to me and read to me about low riders, I was able to say at the IEP meeting, from experience, that Manuel had stronger reading abilities and needed to be pushed. Manuel later informed me that he loved this comment. When Manuel's Caucasian probation officer noted her suspicions to me about his African American foster mother, I considered the possibility that racism played a role in her assessment and made a personal commitment to suspend judgment of Manuel's foster mother.

As with culture, I learned about the meaning of other issues that were significant in this case. What did the parenting style of his parents mean to him (though many times he would hesitate in revealing this information); what did he experience and what did he learn when he was locked up; what was it like to beat up others; how did the experiences affect him now; what did carrying a knife do for him; what was it like when the manager at McDonald's criticized his work; whom did he love or care about, and who did he believe cared about him.

Knowledge about Latinos, foster children, violent youth, abused children, poor children, low-achieving children were lenses that I did my best to avoid while I was working with Manuel. In seeking an emic understanding, this knowledge was put on the back burner. At times it helped in the exploration of Manuel's story; at times the knowledge served as a reference point or a map so I would not get too lost. The knowledge did not become utilized in order to impose a universal or etic construct or story line on Manuel's life. Such constructs are not only inaccurate and objectifying, but they serve to enhance the distance between two human beings.

The Ethnographic Perspective and Love

Love is a "sloppy construct" and a topic not often discussed or written about in social work. With the majority of ethical violations occurring as a result of sexual improprieties, it is no wonder that the discussion on the "relevance of love in social work" is taboo. Without trying to pin an academic definition on love, practitioners can appreciate the role that love has in their willingness to extend themselves on behalf of another and the willingness to allow their clients to inspire and teach them (Faiver et al., 2001).

With love comes a deeply experienced commitment that reinforces and at the same time transcends the admonishments from the NASW Code of Ethics about the "primacy of client interests" (National Association of Social Workers [NASW], 1998). With love for their clients, practitioners resist society's pressures to categorize and write people off and, instead, see them as sources of strength, light, and worthiness.

Love helps social workers move from *tolerance* of their clients to *appreciation* of them. Workers can invoke an ethnographic perspective and tolerate their clients, but their clients may experience that the worker does not truly care or enjoy being with them. Workers who appreciate their clients embrace them. They may work with people on changing certain behavior, but they fundamentally accept their clients as human beings. Their love for people with whom they work comes from a fundamental sense of mutual connectedness (or a common source of divinity, for some traditions) and is not sexualized.

Commitment to being present emerges from this intangible love. Being present does not mean occupying space in a shared location; instead, being present means calming their own concepts, opinions, projections, fears, racist, sexist, or homophobic notions, judgments, and personal internal dialogue so that they can truly hear and be with their clients. When workers suggest or formulate intervention, they are aware that the plan is directed toward the client's well-being and desires, rather than toward an attempt to fix the client in the worker's own image. When workers become aware of getting restless, impatient, or angry, they shine the light of mindfulness or awareness on the process and consciously utilize the feelings or let them go. The goal is to always come back to the here and now. (See Nhat Hanh, 1976, for a Zen approach to cultivating mindfulness.) In the here and now, the worker allows his or her heart to be touched by the client's life and to be moved by the client's strengths and the client's story.

Case Example—Love and Mindfulness

In work with Manuel, a deep caring and respect developed. One time, I was coughing a lot, and he reached out, put his hand on my shoulder, and asked if I was O.K. Then he offered potential remedies that I might take. After considerable distrust at the outset, Manuel stated that he regarded our relationship as very important and, in fact, made sure that we had an appointment on his birthday. I, myself, felt caring and loving toward Manuel. I celebrated his victories and could see and point out his strengths. I maintained mindfulness during those times when I was feeling lazy about meeting him or when I was distracted while I was with him. I felt and continue to feel fortunate that he came into my life.

The ethnographic perspective has merit, even excluding the issues emphasized here regarding spiritual connectedness, suspension of knowledge, and practitioner love and mindfulness. However, it is apparent that stripped down, ethnographic work is vulnerable to some of the same dynamics of practitioner stereotyping, disrespect, insensitivity, and ineffectiveness that originated the development of ethnographic theory for social work.

The Ethnographic Perspective and Compassion

After deep understanding and love, compassion is the final ingredient of a spiritual ethnographic approach. I can learn about someone's life who is culturally different from me, I can appreciate our interconnections, interdependence and the sacredness of the time that I am with the individual, I can genuinely accept and appreciate who the person is and maintain mindful presence when I am with him or her; however, if *compassion* is not present, my commitment to take action on behalf of the client may be limited. Compassion, in Buddhist thinking, is one's *generous* inclinations and commitment to relieve another's pain or suffering. It is the ingredient that spurs the social worker to advocate, go the extra mile, in essence, *take action* in order to improve the life of the client. In the absence of deep, ethnographic understanding though, uninformed compassion can lead to patronizing and disempowering actions on the part of the worker.

Compassionate actions on behalf of the worker include letting go (whether it involves a desire to control outcomes, or saying good-bye), trusting the client's ability to find and work toward solutions, allowing the client to lean on the worker, and taking concrete steps to move things forward (even when those steps require risk or extra work).

Case Example—Compassion

Working from an ethnographic perspective became more complete when I made the compassionate decision to work on issues that Manuel had not initially identified as goals. Although there was already sufficient grist for the mill in our sessions—Manuel's past abuse and violent episodes, his current adjustment to being employed, a girlfriend, and foster home—Manuel's level of worry and generalized anxiety had not been directly addressed. Although I knew it would be a risk, I told Manuel that I was going to teach him relaxation skills and began taking him through relaxation and breathing exercises. Manuel balked at first. He was uncomfortable closing his eyes and he thought the whole idea to be stupid and a waste of time. I persevered and insisted that this could provide major relief for him and that the experience obtained while doing the exercises as well as the exercises themselves could be drawn upon during the course of his life outside of the sessions. Manuel relented. He participated in the exercises and enjoyed the effects immensely. He wanted every session to include relaxation exercises and has since indicated that these exercises have been very beneficial.

Compassion had been a source of my risking the introduction of the exercises as well as the impetus to attend Manuel's IEP meeting and speak on his behalf, advocate for him with his probation officer, and connect with his foster mother.

Conclusion

There is perhaps no literature regarding the utilization of relaxation skills with high-risk Latino youth; however, in our ethnographic, spiritual journey this intervention was arrived at and was appropriate. This chapter has outlined the ethnographic perspective and summarized the outstanding contributions of James Green in bringing ethnography to social work practice. The ethnographic perspective orients social workers to pursue an emic understanding of their clients in terms of the clients' culture and ethnicity, and the meaning that events, conditions and relationships have for their lives. The chapter addressed contradictions that existed in the approach, such as the injection of stereotypes regarding how clients of color supposedly seek help or how feeling-content should be de-emphasized.

An ethnographic perspective with spiritual principles was advanced, and a case example was used to illustrate its dynamics. Because of the infancy of spiritual discussions within social work, the model may appear to be unrefined. The intent of this chapter is to generate discussion and to bolster an approach—ethnographic—that my students and I have found, in California's diverse practitioner and clientele environment, to be effective, empowering, and respectful. I would appreciate continued dialogue concerning the content in this chapter.

Questions for Critical Thinking

1. The need for greater tolerance is often extolled as one of the highest societal pursuits. What does *tolerance* mean to you?

2. In addition to codependence, what other etic concepts interfere with the ability to understand clients from an emic perspective?

3. To what degree has your education, thus far, emphasized cultural traits or "things to watch for"? Describe the helpfulness of this approach for your work with diverse clients.

4. Discuss whether you agree or disagree with the idea that theory can interfere with the ability to understand diverse clients.

5. What does it mean to be in a *sacred encounter* with a client or clients? What are the implications of cultivating this kind of spiritual approach in your work?

6. Do you believe that it is, in fact, helpful for social workers to acknowledge parts of themselves that are capable of some of the acts that their clients engage in? Please discuss.

7. When did knowledge about racial or ethnic dynamics serve to enhance the practitioner's understanding of Manuel's situation?

8. What was your impression of the discussion on love for your clients? Does love have a place in social work?

9. What does "being present" mean in terms of your effectiveness with diverse clients? How do you overcome your own laziness or distraction that can interfere with your being present?

Sources for Further Study

Green, J. (1999). *Cultural awareness in the human services: A multi-ethnic approach* (3rd ed.). Boston: Allyn & Bacon. The evolution of the ethnographic approach and the application for social work is explored here. The distinction between a categorical and transactional concept of ethnicity is particularly useful as are sections regarding the components of emic interviewing and understanding client meaning.

Guadalupe, J. L. (1999). The challenge: Development of a curriculum to address diversity content without perpetuating stereotypes. Dissertation—University of South Carolina. This dissertation deconstructs assumptions underlying social work approaches and academic discourse on diversity. The embedded link between diversity and oppression is presented as well as the limitations of this link. Questions are raised concerning the degree to which multicultural frameworks perpetuate stereotypes and undermine emic understanding.

Leigh, J. W. (1998). *Communicating for cultural competence*. Boston: Allyn & Bacon. Ethnographic communication exchanges are framed as "social worker as stranger." The social worker is portrayed as a spectator at a play whose aim is to enter into the world of the actors (clients). The challenge for the social worker is that she or he does not intimately know "the plot, the language, or the actors well enough to become an equal player" (p. 51). Specific communication skills are offered to assist the social worker's development of an empathic connection and cultural competence.

Nhat Hanh, Thich (1993). *Love in action.* Berkeley: Parallax Press. Whether we are protesting large-scale injustice or are engaging with individuals, our effectiveness begins with our ability to cultivate inner peace, compassion and love. We are encouraged to learn about and free ourselves from our own fear, anxiety, despair and dispersion of mind so that we can meaningfully help others. Concepts and notions that beings create to describe and define self and the other are viewed as interfering with genuine human understanding.

References

Bein, A., & Allen, K. (1999). Hand in glove? It fits better than you think. *Social Work, 44,* 274–277.

Bein, A., & Lum, D. (1999). Inductive learning. In D. Lum (Ed.), *Culturally competent practice: A framework for growth and action* (pp. 145–172). Pacific Grove, CA: Brooks/Cole.

Bein, A., Torres, S., & Kurilla, V. (2000). Service delivery issues in early termination of Latino clients. *Human Behavior in the Social Environment, 3,* 43–59.

Faiver, C., Ingersoll, R., O'Brien, E., & McNally, C. (2001). *Explorations in counseling and spirituality.* Belmont, CA: Brooks/Cole.

Green, J. (1982). *Cultural awareness in the human services: A multi-ethnic approach* (1st ed.). Boston: Allyn & Bacon.

Green, J. (1999). *Cultural awareness in the human services: A multi-ethnic approach* (3rd ed.). Boston: Allyn & Bacon.

Guadalupe, J. (2000). *The challenge: Development of a curriculum to address diversity content without perpetuating stereotypes.* Ann Arbor, MI: UMI Company.

McMiller, W., & Weisz, J. (1996). Help-seeking preceding mental health clinic intake among African-American, Latino, and Caucasian youths. *Journal of the American Academy of Child and Adolescent Psychiatry.*

National Association of Social Workers. (1998). *Code of Ethics.* Washington, D.C.: NASW.

Nhat Hanh, T. (1976). *The miracle of mindfulness.* Boston: Beacon Press.

Nhat Hanh, T. (1988). *The sun my heart.* Berkeley: Parallax Press.

Nhat Hanh, T. (1998). *Interbeing: Fourteen guidelines for engaged Buddhism.* Berkeley: Parallax Press.

Sue, S., & Zane, N. (1987). The role of culture and cultural techniques in psychotherapy: A critique and reformulation. *American Psychologist, 42,* 37–45.

11

Communication Framework

Chrystal C. Ramirez Barranti

Through communication we can facilitate others personal growth or destroy them.

—William B. Gudykunst

I look out into my classroom filled with fifteen eager and anticipating faces. I am struck by the incredible mosaic of color that sits before me. Women, men, younger and older, various shapes and sizes, abled and differently abled, American born, immigrants, and sons and daughters of new arrivals. I myself am a combination of ethnicities—Mexican, Italian, a daughter of immigrant and first-generation parents, female, and lesbian. I am looking forward to discovering the strengths in diversity that make up this new classroom community of foundation social work practice students, a microcosm of communities at large. The learning of practicing competent social work begins right here among us and will be carried out into practicum sites and eventual professional work. Where to begin? How to insure competently skilled social work practitioners in a society of such immense and glorious variety, diversity, difference, and yet inherent interrelatedness?

Such questions represent one of the most profound challenges facing our profession in light of the growing richness of diversity in our country (Green, 1999; Leigh, 1998). In fact, these questions take on even greater importance in light of the necessary challenge to move beyond traditional and unidimensional categorizations of diversity such as ethnicity, race, and culture and to include more complex and multidimensional considerations of the vast variations in diversity such as sexual orientation, physical ability, mental ability, age, gender, generational cohort, socioeconomic class, religious beliefs, minority status, regionality, citizenship status, and so on (Appleby, Colon, & Hamilton, 2001; Green, 1994). This emerging multidimensional conceptualization of diversity can be thought of as simultaneously viewing the "diversity within the person" and the "person within culture" dynamically transacting with the environment.

This chapter invites the reader to join in exploring what may be at the heart of truly competent social work practice for today and for the future, as we become an ever-increasing global and diverse society. Perhaps Leigh (1998) expresses best what lies at the heart of competent social work practice when he writes,

> I believe that the profession of social work should focus on (1) how well the two parties in the helping encounter understand each other, and (2) what methods the social worker can use to strive for this understanding. *The key may lie in paying attention to the communication procedures through which the social worker may well develop an interactive skill that leads toward understanding a client who is culturally, racially, and ethnically different.* (italics mine, pp. 4–5)

Like Leigh, it is this author's belief that mutually creating an honoring, respectful, and caring relationship through communicative competence is at the heart of effective social work practice with the great variety of those experiencing vulnerable life conditions.

In the pages that follow, a model of communicating through a dynamics of difference, "communicating with strangers" (Gudykunst, 1998; Gudykunst & Kim, 1997) is presented as a process of communication that can bring social workers beyond a unidimensional and general cultural competence and into a multidimensional cultural competence. In preparation for this communication model and its place in social work, it is important that a brief look at the history of social work's journey in addressing issues of diversity be provided. Cultural influences on the process of communication will also be identified. Finally, the significance of the etic and the emic in communicative competence will be discussed.

A Look at Where Social Work Has Been

Although the profession of social work was born out of service to those in need, it has long struggled to address the critical issues of diversity (Leigh, 1998). Despite the ethnic, racial, and culturally diverse make-up of the poor, oppressed, and needy who have been the focus of social work efforts, it was not until the Civil Rights Movement of the 1960s that social work education began to address the significance of diversity and difference in the experience of those most vulnerable as well as in the process of practice and the delivery of services (Fong & Furuto, 2001; Leigh, 1998). Lum (2000) has reviewed the last twenty-five years of social work literature, and although he has found an increase in research on the issues of race, ethnicity, and culture as it related to social work practice, overall, research on multidiversity issues has accounted for only eight percent of the articles in the three leading social work journals (*Families in Society, Social Work,* and *Social Service Review*) and only three percent of the total pages in social work practice texts. Given both the central mission of the social work profession and the growing multidimensional complexity of diversity, the profession is called to focus more research in this critical area if we are to move forward with professional integrity and meet the needs of all persons in their environments.

Communication frameworks in social work with diverse populations are embedded in the models for practice that have been presented over the last twenty-five years. Such models of practice have been developed with the intentions of providing frameworks for developing "cultural competency" in social workers. These practice models include, among others, Norton's (1978) dual perspective, Devore's & Schlesinger's (1999) ethnic-sensitive practice model, Lum's (2000) process-stage approach with people of color, Pinderhughes's (1995) cultural competence as an empowerment strategy, Fong, Boyd, & Browne's (1999) biculturalization of interventions, Falicov's (1998) multidimensional ecosystemic comparative approach (MECA), and Green's (1999) cultural competence model. Like viewing a multifaceted crystal from several different points of view, each of these models has offered varying perspectives on culturally competent social work practice.

Perhaps the most helpful definition of cultural competence is provided by Doman Lum (1999). He writes, "From a social work perspective, the term cultural competency denotes the ability to understand the dimensions of culture and cultural practice and apply them to the client and the cultural/social environment" (p. 29). Lum identified four interacting components of cultural competence that can be helpful when considering a communication framework (p. 30).

> ***Cultural Awareness:*** Personal and professional awareness of ethnic persons and events that have been a part of the upbringing and education of the worker.
>
> ***Knowledge Acquisition:*** Knowledge acquisition related to culturally diverse practice.
>
> ***Skill Development:*** Skill development related to working with the culturally diverse client.
>
> ***Inductive Learning:*** Inductive learning that forms a continuum of heuristic information on culturally diverse persons, events, and places.

Falicov (1983) has offered a multidimensional definition of culture that can help us to expand Lum's cultural-competency model to include necessary factors for broadening what has been a fairly unidemensional view of communication skills in practice. She writes:

> Culture is those sets of shared worldviews, meanings, and adaptive behaviors derived from simultaneous membership and participation in a variety of contexts such as language; rural, urban, or suburban setting; race, ethnicity, and socioeconomic status; age, gender, religion, nationality; employment, education, and occupation, political ideology, stage of acculturation. (pp. xiv–xv)

Expanding definitions of the four components to include the more complex and multidimensional view of culture and diversity will make them more effective when considering communications competency with diverse others. For example, including personal and professional awareness of the multidimensional components of "the diversity/culture within the person" and the "person within the culture" is an ongoing life-learning process. A deeply integrated understanding and awareness of one's own multiple cultural contexts is critical for effective communication with those who are in some ways different and some ways similar (Falicov, 1998). Such an understanding of self and others enables a worker to journey into what Rosaldo (1989) has described as "cultural borderlands" or overlapping zones of differences and similarities within and between cultures. Falicov (1998) describes the cultural borderland as a dynamically interactive and contextual zone in which human beings can encounter one another in full appreciation of similarities and differences without falling prey to stereotyping and generalizations. Expanding on Rosaldo's (1989) concept of cultural borderlands, Falicov (1998) writes,

> They give rise to internal inconsistencies, conflicts, and contradictions as well as commonalities and resonances among groups and individuals. Borderlands occur at the edges of "officially" recognized cultural groups, such as being an Argentine, a Jew, and a U.S. citizen. Other borderlands occur at less formal intersections—being raised a traditional girl (gender) in a family of poor immigrants (class and migration) of limited schooling (education), encountering a different world (and values) through advanced education, and acquiring higher social status through marriage. The idea of cultural borderlands captures more accurately the "encounters with difference" or "communities of difference.". . . (pp. 14–15)

Expanding beyond general cultural characteristics to include the complexity of the individual within the group, varying group memberships, and contextual realities is necessary. While cultural borderlands are both formal and individual, they can be the places, if you will, where human beings can encounter one another in all their individual complexities and cultural identity and do so with great appreciation and open heartedness. Building on the concept of cultural borderlands, Falicov (1998) has proposed a multidimensional view of culture, which beautifully integrates the significance of general culture and individual complexity and contextualism.

> Each person has a culture comprised of a number of collective identities—groups of belonging, participation, and identification that make up his or her "ecological niche." This ecological niche shares "cultural borderlands" or zones of overlap with others by virtue of race, ethnicity, religion, occupation, or social class. . . . Rather than restricting ourselves to one cultural identity, we can talk about multicultural identities. (p. 7)

An applied knowledge and skill base of post-modernism social constructivism would be critical for laying a framework for affirmative practice that supports adventures of cultural borderlands and multidimensional identities. Constructivism views reality as being holistic, changing, multiple, and dynamically sensitive to context (Burris & Guadalupe, 2003). From a constructivist view, reality is socially constructed through dialogue, observation, and experience (Gergen, 1999). A social constructivist-informed practice enables effective communication through focus on attending to narratives, recognizing language as creational and social, and engaging in collaborative conversation in which the client is expert.

Perhaps one of the most helpful concepts that has reached practice through postmodern-based solution-oriented approaches is the concept of inclusion, or "both/and" logic (Lipchick, 1993; Rowan & O'Hanlon, 1999). Moving away from the traditional medical model of "either/or" logic, "both/and" logic opens up the rich possibilities of exploring, honoring, celebrating, and understanding both the inherent truth of the interconnectedness of all human beings and the great multidimensional diversity of each individual. It is through communicative competence that the concept of inclusion opens up the unidimensional diversity view of others in the world as being "either" the same "or" different from the viewer. Working with "both/and" logic allows one to go into the cultural borderlands to meet both the similarities and differences of all involved in the communication process.

Skill development further expands beyond the limitations of traditional cultural-competence skills to include competence in diversity communication through the "communicating with strangers" model (Gudykunst, 1998; Gudykunst & Kim, 1997). The ethnographic framework, which includes attention to the dynamic interaction of the etic and the emic, would broaden the inductive learning component while enhancing skill and effectiveness in communication with diverse others.

Core Concepts

Gudykunst's "Communicating with Strangers" Model of Communicative Competence

William Gudykunst, a professor of speech communication, has devoted a lifetime to the study of effective communication within and across cultures and diverse groups. He writes, "communication is a process involving the exchange of messages and the creation of meaning. . . . Communication is effective to the extent that we are able to minimize misunderstandings (Gudykunst, 1998, p. 26). A deceivingly simple definition, as there is a great deal that goes into communicating effectively through minimizing misunderstandings. The "communicating with strangers" model provides a framework for practicing effective communication with others who are both the same and different.

Gudykunst's (1995; 1998) communication model is based on the premise that the actual processes of communication are the same when communicating with those from a different culture as they are when communicating with others within the same culture. He and his colleagues have used the concept of "stranger" in reference to others who are from a different culture than oneself. More specifically, "stranger" is defined as "anyone entering a relatively unknown or unfamiliar environment" (Gudykunst & Kim, 1997). The use of the "stranger" concept opens up unidimensional categories of intercultural or cross-cultural communication to include all multidimensional realities of intergroup communications. In a strong sense Gudykunst's (1983; 1998) concept of "stranger" fits very well with Falicov's (1998) multidimensional definition of culture on which this chapter is based.

The ability to communicate effectively will, it is hoped, be perceived as communicative competence. According to this model, communicative competence is made up of three components: Motivation, knowledge, and skills (Gudykunst & Kim, 1997). Motivation is viewed as the desire to communicate effectively with others. Knowledge refers to a knowledge base and awareness of what needs to be done to communicate effectively. Skills include the behaviors and the ability to employ these for effective communication. These components interact interdependently with the environment and the "stranger" to result in perceived communicative competence. These three components integrate easily with Lum's (1999) four components of cultural competence, discussed earlier in the chapter, while adding a critical component—motivation. There is no doubt that effective communication demands a strong motivation and deep desire to truly connect with others. In fact, without motivation, cultural self-awareness, knowledge acquisition, skill development, and inductive learning are lifeless. What is your level of motivation to meet the other in the cultural borderlands?

While motivation is a driving energy behind cultural competence and all of its components, research has identified several intervening variables that influence effective communication in the cultural borderlands (Gudykunst, 1998; Gudykunst & Kim, 1997). In the two sections that follow, these intervening and influencing factors are described. One's ability to recognize and work with such variables facilitates effective communication.

Anxiety and Uncertainty: Intervening Variables in Effective Communication. Communication at its best is the meeting of two or more in shared meaning and exchange. It is not surprising then, that reactions to the uncertainty inherent in meeting others in the cultural borderlands can and does result in anxiety. The ability to manage levels of anxiety related to experiences of uncertainty in interacting with strangers has direct effects on abilities to communicate effectively (Gudykunst, 1995; Gudykunst & Kim, 1997). Levels of uncertainty and consequent anxiety are impacted by the ability to predict and explain another's behavior and interaction patterns. Levels of uncertainty and anxiety tend to be lower when one interacts with familiar others and others of similar cultures and groups as one's own. When communicating with a stranger or a member of a group that is different from groups one identifies with, levels of uncertainty and anxiety tend to be high. To communicate effectively, levels of uncertainty and anxiety need to stay above minimum thresholds and below maximum thresholds. Such thresholds are uniquely tied to the individual communicator. If anxiety and/or uncertainty are above maximum levels or below minimum levels, conscious management of uncertainty and anxiety must be undertaken to ensure effective communication. For example, if another's behavior is seen as highly predictable (i.e., based on stereotypes), anxiety is low, and there is a high likelihood of misinterpreted messages and hence failed communication. Likewise, if uncertainty is above a maximum threshold, a lack of confidence in predictions and explanations of another's behavior can result in great discomfort and interfere with communication (Gudykunst & Kim, 1997). What is your level of anxiety like when interacting with those who are familiar and those who are different from yourself?

The greater the difference between strangers and/or the less strangers know about each other's group, the greater the potential for higher levels of uncertainty. Similarly, the greater the similarity between strangers and the more strangers know about each other's group, the greater the potential for lower levels of uncertainty. When uncertainty and anxiety thresholds fall below the minimum or rise above the maximum thresholds, interactions and messages can be processed simplistically or unidimensionally and lead to reliance on stereotypes. Most often in high-anxiety and high-uncertainty interactions when knowledge and awareness are low, the potential for the induction of negative stereotypes is also high. Consequently, the potential for misinterpretation, misunderstanding, and unaffirming communication outcomes are also high.

Becoming communicatively competent requires a highly conscious awareness of one's own communication processes when interacting with strangers (cultural awareness). It demands a high "consciousness competency" (Gudykunst, 1998) including self-awareness and self-knowledge. These are two necessary building blocks to effective communication that relate to Lum's (1999) four components of cultural competence: cultural awareness, knowledge, skill development, and inductive learning.

Mindfully Managing Influencing Factors in Communicative Behavior.   While the processes of communicating with strangers and those who are familiar are the same, several factors differ in significance (Gudykunst & Kim, 1997). These include communicative predictions, social identities, and sources of communicative behavior (habits, intentions, and emotions) (Gudykunst, 1998).

Habitual behaviors develop from repeated experiences and interactions and require little conscious attention to what one is saying, doing, or hearing. Habitual behavior relies on cultural scripts, which provide shared interpretations of behavior, enabling predictions about how others will behave. For example, in the southern United States, people greet each other in passing with, "hey." It is a predictable script such that southerners know that, when they greet a stranger on the street with "hey," the stranger will respond in a similar way. In New York, however, people passing in the street do not greet one another, and this, as a regional cultural script, creates little to no anxiety for New Yorkers. All of this occurs in an automatic-response fashion. In other words, in familiar and common situations in which another's behavior matches predictions, an automatic-pilot level of consciousness may be sufficient for effective interaction.

However, when another's behavior does not follow predictions, anxiety and uncertainty are often generated. Without conscious attention to managing the anxiety and the sense of uncertainty that arise in such a situation, communication may be doomed to fail. Managing anxiety and uncertainty requires that we cultivate a mindfulness about the very process of communication we engage in. Developing a mindfulness about how and what we are communicating is a key ingredient to communicating effectively.

> Focusing on the process (i.e., how we do something) allows us to be mindful of our behavior and pay attention to the situations in which we find ourselves. It is only when we are mindful of the process of our communication that we can determine how our interpretations differ from strangers' interpretations of those messages. To be mindful, we must also recognize that there is *more than one perspective* that can be used to understand or explain our interactions with others. (Gudykunst, 1998, pp. 32–33)

Intentions provide direction for how to communicate effectively with others (Gudykunst, 1998). Mindfulness about how messages are sent and how they may be interpreted is at the heart of effective communication. In other words, a thoughtfulness and awareness is required for communication that is enriching and connecting. How mindful are you in your everyday communication with others?

While intentions operate at a cognitive level, emotional basis for communicative behavior operates at the affective or feeling level. Emotions such as fear and anxiety can and do influence communicative behavior. When one is fearful or feeling threatened, it is near to impossible to communicate with others. Mindfulness and a cognitive management of fearful emotions help a person to communicate competently (Gudykunst, 1998).

An individual's identity is another factor that has direct influence on communicative behavior. As an influence on communication, identity consists of three types of identities

(Turner, 1987, as cited in Gudykunst, 1998). Human, social, and personal identities incorporate views of oneself as a member of a group and as participating in various interactions and settings. *Human identity* relates to the views that all people have of themselves; for example, needing to be loved, to be valued, and to have a sense of belonging. Human identity is a sense of being interconnected with all. *Social identity*, on the other hand, reflects how people view themselves based on their group memberships. Roles they play, organizations they belong to, and demographic characteristics that define them are examples of where people derive their views to make up their social identities. Defining people even further is *personal identity*, the way people view themselves based on their unique characteristics and qualities (personality characteristics, temperament, intelligence, etc.). Everyone involved in interacting within cultural borderlands brings along his or her unique human, social, personal identities.

People are a human, social, and personal identity all at the same time. For instance, I am aware that I am part of all of life on earth, inherently interconnected with all human beings. I am a middle-aged, first generation Mexican-Italian lesbian woman who is an assistant professor and a Democrat. I am middle class and have access to many social resources. I was raised Roman Catholic and have a strong spiritual base. I am a warm and friendly individual who finds it easy to make friends. How about you? What are your identities?

People's identities influence their communication behaviors; however, one identity may predominate depending on the particular setting a person is in (Gudykunst, 1998). Because people rely most on group memberships when social identities predominate in an interaction, they are more likely to interpret another's behaviors based on that person's group memberships. In such interactions, there is a greater chance of misinterpretation. The need for mindful awareness regarding this potential is important in order to avoid ineffective communication. Simultaneously realizing people's interconnectedness and differences is significant to communicating effectively in the cultural borderlands (Falicov, 1998; Gudykunst, 1998).

When people communicate, they make some kind of prediction about the outcome of their communication. Three types of information are used to help make these predictions and include cultural, social, and personal or psychological information (Gudykunst, 1998; Gudykunst & Kim, 1997). The environmental context in which communication occurs is an additional source of information influencing communicative behavior. Cultural, social, personal, and environmental influences can be viewed as conceptual filters that determine how messages are sent and interpreted (Gudykunst, 1998; Gudykunst & Kim, 1997).

When people rely on cultural information to predict behavior, the norms, rules, values, and beliefs shared by a culture enable regularity of behavior (i.e., cultural scripts— common behaviors). Accuracy of predictions that support effective communication are influenced by the degree of knowledge and experience people have of each other's culture. The more knowledge and experience, the greater probability for accurate predictions and effective communication. The cultural competence components of cultural awareness and knowledge are significant building blocks.

People use social information predominantly when making prediction about outcomes of communication with those who are from their own culture. Social class, ableness, gender, sexual orientation, ethnicity, marital status, religious affiliations, and social roles are examples of group membership information used to make social predictions (Gudykunst, 1998). Encompassing the whole ecological system of people communicating includes considering the multidimensional complexity (familiar and unfamiliar) of all the group memberships represented. These informal intersections of cultural borderlands are where people can sensitively and thoughtfully take in the rich information that exists in the overlapping zones of similarities and differences—be it individuals, families, or groups who are engaged in the communication.

> In fact, the unique combination of multiple contexts and partial perspectives that defines each family's culture can be thought of as their "ecological niche." A family's values form and evolve over time by their participation in these multiple contexts. The experience of dominant or marginalized access to resources, of entitlement and powerlessness, also derive from one's ecological place and experiences in various contexts. It is critical that therapists be aware of the family's holistic membership in these many, varied groups. (Falicov, 1998, p. 15)

Predicting communication outcomes on social or cultural information involves placing people in social categories. When people place those with whom they are communicating in social categories, they are more likely to assume that all persons in such categories are alike, and more likely to predict erroneously based on stereotypes (negative and positive). Without conscious and well-cultivated mindfulness, it is easy to use "either/or" logic and focus solely on the homogeneous similarity of all who belong to the particular category they have been assigned to. Automatic-pilot consciousness can leave people prey to the confines of "either/or" logic. Mindful use of personal information facilitates predictions that are based on "both/and" logic, which allows for the recognition of both the similarities and individual uniqueness of a particular person. Are you mindfully aware, compassionately curious of all persons you encounter?

Social work is certainly familiar with the significance of people's environmental factors when interaction is considered. The person-in-environment perspective is a defining framework for the profession. When considering conceptual filters influencing communication effectiveness, additional environmental factors such as geography, climate, and even architectural settings play an important role in impacting communicative behavior (Gudykunst & Kim, 1997).

The Organizing Model of Communication.   Effective communication among people who are familiar with one another and among those who are not is highly influenced by the ability of the communicators to mindfully manage anxiety and uncertainty. Mindful awareness of influencing factors—degree of predictability, human, social, and personal identities, group memberships, habitual scripts, intentions, and emotions—is critical for successful communication in the cultural borderlands. The actual sending and receiving of messages can be thought of as being filtered through cultural, social, personal, and environmental influences (Gudykunst and Kim, 1997). Cultural self awareness and knowledge of the "stranger's" cultural, social, personal, and environmental filters is essential in making accurate predictive outcomes of communicative behavior. Figure 11.1 attempts to offer a visual presentation of the process of communication within cultural borderlands.

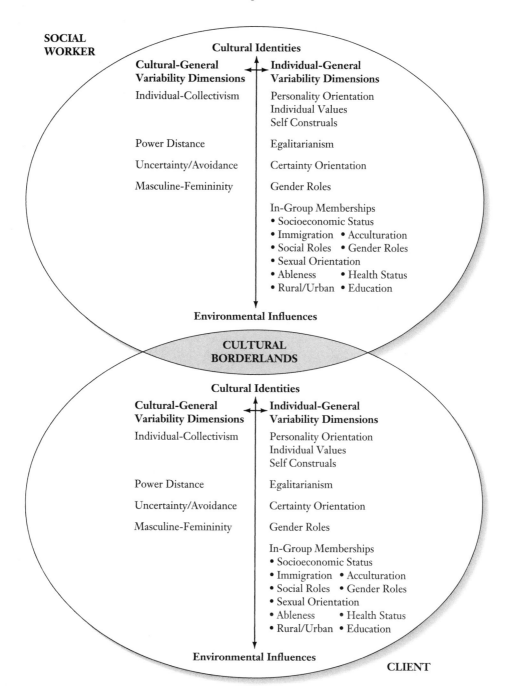

FIGURE 11.1 *Communication Framework*

The Importance of the Etic: Taking a Look at the Influences of Group Membership and Culture on the Processes of Communication

One of the critical roles that culture plays in the communication process is that it provides its members with the fundamental knowledge base for communication. Understanding and knowledge of cultures provides an important but not exclusive tool in effective communication. General cultural knowledge must be considered in dynamic relation to the unique characteristics and personality of the individual member with whom one is communicating. The ethnographic approach to communicating with others from different cultures and even different groups from oneself offers a helpful framework for thinking about the culture-wide information (etic) and individual/culture specific information (emic) (Leigh, 1998; Lum, 2000). The dynamic interplay of the etic and the emic can help people consider important influences on communication processes while they honor and learn from the unique individual person with whom they are communicating (Gudykunst, 1998; Lum, 2000). Each person is an individual and a member of a culture and other groups.

Etic in a broad sense refers to universal human commonalities that exist for everyone, such as basic human needs for belonging, acceptance, and love. An etic perspective helps people keep in mind the ways in which all are similar and interconnected. In addition, when considering etic influences on communication, one is considering what Lum (2000) describes as "culture-common characteristics" of a particular culture and/or group. Falicov (1998) speaks of these as the formal recognized cultural borderlands. Several dimensions can be thought about in considering the etic of a particular culture, or the culture-common of a particular group. Gudykunst (1998) describes these influencing dimensions as dimensions of cultural variability. Helpful dimensions of cultural variability have been identified by Hall (1976), Hofstede (1980), and The Chinese Culture Connection (1987).

Hall's Individualism–Collectivism and High–Low Contextual Patterns

The individualism–collectivism dimension first identified by Edward T. Hall (1976) is one of the primary cultural variability factors helpful in understanding differences in communication across cultures. Hall contends that a major role of culture is to provide a screen between the individual and the myriad of perceptual stimuli that one is constantly exposed to. In other words, this culture-specific screen selectively filters in particular perceptions and provides a particular system for interpretation of what is filtered in. Specific cultures vary on a continuum of high to low on both individualism and collectivism as well as on the relative significance of context in communication.

Individualistic cultures value individual goals, individual initiative, and individual achievement over group goals, initiative, and group achievement. On the other hand, collectivist cultures place a primary emphasis on group membership, cooperation, group goals and group needs. While in both individualistic and collectivistic cultures individuals belong to in-groups (family, church, community, university, company, etc.), the role of the in-group varies. Within collectivist cultures in-groups have a greater influence on individual behavior across all situations (Gudykunst, 1998) than in individualistic cultures. In such cultures there is a greater psychological distance from those who are not a member of the in-group (Lustig & Koester, 1999). Among collectivist cultures, different in-groups have priority. For example, the family is the primary in-group in Latin American families, while community is the primary in-group in many African cultures. In-groups are also important in individualistic; however, the influence of the in-group is specific rather than general as it is in collectivistic cultures (Gudykunst, 1998). For individualistic cultures, there is a weaker connection to and within in-groups than there is for collectivistic cultures (Lustig & Koester, 1999) Similarly, there is a stronger connection to out-groups for individualistic cultures than there is among collectivistic cultures (Lustig & Koester, 1999).

In addition to considering culture variability along dimensions of individualism–collectivism, cultures can differ in how relationships among people are viewed and experienced. Cultures can be described as being either horizontal or vertical (Gudykunst, 1998). In horizontal cultures, there is an emphasis on equality and blending in; whereas in vertical cultures, equality is not valued highly and individuals are expected to stand out and be different. Table 1 provides examples of cultural variability along both the individualism–collectivism and horizontal–vertical dimensions.

Using Hall's (1976) continuum of high–low context, cultures can be organized according to how much information in communication processes is implied in the setting or context of the interaction irrespective of actual words or language used. In high-context (HC) cultures, high-context messages are used and the actual meaning of the message is implied in the setting and/or in the presumed values, norms, and beliefs of the individuals involved (Hall, 1976). In high-context cultures there is a presumption of shared meanings. Non-verbal cues are heavily relied upon, and much less of the meaning of the communication is provided in the spoken words. High-context communication can be described as indirect, implicit, and less precise. Low-context (LC) communication contains a majority of the meaning of the message in the actual words spoken. Spoken words are relied upon to express the actual meaning of the message, and communication is more precise and clearly

TABLE 11.1 *Cultural variations along the individual–collectivism and horizontal–vertical dimensions*

	Individualism "I"	Collectivism "We"
Horizontal "same as"	Be an individual	Don't stand out
	Don't stand out	High value on equality
	High value on equality	Low value on freedom
	High value on freedom	
Vertical "different from"	Stand out from group	Fit into the group **and** stand out in the group
	Low value on equality	Low value on equality
	High value on freedom	Low value on freedom

Summarized from Gudykunst, 1998; Triandis, 1995

TABLE 2 *Low- and High-Context Cultural Characteristics*

High-Context	Low-Context
Implicit and Indirect	Precise and Explicit
Setting and Situation Important	Meaning in Words
Shared Internalized Meanings	Detailed Information Shared
Reactions Reserved	Reactions Expressed
Nonverbal Coding	Specifics Verbalized
Strong In-group Bonds	In-group Bonds
Distinct In-groups & Out-groups	Less Distinct In-groups and Out-groups
"We" focused	"I" focused

Summarized from Fong & Furuto, 2001; Gudykunst, 1998; Lustig & Koester, 1999

direct. It is characteristic for individualistic cultures to predominantly use low-context communication and collectivistic cultures to most often use high-context communication processes. However, this is an opportunity to be ware of "either/or" logic and to keep in mind that both high- and low-context communication processes are used in both individualistic and collectivistic cultures (Gudykunst, 1998). Likewise, while cultures tend to be predominately individualistic or collectivistic, individualism and collectivism exist in all cultures (Gudykunst, 1998). What might high-context and low-context characteristics look like? Some of these are summarized in Table 2.

Hofstede's Dimensions of Cultural Variability

Extensive studies of cultural differences in value orientation were done by Geert Hofstede (1980). Four dimensions were identified that include individualism–collectivism, power distance, uncertainty avoidance, and masculinity–femininity (Hofstede, 1980). Although originally derived as work-related values, further research supports application to general cultural values (Lustig & Koester, 1999). Since individualism–collectivism was discussed above, the focus here will be on the additional three dimensions.

The power distance dimension defines a culture's value orientation on the significance and appropriateness of status and social hierarchies (Hofstede, 1980). The power distance dimension describes the extent to which a culture believes that power should be equally or unequally distributed and the extent to which decisions made by those in power should be challenged or not (Lustig & Koester, 1999). Hofstede (1980) devised a power distance index (PDI) to assess and identify a culture's power distance dimension. Cultures who are on the low end of the PDI endorse small power distances, support social and economic equality, believe in challenging authority and using power ethically (Lustig & Koester, 1999). When a culture is on the high end of the PDI, there is a preference for large power distances; social and economic inequality are viewed as the norm; authority should not be challenged; and power is to be used by those with social status. Those from high-PDI cultures would not consider challenging superiors, while those from low PDI cultures would (Gudykunst, 1998). While either a low or high power distance dimension predominates in a given culture, keep in mind that both low and high power distance dimensions are also present (Gudykunst, 1998).

The experience of change and ambiguity is universally experienced by all human beings in every culture. Considering how particular cultures interact with the unpredictability and anxiety associated with change and ambiguity is a cultural pattern influential in communication processes (Gudykunst, 1998; Lustig & Koester, 1999).

Hofstede (1980) has developed an uncertainty avoidance index (UAI) to help identify to what degree a culture responds to unpredictability and ambiguity by creating more structure (Lustig & Koester, 1999). For instance, cultures that are high in uncertainty have a greater need for social consensus, formal rules and regulations, and have little tolerance for diversity. Keeping in mind that this is cultural general, Gudykunst (1998) describes high-uncertainty-avoidance cultures as being more emotionally expressive, having stronger superegos, and having little tolerance for what is non-normative behavior than do members of cultures with low-uncertainty avoidance. In other words, high-uncertainty-avoidance cultures experience high anxiety in the face of unpredictability and ambiguity while low-uncertainty-avoidance cultures experience less anxiety when confronted with change and difference. Like the other dimensions of cultural variability, there is a range of uncertainty-avoidance patterns from high to low among individuals in cultures, while the culture general itself tends to embrace either a high or low uncertainty-avoidance pattern (Gudykunst, 1998).

Gender roles in a culture are also significant patterns to consider in effective communication with others. The masculine–feminine dimension helps to conceptualize how a culture values achievement, assertiveness, nurturance, and social support. For example, a culture high in masculinity primarily embraces achievement, competitiveness, and assertiveness. Such cultures are more likely to value "machismo" and have more defined sex roles. They are less likely to operate on a belief in equality between the genders (Lustig & Koester, 1999). As with the dimensions of power distance and uncertainty avoidance, Hofstede (1980) has developed the masculinity assessment scale (MAS) to identify where cultures fall on this dimension.

Bond's Confucian Work Dynamism

Hofstede's (1980) work has been well documented, and many additional studies have supported the cultural dimensions he has identified (Lustig & Koester, 1999). It is important to recognize, however, that Hofstede's work was based on samples from a large multinational company and may include a western bias (Gudykunst & Kim, 1997). Michael Bond from the Chinese University of Hong Kong and a group of researchers known as the Chinese Culture Connection (1987) applied Hofstede's methodology. Working from an intentional Chinese bias, the researchers surveyed Chinese respondents residing in different cultures and identified four cultural variability dimensions: Confucian work dynamism, integration, human-heartedness, and moral discipline. Integration, moral discipline, and human-heartedness were found to correlate with Hofstede's individualism, power distance, and masculinity–femininity (Gudykunst & Kim, 1997).

Eight values make up the Confucian work dynamism that did not correlate with any of Hofstede's dimensions (Gudykunst & Kim, 1997). Ordering relationships, thrift, persistence, and sense of shame were four values that were found to correlate positively with the Confucian work dynamism dimensions and reflect hierarchical aspects of Chinese culture. Describing the other end of the dimension were the four values that negatively correlated with the Chinese work dynamism: protecting one's face, personal steadiness, respect for tradition, and reciprocation (Gudykunst & Kim, 1997).

Closely related to Hofstede's individualism–collectivism dimension, the integration dimension describes social stability. Such values as group solidarity, tolerance, non-competitiveness and interpersonal harmony are indicative of high integration (Lustig & Koester, 1999). The human-heartedness dimension conceptualizes a sense of compassion and gentleness and is correlated with Hofstede's masculinity–femininity dimension. Kindness, compassion, courtesy, and patience are embraced by those high on human-heartedness. Finally, the moral discipline dimension that conceptualizes a sense of restraint and moderation in daily activities correlates with the power distance dimension. High moral discipline is reflected in detachment and purity (Lustig & Koester, 1999).

Core Principles for Practice

Communicating with the "Other": The Importance of the Emic

This chapter has explored concepts of cultural variability that are significant to effective communication with strangers from the etic perspective or cultural general view. It has also kept in mind the significance of the individual's unique integration and expressions of the "culture within the person." "To understand an individual's behavior, we must understand the individual's characteristics that mediate the influence of cultural-level tendencies on individual communication" (Gudykunst & Kim, 1997, p. 56). Both/and logic brings recognition of the interactive importance of the etic and the significance of the emic and allows for a truly multidimensional consideration of self and other. The emic perspective brings attention to individuals in all their complexity, individuality, and universality and focuses on learning from individuals about their unique experience. Everyone, although living within a common culture, experiences variability in how he or she is socialized. The emic perspective invites each person to be a "teacher" or "guide" in learning and sharing through communication.

> Families partake of and combine features of all of these contexts. The contexts provide particular experiences and bestow certain values. It is the combination of multiple contexts and partial perspectives that shape and define each family's culture, rather than any of those separately. Nor does some monolithic "culture" exert an inexorable influence upon the individual. Each person is raised in a "plurality of cultural subgroups" that exert a "multiplicity of influences" depending on the degree of contact with each subcultural context (Falicov, 1998, p. 14)

Gudykunst (1998) has identified several individual or emic factors that mediate the influence of the etic perspective of cultural variability dimensions. For example, one's personality orientation, individual values, and self construals influence how an individual integrates and expresses the individualism–collectivism dimension of culture through communication (Hall, 1976; Hofstede, 1980). Personality orientations have been discussed in terms of allocentrism (personality orientation of social support and collectivism) and idiocentricism (personality orientation of achievement and individualism). Allocentric and idiocentric personality orientations can be found in either collectivistic or individualistic cultures. For instance, allocentric individuals in an individualistic culture are concerned about the in-groups they belong to while idiocentric individuals are most concerned with "me" and "I" rather than "we" (Gudykunst, 1998). Likewise, individual values reflecting individualism and/or collectivism filter how the cultural dimension of individualism–collectivism influences communication processes. Similarly, how one thinks of oneself, or one's self construals, impacts behavior and consequently communication in various situations. Independent self construals, which tend to predominate in individualistic cultures, influence a tendency toward clear and direct communication, while interdependent self construals which predominate in collectivistic cultures, influence a tendency toward communication that maintains support and avoids discord (Gudykunst, 1998).

There are several cultural variability dimensions in addition to the significant dimension of individualism–collectivism. These include power distance, uncertainty avoidance, gender roles, and cultural identity. The influence of power distance is mediated by an individual's level of belief in egalitarianism (Gudykunst, 1998). For instance, low egalitarianism is often related to high power distance. Cultural uncertainty avoidance is influenced on the individual level by one's certainty orientation (Gudykunst, 1998). Low uncertainty avoidance is reflected in an openness to and curiosity about differences. One's psychological sex roles orientation mediates the influence of the cultural dimension of masculinity-femininity and influences experiences of same as well as opposite sex communications.

An additional individual dimension that mediates culture general influences on communication is one's cultural identity (Gudykunst, 1998). The strength of identification with one's cultural identity influences the extent to which one expects others to adhere to one's own cultural norms and values. The stronger the cultural identity, the greater potential for ethnocentrism. While strength of cultural identity is influential in communication processes, so, too is the actual content of one's cultural identity. The content of one's cultural identity consists of the dimensions of cultural variability discussed above and the unique combination of multidimensional cultural borderlands that make up the individual.

A Ripple in a Great Pond: Building Community One by One

Communicative competence has all too often been viewed rather narrowly as a micro practice skill; however, if one looks closely enough, one can easily see the impact that ineffective communication processes have on all communities, local and global. Conflict, oppression, social injustice, prejudice alike are kept alive by individuals, groups, communities themselves, and political structures that refuse to see the universality and the uniqueness of every being. Communicative competence can and does have a significant impact on the nature and quality of the communities that one participates in and contributes to. Communicative competence is an intervention tool that provides material for building bridges across differences and enriching and honoring journeys into the cultural borderlands. Building community is about building relationships. Through communicative competence people can build community one by one. Table 3 offers a summary of community-building principles.

TABLE 11.3 *A summary of community-building principles*

Principles for Building Community

Principle One: Be Committed
- Be committed to the value of community.
- Be committed to relationships with "strangers."
- Be committed to dialogue as a way of problem solving.
- Be committed to lifelong learning.

Principle Two: Be Mindful
- Pay attention to what you say and do.
- Focus on the process of communication, not the outcome.
- Give full attention and avoid "automatic pilot."
- Seek to truly understand with genuine curiosity.
- Use an ethnographic and constructivist-based approach.
- Remain committed.

Principle Three: Be Unconditionally Accepting
- Accept and appreciate strangers for all their uniqueness.
- Accept and welcome a stranger's multidimensional cultures.
- Trust strangers, a necessary ingredient for community building.
- Remember that strangers are the expert on their multidimensional identity.
- Use diversity-competent communication skills.
- Be mindful.

Principle Four: Be Concerned for Yourself and Others
- Be inclusive.
- Be concerned with and welcome both your own and strangers' multidimensional cultures.
- Take responsibility for including all.
- Employ principles of social justice to all.
- Take the journey into the cultural borderlands of yourself and others.

Principle Five: Be Understanding
- Be committed to understanding strangers from their perspective.
- Appreciate and celebrate the differences and similarities of yourself and others.

Principle Six: Be Ethical
- Cultivate genuine compassion and care for strangers.
- Act with integrity.
- Support the dignity and respect of strangers.
- Be true to moral and ethical principles.

Principle Seven: Be Peaceful
- Strive for internal harmony.
- Work to develop personal peace in thought, word, and action.
- Embrace non-violence.
- Be honest.
- Remain true to commitments.
- Work for peace.

Adapted from Gudykunst, 1998, and Gudykunst & Kim, 1997

Working in the Cultural Borderlands: Social Work
Principles for Communicative Competence

It may have become clear to the reader by now that the development of communicative competence requires a dedicated and lifelong effort. It is a complex process, so often taken for granted, that requires a purposeful mindfulness if the journey into cultural borderlands is to be meaningful, empowering, and healing for social work clients. Communicative competence is an essential element in all social work, for without it practitioners never make true contact or have meaningful life-affirming exchange with others. There are several principles for practice that a social worker is ethically bound to consider in developing and applying communicative competence.

1. An ongoing learning and development of one's own cultural borderlands is a prerequisite for developing communicative competence.
2. Integrating the social constructivist perspective of "both/and" logic facilitates an increasing appreciation for the simultaneous and dynamic coexistence of universality and uniqueness of self and others.
3. Bringing the dynamic interactive perspective of both the etic and the emic offers an additional lens through which social workers can experience the multidimensional cultural identities of self and others.
4. Cultivating a deepening conscious mindfulness of internal and external processes of communication provides a significant tool for managing anxiety and ambiguity, avoiding habitual scripts, and appreciating the unique characteristics of each individual.
5. Operationalizing the ethnographic perspective, recognizing that clients are the true experts about their lives and experiences. Taking a "not knowing" stance with genuine curiosity conveys honor, respect, and reverence for others as they teach practitioners about their cultural borderland experiences.
6. This is an ongoing and lifelong process that calls practitioners to continual personal growth and transformation.

Case Example

Lila, a seventy-eight-year-old retired elementary school teacher, had been socially withdrawn, almost non-verbal, and unable to eat. She had been a resident at the senior living housing community for about three months when I was called by the community's social worker for help in intervening with Lila.

The social worker, Insoo, was a young, newly married woman who had recently graduated with her MSW from the nearby state university. When she called, she had shared that she had tried to make a connection with Lila but had been unable to establish an engaging relationship with her. She was concerned because she had seen Lila's depression worsen over the preceding three months. Insoo noted that Lila's friend had died about five months ago. Insoo was concerned because she thought that Lila was experiencing an extreme grief reaction in relation to the loss since it was only a friend that Lila had lost, not a husband or child.

Little was known about Lila's life history. She had come to the senior community to live after the sale of the home she had lived in for over fifty years. Details were sketchy, but it appeared that she did not own the home she had lived in most of her adult life. She had no children and had not married. Insoo had identified a distant niece who lived in another state; but other than the niece, it did not seem that Lila had any extended family for support. Lila had mentioned that she had shared the home with a roommate, Mary. Mary had died after long bout with cancer two months before Lila moved to the community residence.

When I first met Lila, I was struck by the depth of her apparent grief. There was a deep sadness in her eyes that was mirrored in the flat tone of her voice, the slowed movement of her body, and the lack of expression in her face. I noticed that there was little furniture in her one-bedroom apartment. A few pictures were leaned up against the wall and had not yet been put up. I spotted a beautiful figurine of a ballet dancer on the one table in the living room where we sat together.

We began a gentle conversation in which Lila mostly nodded and responded with a word or two. I approached Lila from a "not-knowing" stance so that we could move at her pace and she could, as she wished, tell her story and be my guide to her world and experience. I paid close attention, careful not to assume that I knew the life experience of a woman of Lila's age cohort who had spent her life teaching and living an almost middle-class life. I was genuinely curious about Lila. What was her story? What was her experience of loss? What was at the heart of her deep and consuming grief? I asked Lila how I might be of help to her.

Gradually, over many visits, Lila began to share more about her life. First, she began to open up about her life experiences teaching in what she called "grammar" school. I began to learn more about how she viewed the world and how she had experienced her contributions and made meaning out of her life. Lila slowly began to speak more during our time together.

During one visit, I asked about the beautiful ballet figurine that she kept on her table. I wondered what the story was about the glass figure. For a moment, Lila's eyes came alive and then sunk back into sadness. She shared that the figure was one of the few items she had left from her home of fifty years. It was one of a large collection of ballet dancers that her roommate Mary had collected. Mary loved ballet and had been a dancer. Lila had given this particular figure to Mary for Mary's sixtieth birthday. This was the most that Lila had ventured to say about Mary since we had begun to meet together. I asked about the other figurines, and Lila tearfully began to tell the story of her great loss.

Our talk about the figurine had been the doorway to Lila's real world, one might say. Over the next three months, Lila began first to tell the story of losing the figurine collection after Mary's death. Mary's family had come to the house and had taken the collection, along with most of the furniture and other items they assumed belonged only to Mary. Lila was told she could pick out one figurine to keep. Mary's family decided to sell the house she and Mary had lived in for over fifty years. The house was in Mary's name, and Mary's family assumed possession of it, and it sold within two months of Mary's death. Lila, expecting to spend the rest of her life in that home, was forced to move.

One day, during our time together, Lila began to talk about a particular ballet that she and Mary had attended. It was the first time they had gone on an "outing" together. The story of Lila and Mary as spouses, lifelong lovers, and companions began to be told. Lila had lost her partner of fifty-five years, and she had carried this deep soul-level loss alone until now. The consequences of homophobia and heterosexism had blinded all those around her to the truth of Lila's real life story. Mary's family did not see and had taken all of the shared effects of their life together, with no reverence or respect for Mary and Lila's life-long relationship. Insoo, the worker, had missed the true meaning of Lila's loss through heterosexist assumptions. And Lila had internalized the prejudices and oppression of a heterosexist culture and the historical context in which she had lived.

Lila and I had ventured into the cultural borderlands of our individual cultural identities. There we were able to meet, gaining trust in an atmosphere of respect, reverence, and honoring of her experience. Lila was my guide into her world.

Questions for Critical Thinking

1. How would you describe your current development in the areas of cultural competence: motivation, cultural awareness, knowledge, skill development, and inductive learning?

2. Who are you in terms of a multidimensional perspective of cultural identities? How would you describe your own cultural borderland?

3. Think of an experience in which you were immersed in an unfamiliar environment and interacting with those whom you assumed to be different from yourself. How did you respond? Where you able to meaningfully communicate? How do you know? How did you manage anxiety?

4. How would you identify your own communication style in terms of individualism–collectivism? Try reflecting on your communication experiences over the next several weeks.

5. Considering Hofstede's dimensions of cultural variability, where do think you fall on power distance, uncertainty avoidance, and masculinity–femininity dimensions? How does this influence your communication processes?

6. What is mindfulness, and how is it important to effective communicative competence? How can you cultivate your own conscious mindfulness?

Sources for Further Study

Appleby, G. A., Colon, E., & Hamilton, J. (2001). *Diversity, Oppression, and Social Functioning*. Boston: Allyn & Bacon. This text provides an approach to developing a culturally sensitive practice competence with diverse and vulnerable populations. An ecological, diversity- and strengths-based perspective is well defined within a strong person-in-environment framework. In fact, the authors use the person-in-environment (PIE) assessment tool developed by Karls and Wendrei in 1994 as a method for conceptualizing client challenges in social role functioning and environmental problems. Culture-specific knowledge is presented and an affirmative practice paradigm discussed.

Falicov, C. J. (1998). *Latino Families in Therapy: A Guide to Multicultural Practice*. New York: The Guilford Press. This is one of the most engaging texts available presenting a multidimensional ecosystem comparative approach (MECA) that is applicable for practice with all. Falicov presents a "both/and" perspective that includes the "not-knowing" stance as well as culture-specific information. The text provides a wonderful discussion of cultural borderlands as an informing concept for communicating with others. In addition, the author provides an informing discussion of the Latino experience from migration, adaptation, family life cycle, belief systems and more. All concepts come alive with exceptional case examples.

Fong, R., & Furuto, S. (2001). *Culturally Competent Practice: Skills, Interventions, and Evaluations.* Boston: Allyn & Bacon. The authors present a culturally competent practice model that is well steeped in ecological, strengths, and empowerment theories. The unique contribution to practice is that the authors refocus the profession on understanding cultural values and emphasize the critical importance of understanding the significance of these values to individual clients. The model espouses a biculturalization of social work interventions that functions through the assessment and intervention stages of social work.

Green, J. W. (1999). *Cultural Awareness in the Human Services: A Multi-Ethnic Approach* (3rd ed.). Boston: Allyn & Bacon. This text is by far one of the most thoughtful and comprehensive presentations of a cross-cultural approach for social work practice. A solid discussion and application of the ethnographic approach is thoroughly reviewed. A significant contribution to communicative competence, the author defines four components to the cultural competence model that includes comparative analysis. Each chapter provides case studies, experiential exercises, and informative annotated bibliographies.

Gudykunst, W. B. (1998). *Bridging Differences: Effective Intergroup Communication* (3rd ed.). Thousand Oaks, CA: Sage. This book provides an excellent in-depth presentation of the "communicating with strangers" model. It fully explains the model in an easy-to-read format. Gudykunst makes a wonderful contribution in this volume by providing many self-assessment scales relating to major concepts in the model. In addition, he suggests experiential activities at the end of every chapter to practice application of the model. *Bridging Differences* will provide the reader with a growth experience and a beginning working knowledge of the "communicating with strangers" model.

Lum, D. (2000). *Social Work Practice and People of Color: A Process-Stage Approach* (4th ed.). Belmont, CA: Brooks/Cole/Thompson Learning. Doman Lum has developed a process-stage approach for working with persons of color that is applicable to work with all who may be considered different from oneself. The model includes five process stages that provide a framework for the three general phases of social work intervention: beginning, middle, and end. The author uses a variety of case examples and follows a single family through the five-stage process.

References

Appleby, G. A., Colon, E., & Hamilton, J. (2001). *Diversity, oppression, and social functioning.* Boston: Allyn & Bacon.

Burris, J., & Guadalupe, K. L. (2003). Constructivism framework. In J. Anderson & R. Carter (Eds.), *Diversity perspectives for social work practice.* Boston: Allyn & Bacon.

Chinese Cultural Connection. (1987). Chinese values and the search for culture free dimensions of culture. *Journal of Cross-cultural Psychology, 18,* 143–164.

Devore, W., & Schlesinger, E. (1999). *Ethnic-sensitive social work practice* (5th ed.). Boston: Allyn & Bacon.

Falicov, C. J. (Ed.). (1983). *Cultural perspectives in family therapy.* Rockville, MD: Aspen.

Falicov, C. J. (1998). *Latino families in therapy: A guide to multicultural practice.* New York: The Guilford Press.

Fong, R., Boyd, T., & Browne, C. (1999). The Ghandi technique: A biculturalization approach for empowering Asian and Pacific Islander families. *Journal of Multicultural Social Work, 7,* 95–110.

Fong, R., & Furuto, S. (2001). *Culturally competent practice: Skills, interventions, and evaluations.* Boston: Allyn & Bacon.

Gergen, K. J. (1999). *An invitation to social construction.* Thousand Oaks, CA: Sage.

Green, J. W. (1999). *Cultural awareness in the human services: A multi-ethnic approach* (3rd ed.). Boston: Allyn & Bacon.

Gudykunst, W. B. (1995). Anxiety/uncertainty management theory. In R. Wiseman (Ed.), *Intercultural communication theory*. Thousand Oaks, CA: Sage.

Gudykunst, W. B. (1998). *Bridging differences: Effective intergroup communication* (3rd ed.). Thousand Oaks, CA: Sage.

Gudykunst, W. B., & Kim, Y. Y. (1997). *Communicating with strangers: An approach to intercultural communication* (3rd ed.). New York: McGraw-Hill Companies.

Hall, E. T. (1976). *Beyond culture*. New York: Doubleday.

Hofstede, G. (1980). *Culture's consequences*. Beverley Hills, CA: Sage.

Leigh, J. W. (1998). *Communicating for cultural competence*. Boston: Allyn & Bacon.

Lipchick, E. (1993). "Both/and" solutions. In S. Friedman (Ed.), *The new language of change: Constructive collaboration in psychotherapy* (pp. 25–49). New York: Guilford.

Lum, D. (1999). *Culturally competent practice: A framework for growth and action*. Pacific Grove, CA: Brooks/Cole.

Lum, D. (2000). *Social work practice and people of color: A process-stage approach* (4th ed.). Belmont, CA: Brooks/Cole/Thompson Learning.

Lustig, M. W., & Koester, J. (1999). *Intercultural competence: Interpersonal communication across cultures* (3rd ed.). New York: Longman.

Norton, D. (1978). *Dual perspectives: The inclusion of ethnic minority content in social work curriculum*. New York: Council on Social Work Education.

Pinderhughes, E. (1995). Empowering diverse populations as a basis of empowerment strategy. *Families in Society, 76*, 131–140.

Rosaldo, R. (1989). *Culture and truth: The remaking of social analysis*. Boston: Beacon Press.

Rowan, T., & O'Hanlon, B. (1999). *Solution-oriented therapy for chronic and severe mental illness*. New York: John Wiley & Sons.

Triandis, H. C. (1995). *Individualism–collectivism*. Boulder: Westview.

Turner, J. H. (1987). Toward a sociological theory of motivation. *American Sociological Review, 52*, 15–27.

Part VI

Vulnerable Life Situations Perspectives

12

Feminist Framework

Susan Taylor
Robin Kennedy

To say that feminist theory is a single, well-defined, and unifying theory would be a misstatement. Feminist theory is not monolithic. It has multiple variations that, although centered in certain key concepts, vary widely in how those concepts are operationalized. Feminist scholarship ranges from a broad societal empowerment perspective encompassing international and national elements, to a more focused view, emphasizing the inherent power differentials between individuals.

In the evolution of oppression and empowerment theories, feminist theory emerged to challenge many of the social, political, and cultural assumptions that limit the experiences of women. In Western societies, feminist and empowerment theory development has coincided with the rise of civil rights movements. This has been particularly true of those theories related to gender, race, and sexual orientation.

Feminist scholarship has primarily concentrated on the ways in which women are disproportionately affected by patriarchal arrangements. Most recent feminist scholarship has expanded feminist discourse toward a more multidimensional frame of reference related to vulnerability, oppression, and injustice. This has resulted in research investigating differentiations across and within categories of race, class, gender, sexual orientation, age, religion, ethnicity, culture, and nationality. Much of this scholarship has been primarily driven by marginalized women (e.g., non-White, non-heterosexual, non-privileged) who, for the most part, were left out of much of the early development of feminist discourse in mainstream publications.

This chapter emphasizes contrasts in diversity within the development of feminist theory as a particular theory within the genre of empowerment and oppression theories. Broadly stated, the historical, cultural, and political components associated with the development are highlighted. Included in the discussion are contrasting and sometimes conflicting opinions and experiences of women engaged in feminist scholarship, commentary, and practice. Analysis by social work and non-social work theorists is included; thus offering diverse resources reflective of theory development and its applicability within diversity discourse.

Voices of marginalized women and their communities are emphasized throughout this chapter. Because of the complex, divergent, and often contrasting perspectives of feminist scholarship across multiple dimensions (e.g., race, ethnicity, class, sexual orientation, age, ableness, nationality, etc.), the authors chose to highlight diversity from race, class, and sociohistorical perspectives. These dimensions center the discussion of diversity and allow for the key conceptualizations of feminist theory and scholarship to emerge. Because scholarship by non-majority women is so diverse and unequal in breadth across groups, the authors chose to concentrate on the voices of those women who have provided the most consistent voice to feminist diversity discourse: White, African American, and Chicanas. This emphasis is not meant to be hierarchical or disparaging of other women's voices; rather it provides a jumping off point for further investigation from a diversity perspective. Where possible, scholarship by other non-majority women has been included and/or referenced for further discussion.

A vignette is presented emphasizing micro, mezzo, and macro components of practice issues. The strengths and limitations of feminist theory and practice will be discussed in relation to the vignette. Discussion questions appear in the final section of the chapter to direct critical analysis and thinking about the implications of feminist theory in social work practice. Bibliographic annotations are also included, highlighting various threads within feminist theory and providing direction for further reading.

Finally, it should also be noted that the use of the terms "women of color" and "non-majority" are not meant to imply homogeneity in terms of experience, specific needs, or particular points of reference (i.e., standpoints). Many scholars writing from a diversity perspective have used the terms to differentiate from White, middle/upper class, heterosexual women; in the United States, those women who have cultural, societal, political, and economic privilege (whether used or not). The use of language and definition of the appropriate terminology are often difficult when attempting to describe experiences of people's lives from a respectful and culturally unbiased lens. Where the authors have failed in this effort, we apologize.

Major Precursors and Developers

The theoretical and methodological components of feminist thought have evolved over the last 150 years. Understanding the historical development of feminism as a philosophy and feminist thinking as a practice provides understanding of how and why women's lives have been deconstructed in the ways in which they have. Most important has been dialogue related to how voices of marginalized women and their contributions to the discourse have been treated within the theoretical, methodological, and practice arenas.

Feminism and feminist theory development is framed within three historical time periods. Referred to as the "three waves of feminism," contemporary scholars (Arneil, 1999; Findlen, 1995; Jaggar & Rothenberg, 1993; Taylor & Whittier, 1993; Walker, 1995) have noted that theory, philosophy, and practice have expanded during each of these three waves, based in large part on the challenges to the white feminist status quo by non-majority women (e.g., women of color, lesbians, bisexual, transgendered, and/or poor). First- and second-wave feminists primarily focused upon social, political, and cultural dichotomies (e.g., women vs. men; public vs. private sphere). Third-wave feminists have used more multidimensional frameworks in their examination of women's experiences. These scholars have concentrated on the intersecting themes of gender, class, race, age, sexuality, religion, nationality, wealth, colonialism, political systems, and the environment in women's lives. The three waves are distinguished by the degree of inclusiveness of ideas from majority (white, middle/upper class), non-majority (e.g., women of color, lesbians, bisexual, transgendered, and/or poor), and indigenous (e.g., American Indian, Chicanas, and third- and fourth-world) women in the discussion and analysis of issues affecting women's lives. Knowledge of the three waves of feminism contributes to an understanding of the fluidity of theory development and the corresponding strengths and limitations of the theory for social work practice.

The first and second waves of feminism are described by scholars in terms that limit the discussion to the United States. Third-wave feminist scholarship includes issues that are both Western in their orientation as well as global. Each of the three waves has been strongly influenced by the social, political, cultural, and economic values and orientations of the time.

First-Wave Feminism

The first wave of feminism is generally considered by feminist scholars (Arneil, 1999; Taylor, 1998) to include the years from 1830 to 1920. Two significant events framed this time period: the Civil War and the suffrage movement. Coinciding with these events was the emancipation of African American men and women from slavery, the establishment of Black colleges, White women gaining access to universities/colleges, and the first national women's conference. Through the various progressive social movements of this period (e.g., abolitionist, suffrage) there was a strong interface of individuals of various social classes, educational backgrounds, and races/ethnicities.

While much has been written in White feminist literature about the contributions of Elizabeth Cady Stanton, Susan B. Anthony, and Jane Addams (all White, upper-class women) to the social feminism of the time period, much less has been written about significant contributions of women of color. This body of literature has been developed primarily by African American (Giddings, 1984; Guy-Sheftall, 1995; hooks, 1981, 1984), Chicana (Hurtado, 2000; Martinez, 2000; Mora & Del Castillo, 1980; Moraga & Anzaldua, 1981), Asian (Brock, 1996; Chan, 1994; Lee, 1991), and Native American (Buchanan, 1986; Child, 1998; Crow Dog, 1990) feminist scholars. This is particularly true of Black feminists who have widely documented the lives of such individuals as Francis Ellen Watkins, Sojourner Truth, Ida B. Wells-Barnett, Mary Church Terrell, and Nannie Burrough, all of whom were extremely active in framing feminist discourse during that time.

The issues of White and Black women dominate feminist first-wave literature. This is predominately due to the involvement of both groups in the abolition and suffragette movements. Yee (1992) writes that "between 1830 and the 1860s black women abolitionists had developed a collective feminist consciousness that reflected their experiences as black women" (p. 151). She also notes the "aspects of sexism they shared with white women" (p. 151) and suggests that this created a desire to engage in a gender equality dialogue. Taylor (1998) notes, however, " in general, African American women activists were often abandoned by White suffragists." This was due in large part to the ingrained racism that was apparent in many of the White women of privilege in the progressive movements. Sojourner Truth's historic "Ain't I a Woman" speech before the 1852 Convention on Women's Rights in Akron, Ohio, emphasizes the overlapping issues of race and gender, a conceptualization that was lost on many White women feminists of the day. Hooks (1981) notes that in spite of the calls by white women to not let her speak, Truth took the stage. Hooks (1981) writes,

> It was no mere coincidence that Sojourner Truth was allowed on stage after a white male spoke against the idea of equal rights for women, basing his argument on the notion that woman was too weak to perform her share of manual labor—that she was innately the physical inferior to man. Sojourner Truth quickly responded to his argument, telling her audience . . . Well, children, whar dar is so much racket dar must be something out o' kilter. I tink dat 'twixt de niggers of the Souf and de women at de Norf all a talking 'bout rights, de white men will be in a fix pretty soon. But what's all dis here talkin' 'bout? Dat man ober dar say dat women needs to be helped into carriages, and lifted ober ditches, and to have de best places . . . ain't I a woman? Look at me! Look at my arm! . . . I have plowed, and planted, and gathered into barns, and no man could head me—and ain't I a woman? I could work as much as any man (when I could get it), and bear de lash as well—ain't I a woman? I have borne five children and I seen 'em mos all sold off into slavery, and when I cried out with a mother's grief, none but Jesus hear—ain't I a woman? (p. 160)

Truth's passionate statements highlight the growing tensions and perceptual differences between White and Black feminists. The interacting variables of race, gender, and class are apparent in Truth's narrative. These are themes that would ironically repeat themselves nearly one hundred years later in the second wave of feminism.

Although Black women continued to be involved in the early suffrage movement, there was a recognition by them that the entire race needed to be represented in voting to change the tone and effect of Jim Crow laws. As such, Black women in particular not only continued their activity in the primarily White suffrage movement but also helped establish the National Association of Colored Women, the National Association for the Advancement of Colored People, and the National Association of Wage Earners. These multi-issue organizations addressed the corresponding overlap of race, gender, and class.

In the same ways their White counterparts philosophically focused their attention on access by women (primarily White) to the public sphere (e.g., employment, the professions, education) and gaining the right to vote, Black women also recognized the value of both. What was different in their perspectives was the recognition of the intersection of overlapping oppressions. Black women understood that the freedom to participate fully in society went well beyond the limitations of gender.

The Puerto Rican Experience.   While different contextually for Latinas, the recognition of overlapping aspects of multiple oppressions was also apparent in the history of women's experience in Puerto Rico. In contrast to what was happening on the U.S. mainland, the early suffragist movement in Puerto Rico suffered similar struggles but revealed itself in a different form. The early twentieth century found women workers in the tobacco industry facing intolerable working conditions with little help from organized labor. By 1904, eight women's labor organizations had been established with over five hundred workers. By 1908 the Federacion Libre de Trabajadores, the main labor union of the Puerto Rican tobacco industry, recognized that they had to help women "get organized in unions, to get an education; they can't be our enemies, they have to be our allies" (Ruiz & DuBois, 2000, p. 270).

In 1917, Ana Roque de Duprey organized the Liga Feminea de Puerto Rico, the Puerto Rican Feminine League. The main objective of this group was to fight for women's rights, specifically the right to education, active participation in society, and particularly the right to vote. Liga Feminea's stance on suffrage differed from the Federacion Libre de Trabajadores in one very important aspect: who should be allowed to vote. The Liga Feminea demanded restricted suffrage. Specifically, voting privileges would be extended only to women aged twenty-one years and over and those who could read and write. Federacion Libre de Trabajadores, however, demanded universal suffrage. Azize-Vargas notes "the majority of the suffragists who favored the restricted vote did not share working women's problems or situation, and avoided involvement in militant demonstrations such as strikes or other kinds of protests" (Ruiz & DuBois, 2000, p. 271).

In 1920, when the United States passed the Nineteenth Amendment, most Puerto Rican women assumed, by virtue of Puerto Rico's status as a territory, they, too, had gained the right to vote. The U.S. Bureau of Insular Affairs, however, ruled that the privileges granted U.S. women by the Nineteenth Amendment were not applicable to the women of Puerto Rico. Once again, this left the suffrage decision to the Puerto Rican Legislature. Literacy became the weapon of the privileged as well as the Liberal Party (the ruling party). Ana Roque summed up the conflict in a 1920 newspaper article: there were potentially three hundred thousand female voters in Puerto Rico; the majority of these women were the working poor and a potential bonanza for the Socialist Party. Seven years of class struggle ensued. Organized labor fought for universal suffrage, while conservatives supported restricted suffrage. In 1929 the Puerto Rican Legislature passed legislation supporting the restricted position, while labor organizations attacked the law as elitist and discriminatory (Azize-Vargas, 2000).

Puerto Rico's suffrage struggles mirrored the conflicts that took place between women of different ethnic, racial, and class groups during a similar period in the U.S. mainland. In much the same way politically oriented and economically oriented groups in the United States organized to maintain or gain power through the suffrage movement, so did those in Puerto Rico. What was unique about the Puerto Rican experience, however, was class and political ideology, as opposed to race, as factors in the discourse. This would continue to be true in the history of women's equality struggles in that territory. This fact also makes Puerto Rico unique in the discourse associated with differentiations between majority and non-majority women.

The Public/Private Duality. A brief discussion of the public/private duality ingrained in first-wave feminism is important in contextualizing what would continue to be issues between White women of privilege and women of color—particularly African American women—across time. In the U.S. mainland, public/private duality is based to a large degree on concepts of class privilege, gender, and race. The concept of race as a contributing factor in differentiations between women makes it unique to the United States. Also important to this time period is the sexualization of some women and not others. This factor would contribute to the tensions among and between women over time. It would also affect the corresponding discussion of heterosexism in the second- and third-wave feminisms.

The distinctions between public and private spheres is historically rooted in the earliest political theories of Aristotle and Plato (Coole, 1988; Okin, 1978) and the later liberal political theories of Hobbes, Locke, Filmer, Mill, and Rousseau (Pateman, 1983; Phillips, 1992; Allen, 1983; Gavison, 1980). Succinctly put, the public and private spheres referred to the inherent rights and responsibilities in the accepted gender-prescribed roles of men and women within the family (private) and society (public). Men (in this case, White men) were the masters of both domains. By the late nineteenth century, however, White feminists argued for the inclusion of women in the public realm, although continuing to advocate for the traditional role of women in the private realm. Levy Simon (1994) distinguishes women's roles in the private sphere as the ". . . sacred duties of mothering, nursing, teaching, and uplifting" (pp. 247–248). Social feminists of the time argued those types of skills made them uniquely qualified to enter a public realm, rescuing society from the problems associated with massive immigration, urbanization, and industrialization—conditions plaguing the country from the late 1800s through the first two decades after the turn of the century (Chambers, 1986; Cohen & Hanagan, 1991; Koven & Michel, 1990; Rendall, 1990). Arneil (1999) argues that this type of thinking was based in "Victorian morality . . . with white middle-class women being more closely associated with reason, culture, and civility and men were more likely to fall victim to the animalistic side of their natures, through instincts such as passion, greed, and lust" (p. 158). As the social construction of the virtues of White women developed, it was also perceived that White women were asexual; a notion that not only developed the "cult of motherhood" but also allowed for the development of Boston marriages (Faderman, 1991).

Sexualization.   Hooks (1981) notes that the conceptual divide began growing between White and Black women through the proliferation of this early cultural myth and the cultural place to which Black women were relegated as a result of the asexualization of their White counterparts. She suggests, "the shift away from the image of white woman as sinful and sexual to that of white women as virtuous lady occurred at the same time as mass sexual exploitation of enslaved black women" (p. 31). Many feminist scholars (Giddings, 1984) have agreed, suggesting that sexualization of Black women while White women were viewed as asexual and virtuous created a hierarchical differential related to race that carried out of the private sphere into public discourse. Black women were not the only groups affected by this cultural myth, however. Feminist scholars note the sexualization of Asian (Lai, 1988) and Chicana (Espin, 1984) women during this same time period.

While scholarship related to first-wave feminism is primarily described in terms of the racial divide of the Black/White dichotomy, period descriptions of the lives of other women of color are beginning to appear in feminist literature. This has included scholarship related to Asian (Brock, 1996; Chan, 1994; Lee, 1991; Liang, 1998; Ling, 1998; Peffer, 1999; Tong, 1994; Yung, 1995), Chicana (Cotera, 1976; Del Castillo, 1989; Del Castillo & Mora, 1980; Deutsch, 1987; Haas, 1995), and Native American (Buchanan, 1986; Child,

1998; Crow Dog, 1990; Devens, 1992; Jacobs, 1999; Perdue, 1998) women. This diversity in scholarship would continue to evolve in the second wave of feminism.

Second-Wave Feminism

The issues apparent in second-wave feminism are in many ways not so dissimilar from the issues associated with the first wave. While White women's sociopolitical position had improved since the beginning of the century, women of color and other marginalized women still faced the burden of overlapping oppressions—racism, sexism, heterosexism, and classism. Like first-wave feminism, second-wave feminism—spanning the late 1950s through the 1980s— developed along with the many progressive social movements of the time. This period was one of tremendous social unrest, giving rise to the Anti-War movement, the Women's Movement, the Black Power and Civil Rights Movements, the Asian American movement, the Chicano movement, the American Indian Movement, the Gay and Lesbian Movement, and the Poor People's Movement, to name only a few. Similar to the first wave, women (and men) of various racial, ethnic, educational, and socioeconomic backgrounds were brought together through the interplay of these movements. What emerged, however, was the contrast of women's experiences and—as with the first wave of feminism—a disregard for the unique issues affecting non-majority women.

The dualities of the public and private spheres again emerged as a focal point for White feminist discourse. The assumption that all women needed emancipation from the private sphere (i.e., the role of housewife) and full equality (with men) in the public sphere contributed to the feminist motto "the personal is political." White feminists, in particular, argued that women and men were innately equal to one another, and that their relationship in both the public and private spheres could and should be interchangeable. Feminists (White, women of color, and lesbians) exposed the sexism apparent both within the family (private) and society (public), challenging the many ways in which men controlled their lives both within the private and public spheres. Arneil (1999) notes that this patriarchal coercion affected "the everyday lives of women: what they wore, what they ate, how they acted, all related to the way in which 'femininity' had been constructed" (p. 165). In addition, second-wave feminists (in general) also saw the need for state intervention in the economic, political, and the social domination of women in the private sphere; specifically, through the prevention of domestic violence and marital rape, access to child care and senior care, and reproductive freedom.

Driven by the early writings of White feminists Betty Friedan, Simone de Beauvoir, Sheila Rowbotham, Juliet Mitchell, and Kate Millet, the Women's Movement emphasized primarily the needs of middle-class White heterosexual housewives. This fact became an increasing point of contention between White feminists and feminists of color, lesbians, and poor and working-class women. Due to this fact, non-majority women began writing about their experiences separate from and in contrast to White feminist scholarship—which for the most part did not include their perspectives.

Black women engaged in discourse about their lives both through the popular press and the academy. Early essays and commentaries by Black women took both pro-feminist (Chisholm, 1971; Ware, 1970) and anti-feminist (Ladner, 1972) stances. In general, though, hooks (1981) notes that Black women initially approached the (primarily White) Women's

Movement with a hopefulness that women working together could end sexism. Just as Sojourner Truth found in the first wave, hooks notes, "we were disappointed and disillusioned when we discovered that white women in the movement had little knowledge or concern for the problems of lower class and poor women or the particular problems of non-white women from all classes" (p. 188). Further, "those of us who were active in women's groups found that white feminists lamented the absence of large numbers of non-white participants but were unwilling to change the movement's focus so that it would better address the needs of women from all classes and races" (p. 188).

Taylor (1998) suggests that "black feminist activism during the second wave was similar to that of their foremothers in that they continued to negotiate their activism in what was perceived to be two movements (Black revolution and women's liberation)" (web text). Congressional Representative Shirley Chisholm, often ridiculed for her decision to remain active in the primarily White Women's Movement, argued that her presence as a Black woman was necessary because "white women must realize that black people in America are not yet free" (Chisholm, 1971, p. 19).

The emergence of "womanism" as an alternative to feminism came to the forefront of the Black feminist discourse through the writings of Alice Walker. In her 1983 book, *In Search of Our Mothers' Gardens,* Walker first coined the phrase "womanist." Hill Collins (1996) explains, "taking the term from a Southern folk expression of mother's to female children 'you acting womanish,' Walker suggests that black women's concrete history fosters a womanist worldview accessible primarily and perhaps exclusively to black women." Hill Collins notes,

> 'womanish' girls acted in outrageous, courageous, and willful ways, attributes that freed them from the conventions long limiting white women. Womanish girls wanted to know more and in greater depth than what was considered good for them. They were responsible, in charge, and serious.

Feminist scholars (Hill Collins, 1996; Pinkney, 1976; Van Deburg, 1992) characterize "womanism" as being rooted in Black empowerment and a general universalist perspective.

Walker (1983) broadens the definition of womanist to include "a woman who loves other women, sexually and/or nonsexually" (p. xi). Much like the heterosexism and homophobia apparent among the White feminists in the second wave, Hill Collins notes that these biases are also apparent among some Black feminists and womanists.

> The relative silence of womanists on this dimension of womanism speaks to black women's continued ambivalence in dealing with the links between race, gender, and sexuality, in this case, the "taboo" sexuality of lesbianism. In her essay *The Truth That Never Hurts: Black Lesbians in Fiction in the 1980s,* black feminist critic Barbara Smith (1990) points out that African American women have yet to come to terms with homophobia in African American communities. Smith applauds the growth of black women's fiction in the 1980s, but also observes that within black feminist intellectual production, black lesbians continue to be ignored. Despite the fact that some of the most prominent and powerful black women thinkers claimed by both womanists and black feminists were and are lesbians, this precept often remains unacknowledged in the work of African American writers. (Hill Collins, pp. 9–18)

The issue of sexuality continued to be a point of contention among many feminists—White and Black—throughout the second wave. This factor was a significant departure point for many third-wave feminists.

Much like Black feminism, Chicana feminism came of age during the 1960s (Martinez, 1989; Sandoval, 1990; Segura & Pesquera, 1992; Pesquera & Segura, 1993). Also like Black feminists, many Chicanas had membership across movements. Hurtado (2000) notes, "unlike (mostly male) members of other progressive movements, many Chicana feminists . . . participated simultaneously in more than one of these movements precisely because of their multiple stigmatized group memberships in class, race/ethnicity, gender, and sexuality" (p. 128). She goes on to note, like other marginalized women, "many Chicana feminists disrupted all the movements they participated in: if working within the Chicano movement, they would argue for women's issues; if working with white feminists, they would argue for including ethnicity/race; if working with Chicana women's organizations, they would argue for including gay and lesbian issues" (p. 129). Cordova (1994) notes,

> Chicanas write in opposition to the symbolic representations of the Chicano movement that did not include them. Chicanas write in opposition to a hegemonic feminist discourse that places gender as a variable separate from that of race and class. Chicanas write in opposition to academics, whether mainstream or postmodern, who have never fully recognized them as subjects, as active agents. (p. 194)

For Chicanas the White feminist theoretical developments of the second wave, as well as the scholarship of Black feminists of the same timeframe don't capture Chicana conceptualizations of their experiences. Because of this, Chicana feminists have embarked in another direction. Hurtado (2000) notes that language—Spanish—is unique to the Chicana experience and provides a strongly inclusive point of reference to connect women to their culture; it also acts as a buffer, keeping the brutality of the Anglo world at a distance. Hurtado suggests, within this frame of reference, various methodology has been used to give rise to the Chicana voice.[1] These varying methodologies provide a patchwork of expression associated with the Chicana experience that has placed Chicanas at the forefront in challenging limitations of feminist discourse throughout the second wave and into the third wave.

Scholarship by other women of color and lesbians within each group pushed the primarily White, heterosexual, middle/upper class perspectives beyond the boundaries that were established through the private/public sphere dichotomies in the beginning of the sec-

---

[1]These methods include oral histories, adding the use of different varieties of Spanish (Ruiz, 1987, 1998; Romero, 1992; Zavella, 1997b; Pesquera, 1997; Segura, 1997); creative production, such as poetry, theatrical performance, painting, dance, music (Baca, 1990, 1993; Cisneros, 1994; Cantu, 1995; Perez, 1996; Mora, 1997); the documentation of creative production as evidence of feminism (Broyles, 1986, 1989, 1994; Yarbro-Bejarano, 1985, 1986, 1991, 1994); social science methods (Pesquera & Segura, 1992; Pesquera and Segura, 1993); and a variety of combinations of all of these tools. Examples include the use of creative writing to see Chicanas as "their own ethnographers" (Quintana, 1989, 1996), the use of fables . . . (Hurtado, 1996a), book-length essays drawing on multidisciplinary literature to highlight Chicanas' condition (Castillo, 1995), and multidisciplinary anthologies based on a mixing of genres (Moraga and Anzaldua, 1981; Moraga, 1983; Anzaldua, 1987, 1990; Del Castillo, 1990; Trujillo, 1991, 1998; Alarcon et al., 1993; Del la Torre & Pesquera, 1993).

ond wave. These "marginalized" women gave voice to experiences of the overlapping oppressions that constricted their lives.

Asian women, for example, began exposing practices that stereotyped and exploited them as a group. By the mid 1980s, for example, the mail-order-bride business was flourishing; catalogs such as *Cherry Blossom* and *Love Overseas* offered American men an alternative to the new, liberated American women. These catalogs featured pictures of women, primarily from poor families in Malaysia and the Philippines, and included descriptions such as "Most if not all are very feminine, loyal, loving—and virgins!" and "They love to do things to make their husbands happy" (Lai, 1988, p. 168). The typical mail-order-bride consumer was White, middle-aged, divorced, military veteran (most having served overseas in Asia) and disillusioned by liberated American women.

The mail-order business sold women who were advertised as "unliberated and loyal" commodities attractive to the American business community as well. Profiteering business owners who run low-profile and high-profit operations recruit Asian American workers. Lai (1988) points out, "businesses want docile, subservient workers who will not complain, file grievances, or organize unions . . . Asian American women are also stereotyped as having special dexterity and endurance for routine" (p. 169).

The exploitation of Native American women has also begun to be written about by Native American scholars. Specific attention has been paid to the fact that the survival of Native American women often depends on their daily struggle with the U.S. government, tribal governance, White societal prejudice, as well as the men from their own tribes. In spite of this adversity, Native American women continue to maintain their Indian identity and continue to redefine what that means in the twenty-first century.

From various creative venues, these female scholars have laid the foundation for a third wave of feminism to emerge and push feminist theory and discourse toward a broader, more inclusive reality of women's lives. The recognition of the impact of overlapping oppressions in the third wave has assisted women in conceptualizing the many ways in which multiple social constructions limit their experiences as women. This recognition has contributed to the development of new strategies to assist women in living empowered lives.

Third-Wave Feminism

Third-wave feminist theory emerged in the late 1980s as a response, in part, to the limitations and dualisms inherent in the conceptualizations of second-wave feminism. Although the theoretical frame of reference is still developing, not surprisingly, many of the conceptualizations for the new wave emerged from feminists of color, lesbian feminists, generation Xers, and those conceptualizing queer theory (Heywood & Drake, 1997; Orr, 1997). From a third-wave perspective, gender was no longer the central point of reference from which discourse emerged. Rather, third-wave feminism is much less accepting of the dichotomies of race, gender, sexuality, etc. Arneil (1999) states that third-wave theoretical perspective

> . . . begins with concepts of difference rather than sameness, identity and particularity rather than universality, celebrating the status of other or outsider rather than wanting inside, embodiment rather than the view from nowhere, and finally a relational rather than binary approach (p. 187)

It is the multiplicity of identities rather than "universality" or "sameness"—advocated by second-wave theorists—that speaks to the heart of the third-wave conceptualization of difference. Arneil (1999) notes that everyone possesses numerous identities that coexist as contradictions within the self. As such, ambiguity, contradiction, and the fluidity of experience are celebrated norms in third-wave discourse. Drake (1997) agrees, noting that "what unites the third wave is our negotiation of contradiction, our rejection of dogma, our need to say 'both/and.' " Rebecca Walker (Alice Walker's daughter) (1995) perhaps speaks to the crux of third-wave discourse when she writes,

> . . . for a generation that has grown up transgender, bisexual, interracial, and knowing and loving people who are racist, sexist and otherwise afflicted. We have trouble formulating and perpetuating theories that compartmentalize and divide according to race and gender and all other signifiers. For us the lines between Us and Them are often blurred, and as a result we find ourselves seeking to create identities that accommodate ambiguity and our multiple positionalities. (p. xxxiii)

The metaphor of "borderlands" has often been used to describe the experience of these multiplicities. Conceptualized by Gloria Anzaldua (1987), "borderlands" and "mestizas" are used to describe the experience of those interactions that are faced by many in their daily lives. The borderland includes "borders between nations (Mexico and the United States), borders of identity (race, sexuality, gender), and borders of language and culture" (as cited in Arneil, 1999, p. 214). Anzaldua explains that borderlands are created when two or more cultures come together and when individuals differ in language, ethnicity, race, culture, or class and occupy a common space. The points of intersection exist for all people; but women in particular, because of their unequal relationship to the power structure based upon multiple "isms," face excessive maneuvering of numerous borderlands in their daily lives. How women—and all people—face the difficulties inherent in the borderlands is the challenge that third-wave feminists have embraced.

Bowleg (1995) suggests, "this ability to blend different aspects of our . . . lives is . . . to bridge our different races, ethnicities, nationalities, socio-economic classes, abilities, ages, and sexual preferences and orientations in a manner that is meaningful, noncompromising, and productive" (p. 51). This does not mean that political, social, cultural, and economic limitations are not acknowledged; they are simply not accepted. Heywood and Drake (1997) suggest that coalition activity is the key to intervening in the cycles of multiple oppression, noting the conceptualization of multiplicity of identities also requires vigilance in monitoring the "constantly shifting bases of oppression in relation to the multiple" (p. 3). In embracing the "multiple," third-wave feminists have acknowledged that those who would oppress have diverse targets from which to base their oppression. It requires facing the mechanisms of oppression head on and finding alternatives to countering it. While generalizability is difficult when describing third-wave discourse, what appears to make it unique is its uncompromising commitment to creating an environment void of duality. This, in and of itself, is something that neither the first- or second-wave feminist discourse was able to achieve. Because of this, third-wave feminists are likely to provide a foundation for expanding the notion of what feminist thinking entails and how it is most useful as theory and method.

Core Concepts

As was previously mentioned, there are many schools of feminist thought that have taken key principles of feminist theory and elaborated on them. Particular points of reference have been emphasized that have allowed this scholarship to emerge. These elaborations have included liberal feminism (Jaggar, 1983; Nes & Iadicola, 1989), standpoint feminism (Swigonski, 1993), lesbian feminism (Myron & Bunch, 1975; Rich, 1983), psychoanalytic feminism (Mitchell, 1975; Flax, 1983), Marxist feminism (Hartmann, 1981), radical feminism (Echols, 1989; Eisenstein, 1981; Tong, 1989), eco-feminism, (Adams, 1991; Milwa & Shiva, 1993), global feminism (Bunch, 1993), multiracial feminism (Baca Zinn & Thornton Dill, 1996), and postmodern feminism (Flax, 1990; Sands & Nuccio, 1992; Scott, 1990; Wittig, 1988). These differentiations have added a wealth of perspectives to feminist scholarship that have highlighted different aspects of women's lived experiences. They have also provided contrasts and challenges to one another that have pushed feminist discourse in multiple directions at once.

Feminist Conceptualizations in Social Work

Feminist scholarship has been prevalent in social work literature and practice since the mid-1980s. Texts have appeared that detail feminist theory, method, and practice; emphasizing contextual understanding for the lives of women affected by societal oppressions brought upon them through the mechanisms of racism, sexism, and heterosexism. Bricker-Jenkins and Hooyman's (1986) *Not for Women Only: Social Work Practice for a Feminist Future*; Van Den Bergh and Cooper's (1986) *Feminist Visions for Social Work*; Dominelli and McLeod's (1989) *Feminist Social Work*; Hanmer and Statham's (1989) *Women and Social Work: Towards a Women-Centered Practice*; Bricker-Jenkins, Hooyman, and Gottlieb's (1991) *Feminist Social Work Practice in Clinical Settings*; and Van Den Bergh's (1995) *Feminist Practice in the 21st Century* lead the way in providing insights into the use of a feminist framework in social work practice. While these frameworks have decidedly Eurocentric lenses, they nonetheless provide the foundation for the interface of social work and diversity from a feminist viewpoint.

The broad framework through which feminist theory and method will be considered is through the work of Van Den Bergh and Cooper (1986). Often quoted in feminist discourse, the authors' conceptualizations share compatibility with the early work of Bricker-Jenkins and Hooyman (1986) and are a jumping-off point for later work. Van Den Bergh and Cooper outline five basic constructs that frame their discussion of feminist discourse: "eliminating false dichotomies and artificial separations, reconceptualizing power, valuing process as equally important as product, validating renaming, and believing that the personal is political" (p. 4).

Eliminating false dichotomies and artificial separations is particularly significant for multicultured women. This concept recognizes that it is neither sexism, racism, classism, heterosexism, or any other "ism" that singularly affects the life of a woman experiencing oppression; rather, it is the interface of all or a few "isms" that increases the burden of the oppression. Lorde (1984) eloquently speaks to this issue when she discusses the problems inherent in fractionalizing oneself.

Differences in ourselves as black women are also being misnamed and used to separate us from one another. As a black lesbian feminist comfortable with many different ingredients of identity, and a woman committed to racial and sexual freedom from oppression, I find I am constantly being encouraged to pluck out some aspect of myself and present this as the meaningful whole, eclipsing or denying the other parts of myself. But this is a destructive and fragmenting way to live. My fullest concentration of energy is available to me only when I integrate all the parts of who I am, openly allowing power from particular sources of my living to flow back and forth freely through all my different selves, without restrictions of externally imposed definition. Only then can I bring myself and my energies as a whole to the service of those struggles which I embrace as part of my living. (reprinted with permission, Anderson and Hill Collins, 1992, p. 500)

This same sentiment is highlighted in the work of other women of color (Julia, 2000; Lai, 1988), all of whom speak to the issue of overlapping oppressions and the struggle to maintain personal integrity in the face of it.

The second concept outlined by Van Den Bergh and Cooper is the idea of reconceptualizing power. The authors suggest that power dichotomies are key to maintaining patriarchial arrangements. In these arrangements "power is seen as a finite commodity to be controlled, particularly in determining the distribution of rights, resources and opportunities" (p. 5). In this context, one who can control the power creates the rules, manages and controls information, and dictates acceptable behavior (p. 5).

Feminist and other oppression theorists moved beyond strictly identifying patriarchy as a social limitation and began speaking of "empowerment." Gutierrez and Lewis (1998) suggest that "empowerment is a process of increasing personal, interpersonal, or political power so individuals can take action to improve their lives" (p. 100). Additionally, Gutierrez and Lewis note that "recognizing the way in which power relationships affect daily reality and understanding how individuals can contribute to social change is the process through which empowerment takes place" (p. 100).

Understanding power differentials between and among women, as well as women in relation to society, allows for a recognition of how women have been co-opted by society in an effort to keep each other in their places. Hooks (1984) describes this horizontal oppression in her discussion of a 1979 commencement address by Toni Morrison at Barnard College. Morrison notes,

I want not to ask you but to tell you not to participate in the oppression of your sisters. Mothers who abuse their children are women, and another woman, not an agency, has to be willing to stay their hands. Mothers who set fire to school buses are women, and another woman, not an agency, has to tell them to stay their hands. Women who stop the promotion of other women in careers are women, and another woman must come to the victim's aid. Social and welfare workers who humiliate their clients may be women, and other women colleagues have to deflect their anger.

I am alarmed by the violence that women do to each other; professional violence, competitive violence, emotional violence. I am alarmed at the willingness of women to enslave other women. I am alarmed at a growing absence of decency on the killing floor of professional women's worlds. (as cited in hooks, p. 49)

Morrison reminds us that it is not just patriarchy that subjugates women in societies.

It is also the lack of recognition and responsibility of women toward one another that allows for the socially constructed "isms" to be reinforced.

The third concept put forth by Van Den Bergh and Cooper (1986) is that of valuing process equally with product. The authors note that "only what one achieves tends to be considered, rather than with equal interest, how one arrives at goals" (p. 6). They suggest that "competition, conquest, and individualism are reinforced when the ends are rewarded and the means to those ends are ignored" (p. 7). The process by which one pursues a goal becomes more important than the goal itself. Gutierrez and Lewis reinforce this notion through their description of how consciousness-raising and empowerment are linked in grassroots women's organizations. They note, "consciousness raising contributes to empowerment by helping individuals make the connections between personal problems and political issues" (p. 100). If process were valued more than product, the role of motherhood would actually be valued in society regardless of age, race, socioeconomic status, ethnicity, or sexual orientation. In such a scenario, the process of raising children to be prosperous, happy, loved, and accepted for their own uniqueness would be equally valued and rewarded along with the profits of General Motors.

The fourth concept put forth by Van Den Bergh and Cooper (1986) is the validity of renaming. The authors note the importance of "having the right to name one's own experience" (p. 7). An example of this type of renaming was the articulation of groups with multiple oppressions naming themselves. The authors suggest that, rather than being hyphenated Americans, groups adopted such terms as "Chicano, La Raza, Atzlan, and Pacific Islander to describe their unique cultural identities" (p. 7).

The process of renaming, according to Van Den Bergh and Cooper (1986), includes four processes: "(1) applying new labels (words) to persons, places, and things; (2) changing meanings by altering the format of language; (3) reclaiming archaic definitions; or (4) conceptually broadening the meaning of existing language" (pp. 7–8). Naming oneself, rather than having a society, institution, group, or individual label or categorize, denotes a process of self-empowerment through self-description. Feminists would argue that the act of labeling by those in power automatically oppresses those labeled. To be labeled is to be categorized with socially constructed characteristics whose meanings may not represent the experience or reality of those being labeled.

An example is the limited definition of "family." The conceptualization often does not recognize the bonds between extended family, clan, and kinship that many communities of color and other non-majority communities (e.g., gays and lesbians, immigrant) highly value. In limiting the definition of family by law and rights, many individuals and families find themselves fighting negative stereotypes that have little or nothing to do with the reality of their experience.

Finally, Van Den Bergh and Cooper (1986) suggest the mainstay of feminist thinking: the personal is political. This concept emerged through consciousness-raising and an understanding that it was social, political, economic, and cultural institutions that limited women's lives through narrowly defined gender expectations that better served those institutions than the individuals themselves. The authors suggest that "an underlying assumption of the personal is political is that working to bring about changes within institutions can also alter the course of one's life" (p. 9). Recognizing how institutions limit individual opportunity based on race, gender, class, and so forth is important to this concept. Gutierrez and Lewis (1998) and other scholars (Armott & Matthaei, 1991; Comas-Diaz & Greene, 1994; Zambrana, 1987) note that women of color are "overrepresented in low status occupations, and by a low average of education . . . [they] are underrepresented in positions of power within our government, corporations, and non-profit institutions" (p. 98). These factors represent societal roadblocks that require activism and advocacy to overcome. As such, feminists would argue that social change occurs only when personal experiences are transformed into political action.

Core Principles for Practice

The nine principles recommended as guidelines for social work practice are based on a combination of principles from various feminist theories. These threads include principles from multiracial feminism (Zinn Baca & Thornton Dill, 1996), feminist standpoint theory (Swigonski, 1993), and second-wave feminist theory (Van Den Bergh & Cooper, 1989). The nine principles include

1. Acknowledging the "interlocking matrix of domination" (Zinn Baca & Thornton Dill, 1996)
2. Realizing the relational nature of dominance and subordination (Zinn Baca & Thornton Dill, 1996)
3. Understanding the interplay of social structure and women's agency (Zinn Baca & Thornton Dill, 1996)
4. Recognizing "standpoint" (Swigonski, 1993)
5. Eliminating false dichotomies and artificial separations (Van Den Bergh & Cooper, 1986)
6. Reconceptualizing power (Van Den Bergh & Cooper, 1986)
7. Understanding the validity of renaming (Van Den Bergh & Cooper, 1986)
8. Valuing process equally with product (Van Den Bergh & Cooper, 1986)
9. Reconceptualizing the view of the personal is political (Van Den Bergh & Cooper, 1986)

Acknowledging the interlocking matrix of domination suggests that systems of domination work in conjunction with one another. As the social construction of gender intersects with race, class, sexuality, ethnicity, culture, age, and nationality, particular meaning is given to the life of each woman (Hill Collins, 1990; Baca Zinn & Thornton Dill, 1996).

Realizing the nature of dominance and subordination suggests that power, race, and class have particular meaning in discourse between women. This is particularly true of White women and women of color. Because privilege in these areas has allowed White women to advance in many cases at the expense of women of color (e.g., women of color taking over domestic duties so that white women can pursue careers), the "mutual influence" that one has for the other must be recognized (Gordon, 1991; Zinn Baca & Thornton, 1996).

Understanding the interplay of social structure and women's agency recognizes women's strengths in countering the limitations in their lives based upon mechanisms of oppression related to gender, class, race, and sexual orientation. Through acts of passive and active resistance, women create spaces for themselves in their families and communities that are meaningful and self-assuring (Zinn Baca & Thornton Dill, 1996).

Recognizing standpoint refers to the need for a conscious understanding of social position or location in relationship to social structure and how that affects one's life. Much like the discussion of "borderlands," where a person has interacting locations due to multiple identities, standpoint suggests the need for women to understand how these standpoints (or borderlands) affect their daily lives.

Finally, Van Den Bergh and Cooper's (1986) five constructs are recommended with the exception of a reconceptualization of the concept "the personal is political." It must be acknowledged that while conscious recognition of oppression is important in moving toward taking social action to alleviate such circumstances, many non-majority women feel double binded by this expectation. Role overload and fear of additional loss of privilege or social location prevent some non-majority women from actively engaging in social action. The quiet acts of resistance engaged in by some women must be appreciated and respected equally with active confrontation. In this way, all women can be viewed as participating in their own and collective emancipation.

Case Example

Background

This case centers around Isabella (Izzie), a thirty-two-year-old woman of Mexican descent, her three children, Jesus (thirteen years old), Sally (thirteen years old), Susanna (ten years old), and her husband and father of her children, Ramon.

Izzie and Ramon were both born in the United States, the children of migrant farm workers. Much of their young lives were spent in the nomadic existence of farm workers, traveling from town to town in the hopes of finding work. Izzie was the first of five children; she did not work in the fields with her parents. Her job was to care for her younger siblings while her parents were in the fields. At the age of twelve, she stopped attending school altogether.

Ramon, on the other hand, began working in the fields alongside his mother and father at the age of six and continued farm work until he turned sixteen. The family had established a semi-permanent home in South Texas where Ramon was completing high school. At sixteen he was enrolled in a technical high school where he learned basic mechanics as well some construction skills. Ramon completed high school at eighteen. Ramon and Izzie met at the wedding of a mutual friend while both were visiting family members in Mexico. The couple settled in Northern California. Both Izzie and Ramon's extended families reside in Mexico. Izzie's frequent visits see both of the couple's parents, siblings and grandparents. The couple sends money to both families on a monthly basis.

Four years earlier, Izzie, Ramon and their children resided in a three-bedroom home in an urban area. Izzie was employed as a contract worker for a large construction company performing job-site clean-up services. Ramon was employed only seasonally by the department of transportation where he operated snow-removal equipment during the winter months. The rest of the year, Ramon worked a variety of construction jobs and sometimes supplemented their income with the proceeds of illicit drug sales. Their lives together have included intermittent unemployment, homelessness, recreational drug use, and an intense commitment to one another, their children, and their families.

Approximately three and a half years ago, when Izzie was visiting Mexico, Ramon was arrested in a state police sting operation for the sale of cocaine. Their home and all the family's assets (family car and checking account) were surrendered to authorities and held by the court as drug proceeds. The night of Ramon's arrest, the couple's three children were taken into custody by Child Protective Services. The police raid was a frightening experience for the children, a situation worsened by their separation by CPS. The twins, Jesus and Sally, were taken to a juvenile shelter; their sister Susanna was placed in emergency foster care.

After one week in her emergency foster placement, Susanna, the youngest child, was assigned to a foster placement agency; after three weeks the twins were assigned to a foster placement agency, different from their sister. Although Jesus and Sally had both been assigned to the same foster placement agency, they were placed in different homes. The children were reunited for monthly supervised visits with their mother. Other than this designated time, however, the siblings had no contact with one another.

Upon Izzie's return home, she was repeatedly detained and questioned by police over a period of months. Although the authorities were never able to prove any involvement by Izzie in Ramon's drug operation, the official police statement to family court reported that she was "still a suspect" in felony drug charges. In a signed statement to police officials, Izzie denied any knowledge of Ramon's drug transactions, but did admit to her own "occasional use of cocaine and marijuana."

During this time, Izzie lived with a series of friends and relatives. She spent her days planning the reunification of her family. She continued her work in construction, purchased a car, and saved money for rent. According to her CPS worker, family reunification was contingent on two factors: she had to secure housing, and she had to be in drug treatment. Reunification had been delayed twice due to her inability to locate housing. The Housing Authority did not consider her eligible for public housing unless she had custody of her children; Child Protective Services, however, would not reunify until housing had been secured. Izzie secured additional employment (a paper route) to earn the money needed for an unsubsidized apartment. In addition to her struggles with housing, drug treatment was difficult to find. She was placed on a six-month waiting list for a public outpatient drug treatment program that offered services during a time that would not interfere with her work schedule or her children's visitation schedule.

Izzie's contact with both her and Ramon's families in Mexico had become difficult. She did not have the resources to call or travel to Mexico, and the financial assistance she had been giving to both families was no longer possible. She had not told either family about Ramon's incarceration.

After Izzie had secured housing and successfully completed six months in treatment, and after her children had spent eleven months in the care of CPS, her children were returned to her custody. Izzie spent her days working both jobs, attending outpatient treatment, and re-establishing her family. Izzie began her day at three o'clock in the morning, she picked up the newspapers, prepared the papers for delivery, delivered the papers, and returned home in time to get her children up and off to school. After she dropped her children at school, she drove to the construction company to inquire about work availability. On the days there was work, Izzie was grateful for the money; when there was no work, she was content to go home and sleep. Izzie worried about leaving her young children home alone during the time she delivered newspapers; since the night of Ramon's arrest, all of the children had been showing signs of stress (behavioral problems and declining grades). Susanna, in particular, had been having nightmares combined with frequent incidences of nocturnal enuresis (bed wetting).

Approximately four weeks ago, when Izzie was preparing to leave home to deliver papers, she noticed the smell of smoke. Upon investigation, she noticed billows of smoke pouring out of the windows of the apartment directly under theirs. Izzie quickly gathered her children and escaped the fire shortly before their apartment was engulfed in flames. Once again Izzie found herself homeless. This time, however, she had her children, and she vowed she would not give them up again. She feared, if CPS were to discover her homeless status, she would once again lose her children.

Izzie and her children spent most nights at the homes of family and friends; however, some nights Izzie and one or two of the children slept in the car. Since the fire, Izzie continued to work both jobs and look for housing. Due to the time and energy involved in homeless tasks (e.g., finding showers, restrooms, and a safe place to spend the night), she had not attended drug treatment for three weeks. After Jesus went to school in unlaundered clothes and with a general unkept appearance, one of his teachers made a report to CPS. On the following day, when Izzie arrived at the school to pick up the children, she was asked by the school counselor to come into the school to speak to the CPS worker.

The worker listened to the family's story of the past four weeks. Izzie tearfully confided to the worker she had used cocaine twice in the time she had been out of treatment, but if she could find housing and reunite her family, she was confident she could re-enter treatment and stay clean. The CPS worker told Izzie that, if she made sure her children had temporary housing and she was again in treatment and remained clean, she did not need to fear her children's removal from her custody. Izzie was directed to report to the homeless shelter that night to secure temporary housing for herself and her children. She was also told that outpatient treatment was not optional; she would need to begin treatment again within the week. The CPS worker told her she would visit Izzie the next day at the shelter, and they would together come up with a plan.

Upon the family's arrival at the homeless shelter, Izzie was directed to the women's shelter; however, she was told that her thirteen-year-old son would not be allowed at the shelter. The women's shelter prohibited males over the age of twelve. Her son would need to, once again, be placed at the juvenile shelter.

Izzie's appointment with the CPS worker the next day revealed she was no longer eligible for the outpatient services she had been participating in due to her absence from the program. She would again need to be placed on a waiting list, which could be up to eight months. The worker felt this was too long for Izzie to be out of treatment and presented a solution designed to help Izzie and her family get out of the cycle of addiction and poverty. The CPS worker had managed to get Izzie moved to the top of the waiting list for Family House.

Intervention

Izzie arrived at Family House the next morning for a meeting with the administrator. The administrator described Family House as a residential substance abuse treatment facility that addresses the special needs of women, mothers, and their families. Women and their families reside at Family House for one year, receiving counseling related to substance use and parenting; vocational training and stress management are also required for the female residents. One year of intensive outpatient follows residential treatment, which includes counseling and group therapy; other services such as job placement and anger management workshops are also available as needed.

Unfortunately, Izzie's thirteen-year-old son will not be able to reside with her—he will again be placed in a foster care home, and Izzie's family will be separated. In addition, Izzie will not be allowed to have contact with Ramon for the time she is involved with Family House. She would be "permitted" to write to Ramon; however, this was discouraged.

Currently, Izzie has remained drug-free for nine months. She has successfully completed parenting classes as well as a vocational training program offered by a large computer firm. She is working one job during regular daytime hours and earning more money than the combined income from her past jobs. She gets off work at four o'clock in the afternoon, in time to pick up Susanna and Sally from after-school care. Every day they stop by the home where Jesus is living; they spend time talking, doing homework, and planning for the time when the whole family can be reunited. Although the family living situation is not ideal, Izzie feels secure in her sobriety and her career; in addition, she has re-established a routine that keeps the family in daily contact with one another. All the children's grades have improved, and Susanna's nocturnal enuresis has stopped.

In a recent group session, the leader used the term "role overload." As Izzie listened to the definition, she buried her head in her hands and began to weep. She suddenly had words for her feelings of exhaustion and incompetence. She began to identify all her current roles: mother, wife, employee, client, patient, student, daughter, provider, house member, housekeeper, chauffeur, group member. . . . It had been close to three years since Ramon's arrest; she deeply missed his support and his love; her strongest wish was for Ramon's release from prison and the reuniting of her family.

Reunification

Ramon will be released from prison in three weeks. Izzie has followed the rules of Family House; she has refrained from visiting Ramon in prison; however, she and the children have written to Ramon two to three times a week since his incarceration. She feels she has lived up to all of the expectations she has had of herself as well as all the obligations the system has imposed on her. Izzie has requested to speak with the administrator of Family House to request permission to leave the program early. She explains that she has respected the facility's policy regarding no contact, and she has abided by that policy. She goes on to explain how much her family, her children, and her husband mean to her, and the agony the separation of the past year has caused everybody. She promises to continue the program's outpatient treatment for the required twelve months, but she strongly feels it is in the best interest of her family to reunite after Ramon's release from prison.

The administrator explains to Izzie that, because her commitment to Family House was court-ordered, she would not be allowed to leave the facility prior to the one-year time period. The administrator also explains that the facility's policy prohibiting contact with drug offenders is effective throughout Izzie's contract with Family House—this includes not only her time living in the facility, but also her twelve-month outpatient commitment.

Contributions and Limitations

The Feminist Framework's usefulness in this case example is discussed below. Context for the framework's principles is provided along with an acknowledgement of their interrelationship. The principles are italicized throughout the analysis.

The interlocking matrix of domination is reflected in Izzie's interface with social institutions. Izzie experiences being female through the lens of a lower-middle-class Chicana heterosexual with little formal education. The intersection of gender, race, age, culture, and class (in this case the overlap of wealth and access to formal education) contribute to how the multiple systems to which she has to relate (e.g., child protective service, police, prison, family court, drug treatment, housing authority) affect her daily life (*eliminating false dichotomies and artificial separations*). The extent to which these systems are embedded with bias based upon sexism, racism, and classism affects the degree to which the policy and practice modalities are oppressive. Also, the inability of the multiple systems to differentiate the cultural and age expectations of Izzie as a Chicana in relationship to her family and community also neglects the particular needs she has that reflect her *standpoints*.

The prescribed "professional" stances of the workers who met with Izzie during her interface with various systems (police, CPS, Family House, housing authority) may reflect the *dominance and subordination* expectations of those systems. Compounded by power differentials, racism, sexism, and classism, Izzie may have felt she had no choice but to submit to expectations of those making demands upon her. The extent to which these demands were made by professional women within those systems speaks to the concern expressed by Toni Morrision about the violence of women against one another, and in particular the demands made by majority women on non-majority women. Throughout the case example, Izzie shows tremendous resilience and strength as she navigates the social structures' demands upon her (*reconceptualizing power*). In spite of the restrictive rules of the various systems with which she interfaces, she has created a space for her family to stay connected as a family unit (*interplay of social structure and women's agency*). Additionally, she has made tremendous efforts to meet the expectations of each system with which she has interfaced. In spite of sustained success in meeting the system-prescribed goals, she is rebuffed when she requests flexibility in the rules (a conflict of *the process over product*). In essence, treatment is viewed as time owed the system (a conflict of *the process over product*), and becomes one more mechanism to keep Izzie's family apart.

Izzie's courage to confront the power structure (*personal is political*), however, shows strength of determination, self-direction, and character (*validating renaming*) in spite of the overall system's having labeled her as deviant and in need of rehabilitation. The challenge to her is once again confronting *the matrix of oppression* which confronts her in her daily life. She must choose between the demands of her family and culture, and the systems in which she has become entangled.

Izzie's case highlights the fact that when gender is examined separately, aside from race, class, and culture, situations will be assessed from a White middle-class perspective; the dominant culture becomes the default. If one of the basic tenets of feminist theory—that gender is a social construct—is accepted, the other social constructs of the matrix of domination must be included. Feminist scholars have made considerable progress in deconstructing gender unidimensionally. The challenge is to now deconstruct gender, race, class, and sexuality simultaneously. Feminist social work practice is not a recognition of the oppression of women from strictly a gender perspective; it is the recognition and integration of a number of variables that are included in oppression for all clients. With that recognition, social work practitioners can truly start where the client is.

Sources for Further Study

Andersen, Margaret L. and Hill Collins, Patricia (Eds.). *Race, class, and gender, an anthology.* Belmont, CA: Wadsworth (1992). This is a collection of scholarship analyzing the relationship among gender, race, class, age, religion, and sexual orientation. A more recent edition has been published, which includes a different set of readings. We found this edition particularly helpful for this project. Although a great deal has been written since this edition was published, most is still current today, and other pieces offer a good historical perspective of diversity.

Narayan, Uma and Harding, Sandra (Eds.). *Decentering the center: Philosophy for a multicultural, post-colonial, and feminist world.* Bloomington, IN: Indiana University Press (2000). This collection of scholarship discusses the intersection of race, class, gender, sexual orientation, and nationality in the daily lives of women. Diverse scholarship by leading feminist scholars is represented in this volume.

Ruiz, Vicki L. and DuBois, Ellen Carol (Eds.). *Unequal sisters, a multicultural reader in U.S. women's history* (third edition). New York: Routledge (2000). This is a collection of women's stories spanning time, race, class, religions, and sexual orientations. Feminist discourse includes women's roles in the California Gold Rush, along the Trail of Tears, throughout the history of jazz, as migrant farm workers, and as mail-order brides. This collection offers stories from women's views of oppression across time, focusing not only on the importance of gender, but also of race, class, and sexual orientation as vital pieces in the deconstructing of women's lives.

Saulnier, Christine Flynn. *Feminist theories and social work: Approaches and applications.* Binghamton, NY: Haworth Press (1996). This very thorough and readable book critically reviews nine major feminist theories and their contributions to social work practice. Theories discussed include liberal, radical, socialist, postmodern, lesbian, cultural, eco, global, and womanism. Examples of the application of each theory to practice are given at the end of each chapter.

Taylor, Ula. The historical evolution of black feminist theory and praxis. *Journal of Black Studies* (1998), 29 (2), 234–254. This article provides an historical understanding of the development of Black feminism in the United States. Four unique themes in the construction of Black feminist thought are highlighted, as well as a discussion on the historical tension between African American women and White women across the first two waves of feminism.

Zinn, Maxine Baca and Dill, Bonnie Thornton. Theorizing difference from multiracial feminism. *Feminist Studies, 22* (Summer 1996): 321–332. The article goes beyond discussions of diversity and the differences of women and speaks specifically to the issue of race as it relates to gender issues in feminist thinking. A discussion of multiracial feminism, its theoretical and sociological genesis, as well as its unique presentation of frameworks provide an interesting perspective in new theories generated that highlight the experiences of women of color.

Questions for Critical Thinking _____

What follows are discussion questions to promote critical thinking in learning about and using the Feminist Framework. The questions are broken into theoretical elements of the theory usage as well as issues associated directly with the case example.

THEORETICAL PERSPECTIVE

1. What are the strengths and limitations of feminist theory to social work practice with women of color?

2. In what ways have the three waves of feminism defined the relationships between women across race, gender, class, and sexual orientation?

3. In what ways is the third wave of feminism similar to other theories in regard to discussions about overlapping oppressions?

THE CASE STUDY

4. From a policy perspective, what are some alternatives to the hard line the Family House administrator has given Izzie?

5. Discuss how the combination of race, class, and gender affected Izzie and her family's interactions with the police, CPS, the shelter, the housing authority, and Family House.

6. Identify and discuss the fiscal repercussions of Ramon's arrest and incarceration.

7. Discuss the differences and similarities of Ramon and Izzie's childhood compared to their own children's.

8. When the family is reunified, what cultural, gender, and class issues might arise within the family?

References _____

Adams, M. (1991). Ecofeminism: Anima, animus, animal. In L. Richardson and V. Taylor (Eds.), *Feminist frontiers III* (pp. 522–524). New York: McGraw-Hill.

Allen, A. L. (1983). Women and their privacy: What is at stake? In C. C. Gould (Ed.), *Beyond domination: New perspectives on women and philosophy* (pp. 233–249). Owata, NJ: Rowman and Allanheld Publishers.

Anderson, M. L., & Hill Collins, P. (Eds.). (1992). *Race, class, and gender: An anthology*. Belmont, CA: Wadsworth.

Anzaldua, G. (1987). *Borderlands/La Frontera*. San Francisco, CA: Aunt Lute Books.

Armott, T., & Matthaei, J. (1991). *Race, gender, and work: A multicultural history of women in the United States*. Boston: South End Press.

Arneil, B. (1999). *Politics and feminism*. Malden, MA: Blackwell Publishers, Inc.

Azize-Vargas, Y. (2000). The emergence of feminism in Puerto Rico, 1870–1930. In V. L. Ruiz and E. C. DuBois (Eds.), *Unequal sisters: A multicultural reader in U.S. women's history* (3rd ed.), pp. 268–275, New York: Routledge.

Baca, J. (1990). World wall: A vision of the future without fear. *Frontiers, 14*(2), 81–85.

Bowleg, J. (1995). Weaving an identity tapestry. In Barbara Findlen (Ed.). *Listen up: Voices from the next feminist generation.* Seattle, WA: Seal Press.

Bricker-Jenkins, M., & Hooyman, N. R. (Eds.). (1986). *Not for women only: Social work practice for a feminist future.* Silver Springs, MD: NASW.

Bricker-Jenkins, M., Hooyman, N. R., & Gottlieb, N. (Eds.). (1991). *Feminist social work practice in clinical settings.* Newbury Park, CA: Sage.

Brock, R. N. (1996). Private, public, and somewhere in-between—Lessons from the history of Asian-Pacific-American women. *Journal of Feminist Studies in Religion, 12*(1), 127–132.

Broyles, Y. J. (1986). Women in El Teatro campesino: Apoco estabu molacha la virgen de Guadalupe? In R. Romo (Ed.), *Chicana voices: Intersections of class, race, and gender.* Austin, TX: Center for Mexican Studies, University of Texas.

Broyles, Y. J. (1989). Toward a revision of Chicano theater history: The women of El Teatro campesino. In L. Hart (Ed.), *Making a spectacle: Feminist essays on contemporary theater.* Ann Arbor, MI: University of Michigan Press.

Broyles, Y. J. (1994). *El Teatro campesino: Theater in the Chicano movement.* Austin, TX: University of Texas Press.

Buchanan, K. M. (1986). *Apache women warriors.* El Paso, TX: Texas Western Press.

Bunch, C. (1993). Women's subordination worldwide: Global feminism. In A. M. Jaggar and P. S. Rothenberg (Eds.), *Feminist frameworks* (3rd ed). New York: McGraw-Hill.

Cantu, N. E. (1995). *Canicula: Snapshots of a girlhood en la frontera.* Albuquerque, NM: University of New Mexico Press.

Chambers, C. A. (1986). Women in the creation of the profession of social work. *Social Service Review, 60,* 1–33.

Chan, S. (1994). The exclusion of Chinese women, 1870–1943. *Chinese American, History and Perspectives,* 75–125.

Child, B. J. (1998). *Boarding school seasons: American Indian families, 1900–1940.* Lincoln, NB: University of Nebraska Press.

Chisholm, S. (1971, December). Race, revolution, and women. *The Black Scholar, 22,* 19–26.

Cisneros, S. (1994). *Loose women.* New York: Alfred A. Knopf.

Cohen, M., & Hanagan, M. (1991). The politics of gender and the making of the welfare state, 1900–1940: A comparative perspective. *Journal of Social History, 24,* 469–484.

Comas-Diaz, L., & Greene, B. (1994). *Women of color.* New York: Guilford.

Coole, D. (1988). *Women in political theory: From ancient misogyny to contemporary feminism.* Hemel Hempstead: Harvester Wheatsheaf.

Cordova, T. (1994). The emergent writings of twenty years of Chicana feminist struggles: Roots and resistence. In F. Padilla (Ed.), *The handbook of Hispanic cultures in the United States.* Houston, TX: Arte Publico Press.

Cotera, M. (1976). *Diosa y Hembra: The history and heritage of Chicanas in the U.S.* Austin, TX: Information Systems Development.

Crow Dog, M. (1990). *Lakota woman.* New York: Harper Perennial.

Del Castillo, A. (Ed.). (1989). *Between borders: Essays on Mexicana/Chicana history.* Los Angeles, CA: Floricanto Press.

Del Castillo, A. (Ed.). (1990). *Between borders: Essays on Mexicana/Chicana history.* Encino, CA: Foricanto Press.

Del Castillo, A., & Mora, M. (Eds.). (1980). *Mexican women in the U.S.: Struggles past and present.* Los Angeles, CA: UCLA Chicana Studies Research Center Publications.

De la Torre, A., & Pesquera, B. M. (Eds.). (1993). *Building with our hands: New directions in Chicana studies*. Berkeley, CA: University of California Press.

Deutsch, S. (1987). *No separate refuge: Culture, class, and gender on an Anglo-Hispanic frontier in the American Southwest, 1880–1940*. New York: Oxford University Press.

Devens, C. (1992). *Countering colonization: Native American women and Great Lakes missions, 1630–1900*. Berkeley, CA: University of California Press.

Dominelli, L., & McLeod, E. (1989). *Feminist social work*. Chicago, IL: Lyceum.

Drake, J. (1997, Spring). Third wave feminisms. *Feminist Studies, 23*(1), 97–109.

Echols, A. (1989). *Daring to be bad: Radical feminism in America 1967–1975*. Minneapolis, MN: University of Minnesota Press.

Eisenstein, Z. (1981). *The radical future of liberal feminism*. New York: Longman.

Espin, O. M. (1984). Cultural and historical influences on sexuality in Hispanic/Latin women: Implications for psychotherapy. In C. Vance (Ed.), *Pleasure and danger* (pp. 149–164). Boston: Routledge and Kegan Paul.

Faderman, L. (1991). *Odd girls and twilight lovers: A history of lesbian life in twentieth century America*. New York: Penguin Books.

Findlen, B. (Ed.). (1995). *Listen up: Voices from the next feminist generation*. Seattle, WA: Seal Press.

Flax, J. (1983). The patriarchal unconscious. In S. Harding and M. B. Hintikka (Eds.), *Discovering reality: Feminist perspectives on epistemology, metaphysics, methodology, and philosophy of science* (pp. 245–281). Boston: Reidel Publishing.

Flax, J. (1990). Postmodernism and gender relations. In L. Nicholson (Ed.), *Feminism/Postmodernism* (pp. 39–62). New York: Routledge.

Gavison, R. (1980). Privacy and the limits of the law. *Yale Law Journal, 89*(3), pp. 421–471.

Giddings, P. (1984). *When and where I enter: The impact of black women on race and sex in America*. New York: William Morrow.

Gordon, L. (1991, Spring). On difference. *Genders, 10*, 91–111.

Gutierrez, L., & Lewis, E. A. (1998). A feminist perspective on organizing women of color. In F. G. Rivera and J. L. Erlich (Eds.), *Community organizing in a diverse society* (3rd ed.) (pp. 97–116). Boston: Allyn & Bacon.

Guy-Sheftall, (Ed.). (1995). *Words of fire: An anthology of African American feminist thought*. New York: New Press.

Haas, L. (1995). *Conquests and historical identities in California, 1769–1936*. Berkeley, CA: University of California Press.

Hanmer, J., & Stratham, D. (1989). *Women and social work: Towards a woman-centered practice*. Chicago, IL: Lyceum Books.

Hartmann, H. (1981). The unhappy marriage of Marxism and feminism: Towards a more progressive union. In L. Sargent (Ed.), *Women and revolution: A discussion of the unhappy marriage of Marxism and feminism* (pp. 1–42). Montreal, CN: Black Rose Books.

Heywood, L., & Drake, J. (1997). *Third wave agenda: Being feminist, doing feminism*. Minneapolis, MN: University of Minnesota Press.

Hill Collins, P. (1990). *Black feminist thought: Knowledge, consciousness, and the politics of empowerment*. Boston: Unwin Hyman.

Hill Collins, P. (1996, Winter/Spring). What's in a name? Womanism, Black feminism, and beyond. *Black Scholar, 26*(1), 9–18.

hooks, b. (1981). *Ain't I a woman? Black women and feminism*. Boston: South End Press.

hooks, b. (1984). *Feminist theory: From margin to center*. Boston: South End Press.

Hurtado, A. (2000). Sitios y lenguas: Chicanas theorize feminisms. In U. Narayan and S. Harding (Eds.), *Decentering the center: Philosophy for a multicultural, postcolonial, and feminist world* (pp. 128–155). Bloomington, IN: Indiana University Press.

Jacobs, M. D. (1999). *Engendered encounters: Feminism and pueblo cultures, 1879–1934*. Lincoln, NB: University of Nebraska Press.

Jaggar, A. (1983). *Feminist politics and human nature*. Brighton: Harvester Press.

Jaggar, A. M., & Rothenberg, P. S. (Eds.). (1993). *Feminist frameworks* (3rd ed). New York: McGraw-Hill.

Julia, M. (2000). *Constructing gender: Multicultural perspectives on working with women*. Belmont, CA: Brooks/Cole.

Koven, S., & Michel, S. (1990). Womanly duties: Maternalist policies and the origins of welfare states in France, Germany, and the United States 1880–1920. *American Historical Review, 95*, 1076–1108.

Ladner, J. (1972). *Tomorrow's tomorrow: The black woman*. Garden City, NY: Doubleday.

Lai, T. (1988). Asian American women: Not for sale. In J. W. Cochran, D. Langston, and C. Woodward (Eds.), *Changing our power: An introduction to women's studies* (pp. 120–127). Dubuque, IA: Kendall-Hunt.

Lee, J. F. J. (1991). *Asian American experiences in the United States: Oral histories of first to fourth generation Americans from China, the Philippines, Japan, India, the Pacific islands, Vietnam, and Cambodia*. Jefferson, NC: McFarland.

Levy Simon, B. (1994). Building on the romance of women's innate strengths: Social feminism and its influence at the Henry Street Settlement, 1893–1993. In L. V. Davis (Ed.), *Building on women's strengths: A social work agenda for the twenty-first century* (pp. 247–269). Binghamton, NY: Hawthorn Press.

Liang, H. (1998). Fighting for a new life: Social and patriotic activism of Chinese American women in New York City, 1900 to 1945. *Journal of American Ethnic History, 17*(2), 22–38.

Ling, H. (1998). *Surviving on the gold mountain: A history of Chinese American women and their lives*. Albany, NY: State University of New York Press.

Lorde, A. (1984). *Sister outsider*. Trumansburg, NY: The Crossing Press.

Martínez, E. (1989). That old (white) male magic. *Z Magazine, 27*(8), 48–52.

Martínez, E. S. (1998). De colores means all of us: Latina views for a multi-colored century. Cambridge, MA: South End Press.

Miles, M., & Shiva, V. (1993). *Ecofeminism*. London: Zed Books.

Mitchell, J. (1975). *Psychoanalysis and feminism*. New York: Vintage Books.

Mora, M., & Del Castillo, A. R. (1980). *Mexican women in the United States: Struggles past and present*. Los Angeles, CA: Chicano Studies Research Center, University of California.

Mora, P. (1997). *House of houses*. Boston: Beacon Press.

Moraga, C. (1983). *Loving in the war years: Lo que nunca paso por sus labios*. Boston: South End Press.

Moraga, C., & Anzaldua, G. (Eds.). (1981). *This bridge called my back: Writings by radical women of color*. Watertown, MA: Persephone Press.

Myron, N., & Bunch, C. (Eds.). (1975). *Lesbianism and the women's movement*. Baltimore, MD: Diana Press.

Nes, J., & Iadicola, P. (1989). Toward a definition of feminist social work: A comparison of liberal, radical, and socialist models. *Social Work, 34*, 12–22.

Okin, S. M. (1978). *Women in western political thought*. Princeton, NJ: Princeton University Press.

Orr, C. (1997). Charting the currents of the third wave. *Hypatia, 12*(3), 29–45.

Pateman, C. (1983). Feminist critiques of the public private dichotomy. In S. I. Benn and G. F. Gaus (Eds.), *Public and private in social life* (pp. 281–303). New York: St. Martin's Press.

Peffer, G. A. (1999). *If they don't bring women here: Chinese female immigration before exclusion*. Urbana, IL: University of Illinois Press.

Perdue, T. (1998). *Cherokee women: Gender and culture, 1700–1835*. Lincoln, NB: University of Nebraska Press.

Perez, E. (1996). *Gulf dreams*. Berkeley, CA: Third Woman Press.

Pesquera, B. M., & Segura, D. A. (1993). There is no going back: Chicanas and feminism. In N. Alarcon, R. Castro, E. Perez, B. Pesquera, A. S. Riddell, and P. Zavella (Eds.), *Chicana critical issues*. Berkeley, CA: Third Woman Press.

Phillips, A. (1992). Universal pretensions in political thought. In M. Barrett and A. Phillips (Eds.), *Destabilizing theory: Contemporary feminist debates* (pp. 10–30). Cambridge, MA: Polity Press.

Pinkney, A. (1976). *Red, black, and green: Black nationalism in the United States*. London: Cambridge University Press.

Rendall, J. (1990). *The origins of modern feminism: Women in Britain, France, and the United States, 1780–1860* (2nd ed.). Chicago: Lyceum.

Rich, A. (1983). Compulsory heterosexuality and lesbian existence. In E. Abel and E. K. Abel (Eds.), *The Signs reader: Women, gender, and scholarship* (pp. 139–168). Chicago: University of Chicago Press.

Ruiz, V. L., & DuBois, E. C. (Eds.). (2000). *Unequal sisters: A multicultural reader in U.S. women's history* (3rd ed.). New York: Routledge.

Sandoval, C. (1990). The struggle within: A report on the 1981 N.W.S.A. conference. In G. Anzaldua (Ed.), *Making face, making soul/ haciendo caras/creative and critical perspectives by women of color*. San Francisco, CA: Aunt Lute Books.

Sands, R. G., & Nuccio, K. (1992). Postmodern feminist theory and social work. *Social Work, 37*(6), 489–495.

Scott, J. (1990). Deconstructing equality-versus-difference: Or, the uses of poststructuralist theory for feminism. In M. Hirsch and E. Fox Keller (Eds.), *Conflicts in feminism* (pp. 134–148). New York: Routledge.

Segura, D. A. (1997). Chicanas in white collar jobs. You have to prove yourself more. In L. Lamphere, H. Ragone, and P. Zavella (Eds.), *Situated lives*. New York: Routledge.

Segura, D. A., & Pesquera, B. (1992). Beyond indifference and antipathy: The Chicana movement and Chicana feminist discourse. *Aztlan: The Journal of Chicano Studies, 19*(2), 69–93.

Swigonski, M. E. (1993, Summer). Feminist standpoint theory and questions of social research. *Affilia, 8*(2), 171–183.

Taylor, U. (1998, November). The historical evolution of black feminist theory and praxis. *Journal of Black Studies, 29*(2), 234–254.

Taylor, V., & Whittier, S. (1993). The new feminist movement. In L. Richardson and V. Taylor (Eds.), *Feminist frontiers III* (pp. 533–548). New York: McGraw-Hill.

Tong, B. (1994). *Unsubmissive women: Chinese prostitutes in nineteenth century San Francisco*. Norman, OK: University of Oklahoma Press.

Tong, R. (1989). *Feminist thought: A comprehensive introduction*. Boulder, CO: Westview Press.

Trujillo, C. (Ed.). (1991). *Chicana lesbians: The girls our mothers warned us about*. Berkeley, CA: Third Woman Press.

Trujillo, C. (1998). *Living Chicana theory*. Berkeley, CA: Third Woman Press.

Van Deburg, W. L. (1992). *New day in Babylon: The Black power movement and American culture, 1965–1975*. Chicago: University of Chicago Press.

Van Den Bergh, N. (Ed.). (1995). *Feminist practice in the 21st century*. Washington, DC: NASW Press.

Van Den Bergh, N., & Cooper, L. (Eds.). (1986). *Feminist visions for social work*. Silver Springs, MD: NASW.

Walker, A. (1983). *In search of our mother's gardens*. New York: Harcourt, Brace, Jovanovich.

Walker, R. (Ed.). (1995). *To be real: Telling the truth and changing the face of feminism*. New York: Anchor Books.

Ware, C. (1970). *Woman power: The movement for women's liberation*. New York: Tower Publications.

Wittig, M. (1988). The straight mind. In S. Hoagland and J. Penelope (Eds.), *For lesbians only: A separatist anthology* (pp. 431–438). London: Onlywomen Press.

Yarbro-Bejarano, Y. (1985). Chicana's experience in collective theater: Ideology and form. *Women and Performance, 2*(2), 45–58.

Yarbro-Bejarano, Y. (1986). The female subject in Chicano theater: Sexuality, race, and class. *Theater Journal, 38*(1), 389–407.

Yarbro-Bejarano, Y. (1991). Deconstructing the lesbian body: Cherrie Morega's "Loving in the war years." In C. Trujillo (Ed.), *Chicana lesbians: The girls our mothers warned us about*. Berkeley, CA: Third Woman Press.

Yee, S. (1992). *Black women abolitionist: A study of activism, 1828–1860*. Knoxville, TN: University of Tennessee Press.

Yung, J. (1995). *Unbound feet: A social history of Chinese women in San Francisco*. Berkeley: University of California Press.

Zambrana, R. (1987). A research agenda on issues affecting poor and minority women: A model for understanding their health needs. *Women and Health, 12*, 137–160.

Zinn, M. B., & Dill, B. T. (1996, Summer). Theorizing difference from multiracial feminism. *Feminist Studies, 22*(2), 321–322.

13

Constructivism and the Constructivist Framework

Joyce Burris
Krishna L. Guadalupe

Constructivism is a term that has been variously used in the social sciences to describe one or more of the following overlapping areas of interest:

- A philosophical perspective
- Methods of generating knowledge (constructivist)
- Theoretical perspectives for understanding the development of social forces and institutions (social constructivism or social construction)
- Several theories for understanding the development of individual personality
- Intervention strategies at the micro, meso, and macro levels in social work and in other helping disciplines

It may be that the term *constructivism* is used for many different purposes because the dialogue concerning its definitions and uses is rather new in social work literature and consensus has yet to be established regarding its meaning. As will be discussed later, many of the authors who have, in the past, offered ideas, theoretical perspectives, and social critiques that are now being classified as constructivist by contemporary writers never called themselves constructivists. So, if the term constructivism has become recently more prominent, the ideas themselves have long historical roots, even if the concepts have been reworked and renamed over time.

It is the intent of the authors of this chapter to briefly summarize and critique the five areas of constructivism outlined above and to relate each area to concepts of diversity. In this

*Special thanks to Dr. Brad McKinzie, Professor at the University of Manitoba, for his invaluable feedback, critique, and assistance on an earlier draft of this chapter.

chapter the discussions of micro- to macro-level approaches to theory and practice have been separated for the sake of clarity. This is not meant to reinforce or encourage "either/or" thinking in the readers. In life, constructivists favor and encourage making connections that emphasize the relationships among the many levels of theoretical perspectives and interventions.

Additionally, the authors would like to remind readers that the content in this chapter is shaped by the personal and professional paradigms of the authors, reflecting only two of the multitude of "realities." In this chapter, the evolution of a constructivist lens, the historical development, philosophical underpinnings, assumptions, general principles and various uses of constructivism as it relates to diversity will be explored. Throughout this chapter, various ways that constructivists have tried to illuminate the complexities of diverse experiences and multiple "realities" will be integrated. Uses and implications for social work will also be discussed.

Much of this chapter has to do with the nature of knowledge and its construction. On the surface, it may not be apparent to some readers that there is an inherent connection between constructivism and diversity. The social construction of knowledge as a major part of constructivism has everything to do with diversity. In the social sciences, knowledge—both as a process of construction and as a product—has, until the 1950s and 1960s, primarily been in the hands of intellectuals from a dominant group (cultural, gender, racial, class, etc.). This dominant group created a product that was presented as "objective" and "universal," but which primarily reflected the constructed realities of its own individual and group experiences and lives. This "knowledge" has not been representative of the diverse ways of knowing, being, or emerging as human beings.

Much of this critique of the dominant group's perception has come from a diversity of individuals and groups that include members who identify themselves with one or more of the following: the working-class, women, persons of diverse racial and ethnic backgrounds, persons with disabilities, gays and lesbians, the aged, etc. These critiques and the individuals and groups making them are recently and increasingly being identified as postmodernists or constructionists. According to Neimeyer (1993),

> Perhaps the core of postmodern consciousness is the increasingly widespread awareness that the belief systems and apparent "realities" one indwells are socially constituted rather than "given," and hence can be constituted very differently in various cultures (or subcultures), times, and circumstances, although they might appear to carry the force of necessity to those who inhabit them. (p. 221)

Major Precursors and Developers

Modern science emerged in Western Europe during the fifteenth and sixteenth centuries as scientists challenged the role of the church in controlling knowledge. Since the late eighteenth century, European intellectuals have generally become strong advocates of empiricism or positivism. French sociologist Auguste Compte coined the term positivism in the 1790s. It relates to an approach to knowledge building whereby only "sense" data and only sense experience and its logical and mathematical treatment are capable of testing reality. A closely related term, empiricism, is used to describe knowledge building that is produced by experiment, observation and mathematical analysis of "objective" measures. These terms are today equated with "the scientific method," which is believed to guide the scientists' ability to arrive at an understanding of the universal laws of nature, or the "Truth" (Kuhn, 1970).

This pursuit of Truth is believed to ultimately lead to full understanding, control and prediction of the external phenomena under study. According to this tradition, not only is it believed that discovering Truth is possible, but it is also believed that the only way to discover Truth or reality is through the systematic investigation of quantitative, sense data that can be collected in the external world by value-free and objective observers. Of primary importance is the discovery of presumably linear cause–effect relationships among variables that are controlled during such investigation in order to determine precise associations. It is assumed that reality exists outside the observer for the observer to "discover." Positivism includes "the thesis that empirical knowledge is logically discrepant from the pursuit of moral aims or the implementation of ethical standards" (Giddens, 1978, p. 237). Advocates of this epistemological position have been identified variously as positivists, logical positivists, empiricists, and owing to the extreme popularity of this approach, "scientists."

However, within Western traditions, some have criticized this approach as the only way of knowing: Immanuel Kant, Edmund Husserl, Jurgen Habermas, George Kelly, Paulo Freire, Jean Baker Miller, Sandra Harding, C. Wright Mills, Michel Foucault, Peter Berger and Thomas Luckman, to name only a few. These critics, with a few exceptions, have *not* actually identified themselves with the term "constructivist." Constructivist is a term that is currently appearing in the literature to identify a person who questions the assumptions of the positivists/empiricists in terms of both the exclusive process and product of inquiry. These critics have emerged from many disciplines; most notably they come from philosophy, but also literature, social and behavioral sciences, art, education, music, natural sciences, and physics.

Only within the last ten to fifteen years has the term "constructivism" been used in social work literature, although the sentiments of its critique have been part of dialogues within the profession since its inception (Carpenter, 1996). Regardless of the discipline, constructivists make the case for meanings that are multiple and diverse rather than singular and universal, changing rather than unchanging, responsive to context rather than remaining stable regardless of context, interactive rather than unaffected by interaction and open to interpretation. As earlier noted, constructivism is a term that is currently appearing in the literature to identify those who question the assertions put forward by positivists and offer their own set of approaches. While not totally rejecting empiricism, constructivists include the methods of positivism/empiricism as only one of many ways of investigating, knowing, and knowledge building (Ballou, 1990; Belenky, Clinchy, Goldberger, & Tarule, 1986).

Core Concepts

Carpenter (in Turner, 1996, p. 147) argues that the term *constructivism* is a conceptual framework rather than a practice or treatment theory. Generally that may be true, but there is a family treatment theory and micro practice technique called "constructivism" (Efran, Lukens, & Lukens, 1988), an individual practice theory called "personal construct theory" (Kelly, 1955) and a school of social thought (conflict theory) whose practitioners call themselves "social constructionists" (Berger & Luckman, 1966; McCarthy, 1981; Mills, 1959). Dean (1993) stresses that the emphasis of "constructivist" ". . . is on the individual structural determinants of knowledge . . . , [and the emphasis of 'social constructivists' is] . . . the social aspects of knowing and the influence of cultural, historical, political, and economic conditions. While agreeing with constructivists that we cannot know an objective reality, social constructionists stress the interpersonal rather than the neurological imprints on our ways of knowing the world" (p. 58).

Schriver (2001) in his book *Human Behavior and the Social Environment* presents theories that he divides into two categories of what he calls paradigms. He calls one paradigm "traditional" theories, whose originators generally use positivistic/empirical assumptions and methods of knowledge building. It is pointed out that the theories that culminated from this "traditional" research resemble the lives and experiences of its authors—mainly Eurocentric, White, affluent, heterosexual males. The authors of these "traditional" theories claim that their theories are universal. Schriver calls the second paradigm "alternative" theories, whose originators use methods and assumptions that correspond to descriptions of constructivist knowledge. Schriver himself does not use the term *constructivist* to describe "alternative" ways of knowing, but his definitions for methods that inform these "alternative" theories are consistent with the definitions in the literature of constructivism. The theories that culminate from "alternative" ways of knowing do two things: (1) They criticize traditional theories for rendering women, people of color, gays and lesbians, and people with disabilities either invisible or to an "other" status, and (2) they create theories that explore the humanity and positive nature of human diversity and diverse "realities."

While constructivism is a term applied to a variety of approaches in the social sciences, some commonly expressed principles are used to express those approaches. Constructivists favor naturalistic, experiential, qualitative, and integrative interpretations that include both internal and external realities (personal, intrapersonal, interpersonal, and collective). Constructivists reject the notion of a single "reality" and instead note that there can be many ways of knowing and many realities (Belenky, et al., 1986; Harding, 1991; Richardson & Franklin, 1998). They question the assumptions of empiricists that researchers can be objective, value-free, outside observers (McCarthy, 1981). Constructivists reject the belief that universal Truths exist or that they can be discovered context-free. Critics of positivism observe that, historically, when ideas have been portrayed as "universal," those ideas most often reflect the views and experiences of individuals and groups in positions of privilege and social power (Restivo, 1988), and the diversity of other views and experiences are ignored (Belenky, et al., 1986; Habermas, 1971, 1975; Harding, 1991; Van Den Bergh, 1995).

In that same vein, constructivists reject the use of authoritarian techniques to control, withhold, and mystify knowledge, in both its creation and its dissemination (Freire, 1973; Habermas, 1971; Hartman, 1990; Laird, 1993). They also are intensely interested in the diversity of interpretations, partly because they value subjective experiences and interaction with both internal and external environments and also because they hold value commitments to principles and ethics of equality and social justice. Constructivists view knowledge building as both an intrapersonal and an interactional process and product. Knowing is a holistic experience and requires cognitive, emotional, spiritual and behavioral integration (Gergen, 1999; Robbins, Chatterjee, & Canda, 1998). At heart, constructivists recognize that social interaction is involved in the construction of knowledge, and they favor inclusion of the diverse many in the interactive process of knowledge building. Knowledge creation requires the development of language, meanings, and dialogue to facilitate consensus within a community (Gergen, 1999; Habermas, 1971, 1975; Kuhn, 1970).

Through the constructivist lens, language cannot be taken for granted. Understanding the roles that language (e.g., symbols, signs, words, verbal and nonverbal expressions, lingo) plays in the process of construction, deconstruction, and reconstruction of knowledge and our sense of reality is vital. Constructivists view language as a product of human agreement; for example, a red light means "stop" and a green light means "go" in the current context of the social and legal environment in the United States, but that signal and its meaning represent only one possible way to enhance human safety. In many indigenous nations in the United States, such legal and linguistic rules were historically nonexistent, and the concept of human safety was defined in terms of tribal cohesion. Thus, according to the constructivist's lens, language is contextual.

Taken in context, language often reflects social attitudes as it shapes thoughts, illustrates and guides thinking patterns, and expresses ideas, to mention only a few of its roles. The roles that language plays in human interaction within the context of human diversity can encourage or discourage individual efforts and can influence whether communities maintain or attain optimal health and well-being. For example, within the United States, the terms "White" or "Black" have been used to identify people according to their skin color as well as to present a framework of social experiences often affiliated with issues of "privilege" and "oppression." Experiences of neglect, stereotyping, misinterpretation, and marginalization of individuals and communities are likely to be created and perpetuated with the assistance of language that is used as a weapon rather than as a vehicle of understanding. The inclusion and acceptance of diverse points of view, experiences, narratives and realities help to create more chance for understanding. This above observation has been reflected in social science literature that explores the meaning of human diversity (Guadalupe, 2000). Thus, a constructivist's lens allows one to observe experiences of privilege and oppression not only in terms of "Whites" and "Blacks," but also within the dynamics of individuals who belong to a combination of those and/or other ethnic and racial groups. Add to this an awareness of ways that various combinations of privilege, race, and ethnicity combine with gender, age, disabilities, sexual orientation, country of origin, and religious affiliations, and such considerations can open our understanding of the complexity of human diversity with its implied multiplicity of meanings, interpretations, and effects.

The constructivist's lens emphasizes the importance of taking into account individual narratives in order to reduce misunderstanding of individual experiences. For instance, a tendency exists to generally perceive individuals who are within the "White" category as the "oppressors who hold social privilege" and those in the "Black" category as "oppressed with little to no social privilege." The above interpretation of experiences is a false dichotomy that polarizes two mutually exclusive groups that, in real life, are likely to overlap and play out in complex ways. In employing a constructivist's lens, the roles of language, interpretations, and meanings must be explored in order to increase the understanding of their effects on people's lives.

Various Ways Constructivism May Be Understood and Used

This section discusses the five uses of constructivism listed at the beginning of this chapter. The reader may need to be reminded that these uses are overlapping rather than discrete and separate. Again, the authors would like to emphasize the point that, even though topics relating to level of theory and practice have been separated for clarity and ease of discussion in this section, in reality, micro, meso, and macro theories and interventions inform one another and are interconnected.

Constructivism as a Philosophical Perspective

The term *epistemology* refers to philosophical concerns raised and debated about the nature of knowing and knowledge. The questions of how human beings know something, what the nature of reality is, what the place of values and ethics is in knowledge, what the relationship of authority or power and knowledge are to each other are all those of, though not limited to, philosophers. Philosophers have long been interested in knowledge, both as a product (i.e., a body of knowledge that has been produced) and as a process (i.e., a method or methods for generating knowledge, including all the assumptions and beliefs that accompany the techniques utilized).

This section explores these concepts and summarizes the main points of the debates about knowledge building. We begin with a discussion of root metaphors that is primarily interested in knowledge as product of human creation, and we follow with a subsequent discussion of epistemology that is mainly concerned with the debates surrounding knowledge building as a process.

Root Metaphors and Meta-Theories.   Philosopher Stephen Pepper (1942) argued that, in reviewing knowledge as a product (rather than as a method of inquiry), four root metaphors could be identified that guide the creator's vision of reality (Lyddon, 1989). A root metaphor may be used interchangeably with the terms "paradigm" or "meta-theory" as it is a worldview that embodies unexamined values and unquestioned assumptions that represent the "leap of faith" upon which each set of theories rests. These are super-ordinate philosophies. Pepper makes the point that authors, in describing how they view the world, are unaware of the assumptions they are making about "reality," and therefore he calls these metaphors "meta-theories."

1. *Formistic:* A metaphor for a human personality appearing in a particular form from inception to death and remaining fairly close to that same form over the life span. This view informs theorists who believe that humans are biologically determined and fairly difficult, if not impossible, to change.
2. *Mechanistic:* A metaphor used to describe the human personality as a machine, made up of many parts that contribute to its overall functioning. If a person experiences difficulties in life, it is perceived that some part of the personality has broken down and needs repair.
3. *Organismic:* A metaphor used by theorists who view the human personality as if it were a cell that goes through universal and natural processes of maturation or evolu-

tion that have been programmed into the species. A lot of strength is attributed to the organism's ability to right itself if it gets stuck or finds itself in any kind of trouble. Change is seen to occur in ways similar to evolution. There is an unfolding in the process.

4. ***Contextualist:*** A metaphor used to emphasize that everything that happens to individuals, groups, communities, states, nations, or any other grouping takes place within a social context that includes historical precedent, social, political, cultural, economic, and structural influences, among others. By observing the surrounding context of an interaction, one may gain important information about the interaction. Constructivism explicitly embraces this metaphor (Lyddon, 1987).

Table 13-1 depicts the root metaphors (or meta-theories) and their identifying characteristics. These categories are offered in the spirit of Max Weber's "ideal types," whereby each category is exaggerated somewhat to make the point about the differences between metaphors. The reader is cautioned that there are overlaps in some of the conceptual contents of the theories. In other words, each meta-theory may have characteristics that may indicate that they fit into more than one category. Lyddon (1987), in discussing Pepper, identified the theories of human behavior and/or counseling theories according to the most likely root metaphor indicating the assumptive world of its author.

As can easily be seen, constructivism emanates from the meta-theory that Pepper identifies as "Contextualism," as do most of the theoretical and treatment models presented and discussed in this textbook (e.g., strengths perspective, narrative, empowerment, feminist theory). These theories have in common the belief that contextual factors influence how we are treated, how we experience and perceive our lives, and whether the resources are available to adequately address our needs.

Constructivists view formism and mechanism as metaphors that are socially constructed in such a way as to stereotype and label clients (perhaps unintentionally in some cases), as they ignore contextual influences entirely. Using these worldviews, clients have little chance to speak their own Truth to the professional. Organicism has most recently dominated social work education, particularly in human behavior courses (Human Behavior in a Social Environment).

Organicism suggests a worldview that grants less authority to the practitioner than formism or mechanism, at least on the surface. Constructivists view organicism as a metaphor that fails to adequately recognize diversity, and they would argue that many of the behaviors that are considered "universal and natural" by those using the organicism metaphor are really socially constructed by members of dominant groups and reflect socialization and life experiences of this group. For example, Gilligan (1982) points out that Erikson's life-span development theory, with its emphasis on autonomy, initiative, and separate identity formation, most reflects the socialization of mainstream males in Western cultures. Important lessons in life having to do with sharing, compassion, or interdependence are not even noticed by Erikson, even though these values and skills are highly sought after in females in Western cultures and in both sexes in many non-Western traditions. Feminists, persons of color, gays and lesbians, and people with disabilities argue that, rather than being universal, many of the traditional theories contain a male "construction of reality" based on White, affluent, male socialization in Eurocentric cultures (Gilligan, 1982; Harding, 1991; Miller, 1986, 1991; Schriver, 2001). Critiques do not dismiss the importance of having theories to understand this group of White males, but as Gilligan (1982) explicitly discusses in her book, *In a Different Voice,* when theories do not adequately represent all groups, they should not be used as though they are "universal."

TABLE 13.1   *Meta-Theories and Theories of Human Behavior*

	Formistic *(Metaphor—similarity of form)*	*Mechanistic* *(Metaphor—a machine)*
Defining Belief(s):	Essences or identity categories. Dispositional characteristics (traits). Personality categories (types).	Inter-relationship of working parts that run the machine. Parts exert constraining influence on one another.
Assumptions:	Stable structures exist, regardless of context or temporal features that determine psychological functioning.	Linear cause–effect relationships. Human beings are relatively passive recipients of forces of the machine. Responses are elicited and maintained by antecedent and consequent conditioning or processes.
De-emphasized:	Context and temporal process.	Context and temporal process.
Diagnosis or Assessment:	DSM-IV (Disorders classified by similarity of symptoms or problems that are viewed as "being in the person." Meyers/Briggs test.	Broken parts need to be fixed or strengthened.
Treatment:	Medicate or use appropriate therapy.	Discover malfunction and adjust interworking mechanical parts or alternatively resolve unconscious conflicts and drives.
Counseling Theory:	Match person with "right" occupation or setting.	Work with client so as to reveal unconscious "drives." Discover S–R relationship and interrupt it or use cognitive restructuring to change response.
Example:	Alport's Trait theory. Sheldon's Somatotypes. Jung's personality theory.	Freud's Psychoanalysis Cognitive and Behavioral Theories. Ellis's R-E-T.

(Continued on next page)

TABLE 13.1 *(continued)*

	Organismic (Metaphor—organic processor cell)	Contextualism (Metaphor—transitory historical situation and its many tensions)
Defining Belief(s):	Oppositions that may at first appear to impede development when confronted, actually lead to integration. Core motivating forces and universal principles are stressed.	World events and sociology/psychology phenomena are viewed as a confluence of inseparable factors that depend on one another for their definition. Meaning is tied to its context which is itself in flux.
Assumptions:	Belief in progress and decline is stressed—development over time and some larger unfolding structure emerges into some final integrated whole.	Events or phenomena are not static, but are embedded in a surrounding context that exerts influence as does the event on the context. Reciprocal causality Multi-dimensional/multi-causality.
De-emphasized:	Cultural context.	Stable structures—separation into parts.
Diagnosis or Assessment:	Systems thinking—cell analysis. Look for successive transformation over time—the self constructs and reconstructs itself in "natural" evolution or maturation process.	Holistic nature of sociology/psychology phenomena are inseparable from context— observe, and observe the act of observing, for interactive influence of self and context.
Treatment and Counseling Theory:	Provide rich environment or opportunities to supply resources that make development possible. Fulfill basic human needs, and development naturally occurs.	Humans are active, self-constructing, open, and changing. Use of multidimensional strategies and observations—don't assume the professional knows best. Emphasize relationship building and interaction.
Examples:	Erikson's Eight Stages of Man. Piaget's Cognitive Developmental Theory, Humanism Object Relations Theory. Developmental Life-Span Theories (i.e., Gould, Levinson, Sheehy). Family Systems Theories, Functionalism (from Sociology).	Social interactionists—Sullivan Social Learning—Bandura Symbolic Interactionism Constructivism. Feminist Theory, Narrative Theory, Empowerment, and Strengths-based Theories, and Conflict Theory (from Sociology).

Adapted from William Lyddon's (1989) article, "Root metaphor theory: A philosophical framework for counseling and psychotherapy," *Journal of Counseling and Development. 4:* 67. 42–67.

*This author (Burris) has added social work and sociological theories of which Lyddon, a psychologist, may have lacked familiarity (i.e., functionalism, conflict theory, symbolic interactionism from sociology; strengths-based, narrative, empowerment and feminist theories from social work).

Epistemology.   The eighteenth century philosopher Immanuel Kant wrote *A Critique of Pure Reason* in 1781, claiming that knowledge is the construction of active humans responding to interactions between themselves and their environment (both their internal and external environment). Thus, knowledge, from this point of view, is created by human interaction and is the result of interpretations of experience. The mind is *not* a blank slate neutrally recording the facts, but rather, it is actively involved in creating views that make sense of life and its many experiences (Efran, et al., 1988). Clearly, there can be no single set of universal laws and no single reality, in that the interpretations of individuals and groups vary. These basic ideas are drawn from works of those who are today being called "constructivists."

These views are in direct opposition to philosophers who embraced "empiricism." John Locke, founder of British Empiricism in the eighteenth century viewed knowledge as the result of the careful analysis of observation and measurement of the outside world that rewarded its practitioners with discoveries (Efran, et al., 1988). He saw the mind as a *tabula rasa,* a blank slate on which knowledge and understanding came about through the interplay of the senses and all that they perceived. Rene Descartes proposed that the pursuit of knowledge should be to "study reality," which, of course, he believed exists outside the pursuer. This philosophical perspective inspired people like Isaac Newton and Gregor Mendel who spent much of their lifetimes in empirical pursuits to discover the objective laws of the universe. Their discoveries, among many others, are often used as examples of the superiority of empiricism.

It is important to point out that these scientists researched aspects of the physical world, rather than phenomena in the social sciences. Many have argued that positivism may be a more appropriate method of inquiry in the natural sciences, although that too is disputed (Harding, 1991; Lyddon, 1987). Of these two philosophical approaches, it is clear that Eurocentric cultures, starting in the eighteenth and nineteenth centuries to the present time, have strongly favored the empirical view for both the natural and the social sciences, often to the exclusion of any other perspective.

Empiricists prefer large, randomly selected samples on which to test relationships between or among variables so as to find statistically significant associations. They argue that any one person's private knowledge is irrelevant at best, and, at worst, represents a threat to the goal of discovering Truth due to the subjective bias of personal perception and personal experience. Therefore, personal accounts, while interesting, are discounted as invalid by positivists. This is not at all true for constructivists who favor naturalistic, experiential, and integrative interpretations that include both internal and external realities. While constructivists do not exclude "empirical" evidence, they acknowledge that there are other ways of knowing, and, by utilizing diverse ways of knowing, seek to increase understanding of a diverse world where "empiricism" alone does not enlighten (Ballou, 1990; Belenky, Clinchy, Goldberger, and Tarule, 1986).

Many of these and other positions and concepts in Table 13.2 are discussed in the "Core Concepts" section of this chapter. This table summarizes and extends the perspectives of constructionists and empiricists from various sources. The reader is cautioned that, in use, these two groups may overlap somewhat.

Conceptualized somewhat differently, many of these contrasting concepts are portrayed in textbooks for social work (Jordan and Franklin, 1995, as cited in Robbins, Chat-

TABLE 13.2 *Epistemological Positions of Constructivist and Empiricist Philosophers*

Qualitative/Constructivist	*Quantitative/Empiricist/Positivist*
View of the Nature of Reality	
• Diverse (many realities, multiple meanings)	• Universal—one singular reality
• Changing	• Unchanging
• Sensitive to context	• Unrelated to context
• Holistic	• Fragmented or discrete
• Not created by universal laws	• Created by universal laws
• Subjectively *and* objectively experienced	• Objectively observed
• Perceived internally and externally; socially constructed through dialogue, observation, and experience, as well as observation, measurement, and testing.	• Externally, for observation, measurement, testing, and discovery
• Individual and collective	• Reality is stable so that all may similarly discover through scientific method
• Uncertainty is part of nature of knowing	• Reality can be known with certainty
• Humans are socially adaptable, so immutable scientific laws can't govern behavior and human nature	• Human behavior is material of science, not ethics, or multi-cultural studies
• Human ability to engage in dialogue important; reality is open to interpretation	• Discoveries speak for themselves; Truth is self-evident and unaffected by interaction
• Human communication valued to describe understanding of reality, though math can help	• Math is a medium to describe Truth, though carefully reasoned arguments may help
• Personal accounts are valued	• Personal accounts are devalued as biased
• Diversity is valued	• Assumption of sameness, generalizability, universality
View of the Nature of Logic	
• Multiple	• Linear
• Complex, and dependent on context	• Dualistic—either/or
• Understood through inductive and deductive reasoning	• Deductive reasoning is favored
• Categorizing involves danger of stereotyping	• Categorizing seen as technical process; reality assumed to exist in categories
• Paradox explored as source of wisdom	• Paradox is eliminated
• Knower and known are interactive	• Knower and known are independent
• Human language matters greatly in fostering understanding, insight, and appreciation of diverse realities; action is speech	• Math is primary language of science

(Continued on next page)

TABLE 13.2   *(continued)*

Constructivist	*Empiricist/Positivist*

Role of Values in Investigation

- Separating values from facts is impossible
- Some values are worth pursuing
- Positivists who claim to be value-free are fooling themselves
- Cognitive, emotional, behavioral, and intuitive, spiritual energies integrated in efforts to know and to understand

- Facts exist separate from values
- Values have no place in discovery of reality

- Research and knowing are cognitive activities—avoid emotional, intuitive, spiritual involvement

Methods of Investigation

- Naturalistic, experiential, and integrative use of many methods favored
- Qualitative as well as quantitative methods, phenomenology, Hermeneutics, dialectic construction, deconstruction, reconstruction methods constantly being tried, refined, created and recreated
- Established through a variety of methods
- Defining problem entails values, ethics, politics historical influences, standpoint
- Experts' definitions met with skepticism
- Experts advance knowledge that advances political position of elite few

- Scientific Method only, is favored
- Quantitative methods used—mathematical analysis of sense data

- Discovered through the scientific method
- Defining problems is neutral step in scientific method
- Implicit faith is held in fact-finding expert
- Defining Truth has nothing to do with politics, power, history, or prestige

Goal of Knowledge

- Understand, create community
- Promote well-being, celebrate diversity
- Enhance social justice, support populations at risk, encourage critical thinking
- Satisfy curiosity

- Predict and control
- Improve modern life
- Enhance competitive economy
- Know for the sake of knowledge
- Satisfy curiosity

terjee, & Canda, 1998, p. 297). Lincoln and Guba (1985, p. 37) describe similar comparisons between what they call positivism and naturalistic principles of inquiry. What these authors call "naturalistic" inquiry embodies the approach that is elsewhere called "constructivist." As already mentioned, Schriver (2001) refers to many of these contrasting concepts as "the dominant paradigm" and "the alternative paradigm."

It may be that, with time, the use of the term *constructivism* (used interchangeably with the term *constructivist*) in social work will be limited to the epistemological position identified with methods of the knowledge-building processes rather than as knowledge as product (i.e., theoretical perspectives for understanding the development of social forces, personality, and the other areas listed at the beginning of this chapter such as micro, meso, and macro theoretical perspectives and theories of intervention). In the future, the theories and treatment models may come to have various names, while the process of building theory based on constructivism is recognized.

This is just as *positivism* or *empiricism* are terms used to identify the method of knowledge building, and the theories that result from utilization of this approach are referred to variously as behaviorism, cognitive theory, psychoanalysis, etc. Time will tell if that comes to be.

Constructivism as a Critique of Positivism as a Research Method. There is not sufficient space in this chapter to do service to the critiques of logical positivism. However, a brief summary of some of the main points will be described, as this critique is an important contribution of constructivists. The reader is referred to cited works in this chapter for more detailed arguments.

Almost every claim that is made by positivists has been challenged, and the "social context, social construction and on-site studies of scientific practice and scientific knowledge is increasingly the object of inquiry" (Restivo, 1988, p. 206). For example, the stated ultimate goal of empiricism is to describe reality and to develop theories that reflect Truth. As a critique, Efran, et al. (1988) offer the following:

> The heart of constructivism is the recognition that our hypotheses about the world are not directly provable. To the constructivist, scientific hypotheses persist mainly for two reasons, neither one having much to do with objective truth: first, because "we" find them useful in "our" work (utility); second, because "no one" has yet been able to either disprove them or come up with a better alternative. (p. 28)

Of course, it is important to point out that Karl Popper, a staunch empiricist, made the same observation (Giddens, 1978). The solution that he proposed to this dilemma is "falsifiability," a term he coined to refer to the importance of always trying to disprove a theory (i.e., using the null hypothesis) when carrying out the scientific method. However, Popper recommended continued commitment to work toward capturing Truth through replication and corroboration. According to Popper, corroboration is theory-testing that is done by replication of research by many researchers who are trying to disprove a theory—in order to ultimately shave away what is "false" and thereby, leaving what is "true." Over time, and by the repetition of achieving similar results, researchers make it possible to corroborate a theory and thereby get closer to Truth. Popper argued for the use of the deductive method.

He thought it might be possible to corroborate a theory "falsely" by inductively looking through data with the purpose of "proving" a theory that was not "true." Thus what Popper ultimately recommended is to continue to have faith in the possibility of discovering Truth while recognizing the enormous difficulty of doing so. Critics of Popper are skeptical and want to know upon *what criteria* will the false be separated from truth, and *who* would distinguish what is false from what is true in order to establish Truth during the process of replication.

What is considered true in one context as observed by one group or individual may be seen as false by another individual or group who may see things differently from another context. Popper's suggestion of falsifiability does not even consider what Saleebey (1994) has observed, that experiences and interpretations of truth seem to be sustained through myths or individual and collective interpretations of what gets passed on as reality.

Rejecting Popper's prohibition against using inductive reasoning, constructivists utilize inductive reasoning as a valuable process, along with deduction reasoning. Rather than redoubling the single-minded pursuit of empiricist principles when faced with difficulties in proving hypotheses, constructivists are more inclined to see the impossibility of proving scientific hypotheses as an opportunity for looking at phenomena from many points of view, for exploring diverse perspectives and as a reason to reconnect ethics and values more explicitly to the pursuit of knowledge.

Constructivists do not believe that it is possible to be value-free and argue that empiricists, by claiming to be value-free, blind themselves to the values that they pass along with their "science." Further, empiricists who fail to recognize that, by serving as "science workers" for powerful interests that do take value positions, their claim to neutrality is a thinly veiled misrepresentation of their value-free status (Harding, 1991; Mills, 1959; Restivo, 1988).

Selected Critiques of Knowledge as Product of Positivistic Approaches. The critiques included in this discussion serve to illustrate the point made by constructivists that the products of empirical science do not always reflect progress and increased freedom and democracy as many of those who control institutional resources would have social scientists and the public believe. One rationale for the selection of examples in this section is author familiarity (in other words, other examples might just as easily be used by others who are familiar with other examples). Additionally, the authors tried to select examples that represent a critique of dominant approaches that have been influential in the history of social work.

Constructivists recognize that, along with the good that has resulted from empirical science, there has also come a great deal of harm. Sociologists, by focusing on the social context of knowledge and its "construction," have developed initially in the 1920s what they call the Sociology of Knowledge. Following this tradition, U. S. sociologist C. Wright Mills quickly saw the link between power and science and viewed modern science as subordinate to "the wasteful absurdities of capitalism," the military power, and the nation state. To quote Mills, "science seems to many less a creative ethos and a manner of orientation than a set of Science Machines operated by technicians and military men who neither embody nor understand science as ethos and orientation" (Restivo, 1988, p. 207).

In the helping professions, models of intervention have been developed using positivistic methods, and these models have had their critics. Some of the most egregious examples come from the nineteenth century. We mention, as an example, phrenology, which was the study of bumps on the skull that supposedly indicated personality and behavioral disorders that were believed to lead to criminality. Bumps on the heads of prisoners were surgically removed, rendering extreme hardship or death to the victims of such surgery. This theory and practice, while not utilized by social work, illustrates the misuses of positivism.

In the late twentieth century, the medical model has been subject to critiques from various sources. Thomas Szasz (1961) argued that application of the medical model in treatment of mental illness vests authority and power in the hands of "experts" whose solutions often advantage the mental health practitioner more than the "patient." Further, by fragmenting what is the object of scientific inquiry, enormous social and physical harm is overlooked. For example, Restivo (1988) points out that the . . .

> . . . focus on basic cellular biology in cancer research, for example, assumes a solution that interrupts the carcinogen process in the individual body rather than to rearrange the social order to remove the carcinogen from the environment. The first is called science: the second is called public policy or politics by defenders of the status quo. This alienates the scientist from social processes. (p. 223)

Theorists who might currently be called constructivists recognize that problem definition and problem-solving activities involve political choices as well as "fact-finding" processes. They further recognize the political aspects involved in fact-finding even among scientists who claim to be value-free. Indeed they debunk claims that values and facts are dichotomies and can be separated one from the other. Constructivists are interested in how the social and political past, present, and future affect human perception, experience, cognition, emotion, and action. As noted, they are interested in the human condition in social context.

Survivors of sexual child abuse who manifest signs of clinical depression have traditionally been accused of being stuck in the Oedipus or Electra conflicts of child development and have more recently been accused of having a "false memory syndrome." They are treated within an established framework to feel better (medication can ease the pain), but their concerns are still marginalized. Paulo Freire (1973) would term this type of help oppressive because it fails to inform the client of the ways in which depression is the result of abusive developmental history and oppressive social conditions, and it does nothing to prevent sexual abuse in the nation. It also increases the power and authority of the practitioner at the expense of the person seeking assistance.

Psychoanalytic approaches have been criticized for ignoring almost entirely the social context and for putting all emphasis on individual "social adjustment." Other psychological traditions (e.g., humanists/existentialists and behaviorists) have sustained similar criticisms. Although humanists are often counted as social constructionists owing to their emphasis on individual freedom, it cannot escape notice that humanists fail to recognize that no person constructs his or her own reality without external influences (Berger & Luckman, 1967). Further, in cultures that prize inter-relatedness and group affiliation, concepts like self-actualization and individuation are foreign and represent the threat of shredding apart protective aspects of group cohesion (Miller, 1986; Schriver, 2001). The theorists of constructivism operate with a very different worldview from traditional theorists, whereby old solutions to the human condition (e.g., individuation, separation, oedipus complex, "penis envy," measurable outcomes, individualism, "doing one's thing," family-systems theory, the medical model) become new problems to be solved (Franks, 1986).

Because words matter to constructivists, it is important to be reminded that the way that a problem is defined and conceptualized influences the solutions that are possible and desirable. For example, to define welfare mothers as lazy "pigs at the trough," as Ronald Reagan did when he was in political office, is to suggest one set of solutions to a perceived problem. To define welfare mothers as experiencing poverty due to structural elements in the economy that brings disadvantages to some individuals while bringing advantages to others is to suggest another set of solutions.

Core Principles for Practice

Constructivist Perspective Used to Generate Method of Knowledge Building

Feminist Standpoint Theory has emerged as a research strategy to address the unacknowledged biases of empiricists. The researcher using standpoint theory must ask from whose standpoint is this finding true, and whose standpoint has not even been included in the research. The concept of standpoint involves recognition that reality or knowledge is created from a historical/political/sociological/psychological location or context (Van Den Bergh, 1995). Standpoint does not mean that all points of view are blended into one, but that the actual experience of a particular standpoint must be understood thoroughly within the context of subjective and objective realities of that position.

As a way of knowing, constructivism represents both a critique of the limits of positivism as well as an approach to knowledge generation. Two generations of teachers and students of the Critical School of Frankfurt—from Horkheimer, Adorno, and Marcuse to Habermas—offered a critique of positivism. They observe that what is offered as genuine knowledge often turns out to be a subtle form of ideology and that science and technology have become powerful tools for manipulation, repression, and domination. Habermas sought to approach knowledge that reached "beyond objectivism." The theorists from the Critical School, and contemporary critical theorists, for that matter, do not pretend to be without values; they are committed to social justice.

Habermas and others in the Critical School sought to create the basis for social relations that would remove authoritarianism from social interactions and to create an "ideal" community of equals who could speak their minds freely and seek knowledge together. They were very aware of the political nature of communication and described what they thought was ideal speech—speech free from compulsion, and speaker free from domination (McCarthy, 1981). Both action and discourse are forms of speech and are the basis for knowledge according to Habermas.

Members of the Critical School revived an interest in Hermeneutics, which is the study of understanding, or a way to deal with meaning and interpretation of words used to convey meaning. It was initially used to understand the meaning of spiritual texts (Giddens, 1978) but has received attention more recently as a useful methodology for psychology

(Gergen, 1999). Hermeneutics, and particularly that which is explored by Hans-Georg Gadamer as an approach to understanding, is being currently recommended in social work literature as a way of negotiating between the extreme positions of either "utopian ambition or resigned defeat in modern life" (Richardson & Franklin, 1998, pp. 307–311).

Social Constructivism Used to Critique and Understand Social Forces

Social constructivism is often used as a powerful critique of the forces that seek to normalize oppressive social relations. Functionalism is a macro perspective in sociology that has been used in such normalizing since the 1950s when it was formally introduced into the academy. Functionalism has been introduced into social work HBSE texts in recent years (Hutchison, 1999; Robbins, et al., 1998; Schriver, 2001). It is most often used to illustrate that systems theory, which is the backbone of social work theory, can be interpreted in a way that "blames the victim," to use Ryan's (1971) concept, and, further, that systems may be perceived as closed, unchanging, and blind to human suffering. Both the metaphors of the machine and of the organism from Pepper's typology (Table 13.1) are meta-theories of functionalism.

From this perspective, society is an organism that is similar to the human body system, and it operates in a rather machine-like way. Like the human body, society has various parts (e.g., institutions, norms, and philosophies) that, working together, make the overall organism run smoothly. It is assumed that society is self-contained and determined by immutable, biological-like forces. Functionalists, therefore, argue that if something in society exists (for example, poverty) it must be necessary (otherwise, why would it exist?). It is assumed that "man is rational" and that each person in making a rational choice is "voting" to maintain the system, just as forces of biology work to maintain organic systems. Functionalists argue that the resulting society does the following: (1) Society and its social arrangements represent a "consensus" of opinions regarding its structure and direction. (2) It creates harmony. (3) It benefits everyone (even people living in poverty, because they have "chosen" not to get a good education, work hard, get into the stock market, etc.).

The adherents to functionalism claim to be objective, outside observers who are value-free as they report the functions of various institutions and social norms. For example, functionalists argue that social stratification exists because it rises out of the basic needs of society (still using the analogy of a human organism that has biological needs). The basic need that creates stratification is the need to motivate the most able members to occupy difficult and important positions (Davis, 1949). Regarding stratification, functionalists assume the following:

- People qualified to fill important and difficult positions and jobs are scarce.
- To motivate qualified people to fill these positions, a system of awards must be offered (economic benefits, authority, prestige, etc.).
- Social stratification functions to get the best people into the most difficult jobs and, therefore, is good.
- The resulting inequality is beneficial to all, since individual survival is contingent on the survival of society.

- The well-paid benefit from economic rewards, prestige, etc., and the poor benefit by having a society run by the best people, and because they do not have to put out the effort to get educated and compete for difficult jobs. Therefore, everybody benefits.
- The overall effect is harmony, consensus, and well-being.

Conflict theory is another macro perspective in sociology that follows a tradition that may be characterized as social constructionist. In this chapter, this theory was introduced in the previous discussion regarding the Critical School. Conflict theorists are interested in understanding how power and other important resources are utilized and distributed in society as well as being concerned about the consequences of such arrangements as they exist. Social justice is of primary concern to them.

Conflict theorists offer a critique of functionalism that is almost identical to the constructivist critique of positivists. It includes the following critical points (adapted from Restivo, 1988) in its criticism of functionalism:

- Conflict theorists find functionalists to be far from the objective, value-free, neutral observer representing Truth, that they pretend to be.
- Conflict theorists argue that functionalist arguments, rather than being value-free, are creating "spin" for the rich and powerful and justifying inequality, while claiming to be objective.
- Functionalists use circular reasoning in arguing that "if something exists, it is necessary; otherwise, why would it exist?"
- Functionalists emphasize finding a singular, universal Truth or explanation for social phenomena.
- Functionalists use dichotomous classifications (e.g., deserving–undeserving, facts–values, men–women, Black–White, etc.) that conflict-theorists argue are false dichotomies.
- Functionalists present views that are ahistorical—isolating variables for study from their social context.
- Functionalists engage in nonreflexive use of language as a medium for transmitting thoughts, concepts, and theories.
- Functionalists reinforce competitive individualism when they present society as the sum total of individual "choices." Social problems are seen in terms of individuals making "wrong choices," rather than as social barriers created in a society of unequal power and resource distribution.
- Functionalists are extremely uncomfortable with social change and tend to see it as dangerous. They like slow change, which they equate with evolutionary processes. To try to change society is to go against nature.

It cannot escape the reader's notice that these points are almost identical to the constructivist critique of positivism presented in Table 13.2. Conflict theorists view the functionalist arguments, then, as social constructions that justify the status quo. Remember, conflict theorists always ask the uncomfortable questions about power, its use, and who benefits from any social arrangement. They do not assume that everyone benefits from social arrangements equally, as functionalists do. Conflict theorists recognize that in society there are great differences, disagreements, conflicts, and struggles, and if everyone could safely voice these differences openly, a very different social community may be constructed. Conflict theorists accept that social reality is socially constructed. They urge working toward constructing action and outcome in such a way that optimizes social justice and includes diversity in its many forms. That cannot be done by justifying the status quo, as functionalists do, particularly when the status quo involves growing inequities in income, education, health care, etc.

Constructivist Theories for the Macro Level: Understanding of the Development of Institutions and Institutional Behavior

This discussion is limited to selected highlights of works using the social-construction perspective that has been influential in challenging more traditional assumptions and policies. These works have led to social movements that are highlighted in subsequent sections of this chapter. Social work literature and textbooks have only recently included the work of these authors (Robbins, et al., 1998; Hutchison, 1999); however, their impact in the development of social theory and of social change may be illustrative to social workers as they search for theories of macro practice.

C. Wright Mills, The Sociological Imagination: Conflict theorist C. Wright Mills (1959) invites social workers to have what he calls a sociological imagination. Development of this imagination increases awareness of sociological aspects that surround and constantly influence people without their noticing. In other words, Mills encourages heightened awareness of the social nature of human existence as well as alertness to social contexts in which development occurs. In short, nothing happens without social, political and historical involvement. Society is not like an organism that goes through "evolutionary" changes that require individual acceptance and adjustment, as functionalists describe in their theories. Mills, along with other conflict theorists, argues that changes occur when actual people (usually people who control power and resources) do actual things that create actual results that affect actual others. Understanding of human behavior in the world is tied to context, which is itself in flux. The Sociological Imagination of C. Wright Mills includes the following major points:

1. He encourages people to find the point at which personal biographies intersect with history. In other words, by looking at the historical context at a given time, people discover how social institutions, social structures, attitudes, political climates, norms, etc. have shaped individual choices and perspectives about what is possible.
2. He invites people to find the distinction between "personal troubles" and "public issues." For example, in a city of one million, if only a few children are going to bed hungry, that might be because those children and their families are having personal troubles. However, if one-fourth of the children are hungry, that is a public issue that needs a public response. Politicians may construct a view of hunger as a personal "choice" in order to convince constituents that there is no public issue to attend to. Mills invites a deeper look.

3. He encourages a concern with questions of social structures, the place of societies in the world, social pressures, etc. In other words, he encourages people to notice that nothing happens in the world without happening in a social context.

Peter Berger and Thomas Luckman: The Social Construction of Reality: In the now classic book, *The Social Construction of Reality: A Treatise in the Sociology of Knowledge* (1967) by Peter Berger and Thomas Luckman, the authors describe the mutual social influence of the social forces of a society on the "construction" of the "self" or individual and of the individual, who in concert with other individuals, "constructs" society. The book describes the processes of socialization and re-socialization that take place in intimate and public social interactions that have developed over time as certain behaviors and responses have been ritualized and institutionalized in society. These institutionalized interactions become pre-set definitions of the situation and prescribe behaviors that have become habitualized to the point that they are seen as "natural" and almost biological, as temperament is believed to be. The examples of behaviors and responses are ones that individuals have understood to be "objective" facts by both the individual and observers. Thus, the authors heighten awareness of the social construction of the self. Further, they describe the reciprocal process whereby individuals who refuse to act in expected ways can change social institutions. For example, during the Civil Rights Movement, African Americans refused to leave racially segregated diners during "sit-in" demonstrations in public places, and these actions (along with others) helped to break the back of Jim Crow laws, but these actions gave new meaning to the constructed self-identities of participants in the civil rights struggles.

Erving Goffman, The Presentation of Self in Everyday Life (1959), Asylums (1963a), Stigma (1963b):   Using case studies and meticulous observations, Erving Goffman details several accounts of how individuals "present themselves" socially to communicate or defy the social situation in which they find themselves, or to accomplish a social goal, or to deal with rejection by projecting certain information about themselves. He details ways in which professionals play roles in constructing who becomes "needy," and who is institutionalized, and why. The interactions between staff in asylums and patients show the painful "objectification" process that patients endured. These interactions became institutionalized, and the persons involved as well as bystanders came to see the behaviors as "objective" realities rather than carefully constructed social interactions. Current writings of Michel Foucault contain similar observations through which we are encouraged to make the familiar visible in order to see the "constructed" social order that we do not see when we normalize social situations (Chambon, Irving, & Epstein, 1999; Foucault, 1970).

Use of Constructivism Theories in Intervention Strategies at the Macro Level

Conflict theory is not just a critique of society, but is also an invitation for people to construct new social realities and structures that are more receptive to diversity and its many inherent concerns. The reader is reminded of the Critical School of Frankfurt that sought to explore social knowledge and social actions that would lead to liberating social relations.

The nature of constructivism invites diverse individuals from diverse populations to speak of their own reality, and in doing so, challenge the perceptions of reality put forward by the dominant group. When people do not allow others to define them, and when they speak clearly about their own realities as they see them, social transformation begins. That, of course, is not enough; social structures must also reflect the diverse lives of diverse populations (Chambon, et al., 1999).

Constructionists have influenced feminist theory in the 1970s and onward. It is out of awareness of what C. Wright Mills (1959) calls the "sociological imagination" that the feminist movement adopted the philosophical axiom "the personal is political." In consciousness-raising groups during the '70s, women met and discussed ways in which they had been influenced by socialization that rendered their experiences and lives "invisible." They worked to construct a new social reality that would include gender equality. There were diverse opinions among women about how to achieve gender equality. Many of the leaders and originators of the Women's Movement were blind to diversity (e.g., class, racial and ethnic, sexual orientation, disability) among women, both in terms of how feminism could be defined, but also in terms of the many standpoints within feminism. Certainly, the women's movement is composed of persons with diverse views and constructions of "the problems." Although it is beyond the scope of this chapter to summarize diversity among feminists, Allison Jaggar wrote a wonderful account of the diverse political and philosophical positions within the Women's Movement, to which the reader may refer (Jaggar, 1983).

Deinstitutionalization and independent living facilities for the mentally ill resulted, in part, from the work of Goffman. The movement to deinstitutionalize asylums is incomplete. Part of the plan for that movement was to provide community care facilities which, of course, have not become a reality for the most part. As a result, too many mentally ill are wandering the streets or are institutionalized in jails and prisons and are experiencing a whole new set of social constructions that need to be addressed. However, Goffman did expose the impersonal and, at times, inhumane "care" that had been constructed to maintain institutional control, and Goffman's writings continue to serve as a model for the work that still needs to be done in this area.

Constructivist Theories for Micro-Level Understanding of Personality Development

This section focuses on theories that serve as examples of works that pioneered what has developed as constructivism. The next section summarizes major guidelines that characterize constructivism as an intervention at the micro level.

Symbolic Interactionism is a theoretical perspective from sociology that posits that, as social beings, we create social symbols socially and construct social meanings for those symbols through social interaction. We become human through exchanging social symbols in social interaction. Symbolic Interactionists never described themselves as constructivists, but they describe a process whereby the self is constructed throughout a lifetime of social interactions. Social interactions and social and individual constructions constitute the "stuff" of which the self is made and remade constantly over a life span.

George Herbert Mead called this process socialization, a process whereby individuals, sensitive to the social expectations of others and subject to social pressures, come to see themselves through the lens of the "other." Though individuals exercise their own judgments (which are also subject to others' judgment), they also incorporate the judgments of outsiders into the "self." Self-perceptions and actions, then, become habitualized. Human personality is viewed as social, plastic, adaptable and always in the process of construction and reconstruction. Personality is not just external behavior (as behaviorists posit), but it also includes the internal sense of self and meaning that the individual "constructs" as well (Mead, 1968).

Charles Horton Cooley developed the theory of **"the looking-glass self"** and described a process of self-development as rooted in social behavior that is learned rather than instinctual. According to his views, the self image is the accumulation of images reflected from others' reactions to us or—more importantly—from how we think others respond to us. This includes perceptions of role requirements, position in social groups and society (e.g., racial, gender, age, class, etc.). The looking-glass self contains three elements:

1. the imagination of our appearance to the other person,
2. the imagination of the other's judgment of that appearance, and
3. some sort of self-feeling (such as pride, shame) and action (rejection or acceptance of the judgment).

Development is viewed as a dialectical two-way social negotiation (Cooley, 1964).

George Kelly and Personal Construct Theory.   George Kelly, professor and Director of Clinical Psychology at Ohio State University, wrote two volumes of his book, *The Psychology of Personal Constructs* (1955, 1963), which built a theory with terminology that departed from many of the traditional concepts in psychology. He rejected the empirical Law of Effect, which states that behavior is more likely to reoccur if it has been followed by a positive reinforcer and less likely to be repeated if followed by a negative reinforcer. Kelly (1955, 1963) believed that human behavior is more likely controlled by cognitive "constructions" than by external reinforcements. His interventions included a process of encouraging clients to discover and make clear to themselves the constructions they had developed to guide daily life, to evaluate their effectiveness, and to construct new ways to see themselves that would be more personally satisfying or meaningful. Kelly says this about his work:

> This paper, throughout, deals with half-truths only. Nothing that it contains, or is intended to be, wholly true. The theoretical statements propounded are no more than partially accurate constructions of events that, in turn are no more than partially perceived. Moreover, what we propose, even in its truer aspects, will eventually be overthrown and displaced by something with more truth in it. Indeed, our theory is frankly designed to contribute effectively to its own eventual overthrow and displacement. (as cited in Maher, 1969, "Man's construction of his alternatives," a 1958 conference paper on the assessment of human motives) (p. 66)

Many view Kelly's work as originating constructivism in psychology. Certainly, his work inspired psychologists to create an approach to family therapy that is called "constructivism" and used many of the principles already identified with this tradition (Efran, et al., 1988; Neimeyer, 1993).

Uses of Constructivist Theories in Intervention at the Micro Level

The reader may believe that Kelly's personal-construct theory is equivalent to cognitive approaches. Kelly strongly objected to that characterization. Differences between the two approaches are in the goals of the therapeutic enterprise. Traditional cognitive therapy is used to correct a wrong and eliminate a dysfunction, while constructivist therapies are used to facilitate a better self-understanding within the client in such a way that the individual may transition into a more meaningful personal experience of the self (Neimeyer, 1993). This is often referred to as "growth" or "development." For this to happen, the context, personal narrative, construct system, and one's relationships (interpersonal and intrapersonal) must be explored. In cognitive therapies, the therapist identifies "thought distortions" or "thinking errors," and these become the focus of the directive change efforts, with the therapist being the expert, evaluating "objectively" the level of the client's "success." In constructivist therapy, the client is the "expert" of his or her own experiences and motivation to change. The therapist is aware that personal change is the result of relationship and of building trust and, therefore, takes the role of facilitator, communicator, and cotraveler on the client's journey. The constructivist utilizes dialogue and consensus to evaluate "success."

Constructivism is central to the development of several perspectives for assisting clients at the micro level. Since these interventions are discussed in separate chapters in this book, they will be simply mentioned here: Feminist theory, Strengths Perspective, Empowerment theory and Narrative theory. Assumptions summarized in Table 13.1, in the column entitled "Contextualism," make these theories fall within the family of constructivist approaches. The role of the social worker is one of co-creator of meanings, and of facilitator rather than "expert." The work is more exploratory, less directive, and less structured than traditional methods of intervention. It is assumed that the client is the "expert" of his or her own life (Neimeyer, 1993; Rosen & Kuehlweil, 1996). The belief that individuals are social beings who socially construct and reconstruct meaning and their lives (individually and collectively) guides the work. The social worker learns from the client where the individual is in terms of his or her life's journey and joins with the client in creating that journey's direction. Problems are externalized as a way of creating distance, control, and transformation. It is through relationship and dialogue that the work is accomplished.

Case Example

A wonderful case example comes from the book by Anne Fadiman (1997), *The Spirit Catches You and You Fall Down: A Hmong Child, Her American Doctors, and the Collision of Two Cultures.* Lia Lee is the Hmong child living in Merced, California, in 1982. At the age of three months, she had what American doctors came to diagnose as a serious seizure disorder (epilepsy). However, her Hmong community knew this condition as *qaug dah peg*, which means "the spirit catches you, and you fall down." The Hmong view of it is twofold: On one hand, *qaug dah peg* is considered by the Hmong to be potentially dangerous to its host, and on the other hand, it is a mark of special powers to perceive and to enter trances, which are a prerequisite for the Hmong to enter into the realm of the unseen.

Both Western and the Hmong cultural beliefs have been constructed over many generations, and members of each culture believe that their perspective and the prescriptive care that follows from that worldview will provide for what is in Lia's best interest. The American doctors dismiss the Hmong views about care, as they think that Western views and practices are best for Lia and that their recommendations are based on the only true and objective way of knowing—science. Further, they struggle to make sure that they deliver the best medicine that they can. Their training has been entirely in the medical model, which is at the heart of the mechanistic metaphor from Table 13.1 in this chapter. It has not occurred to them that other legitimate ways of knowing exist, or even that context matters in determining what care Lia needs or in the way they view and behave toward Lia's parents. Their allegiance to mechanism and exclusion of contextualism (the metaphor that guides constructivism) leads to tragic results in the handling of Lia's case.

So as not to spoil it for those who want to read this poignant account of the clash of cultures that follows, these authors will not give away the plot entirely. The book serves as a passionate plea to the medical profession to develop an understanding of the cultural beliefs of immigrants who conceptualize health and the care of the body in totally different ways than Western medicine allows. Also illustrated in the book is the lack of cultural sensitivity shown by the child welfare system. Among one of the most sensitive constructivists, however, is a social worker that becomes trusted by this Hmong family clan, owing to her ability to discover the markers of their cultural constructions and to enter with them into the journey of their lives.

Contributions and Limitations

Traditional developmental theory emphasizes the individual person. Social work distinguishes itself by exploring the "person–environment fit." Most human behavior textbooks explore person and environment separately, with emphasis placed on the individual person. This approach assumes that the person holds the secret and primary responsibility for development. The social context, interactions and mutual inter-relationships between the "person in environment" is still de-emphasized in most texts. However, this is an area in social work where constructivism may prove supportive.

Social workers are showing an interest in theories, not only in psychology, but also in sociology, history, economics, philosophy, religion, world civilization, gay rights, ethnic and women's studies, gerontology, etc. This interest is part of the liberal arts tradition in social work, but it also represents a movement toward increased emphasis on understanding context and constructivist principles in the construction of knowledge. Theories, such as conflict theory, narrative theory, empowerment, feminist theory, multicultural theory explore context to a greater degree than do "traditional theories." Theories may become not only multilevel and multi-modal, but also more multidisciplinary. Such an emphasis increases the likelihood that diverse voices and points of view are integrated in social work theory and practice.

No doubt, constructivism will present limitations that cannot be foreseen. Some critics worry that constructivism encourages passivity or cynicism and thereby accelerates social atomization and personal malaise because it opens the door to relativism (Richardson & Franklin, 1996). It should be pointed out that the so-called "value-free" position required by positivists has its share of consequences in alienation, malaise, and cynicism; however, this is a serious concern, not to be dismissed lightly.

Relativism presents us with the possibility that every reality could be seen and treated as equally valid (e.g., "realities" of hate groups), and thus, all actions could be rendered defensible. What, then, would be the claim to say one point of view or social construction is preferable over another? Certainly, there are no guarantees that the awareness that we socially construct realities, relationships, and social forces will automatically create a better world. Conflict theorists accept that social "reality" is socially constructed, but they see it not as a limitation, but rather as an opportunity. They urge us to construct our actions and work toward goals to deliberately increase the possibility that action and outcome will be "constructed" to embrace values that optimize the appreciation of diverse "realities" and in struggles toward and celebrations of social justice.

Social work is a profession that commits itself to values and ethics that are established in the NASW Code of Ethics. One of the attributes of constructivism is its recognition that the fact–value dichotomy is false. Recognizing that can allow the purposeful integration of values and further encourage practitioners to construct a profession and professional knowledge that embodies the values and ethics that reflect the mission of social work. Saleebey (1990) identified four cornerstones of social work based on his assertion that, before the debate regarding epistemology can be settled in social work, the question regarding the identity of the profession must first be resolved. In other words, he recommends that social workers identify value and ethical positions that serve as principles to use as reference points for everything that social workers do, whether it is building knowledge, critiquing social forces, developing theories, or intervening. These cornerstones include indignation to injustice; inquiry that is participatory and that involves dialogue within community; compassion and caring; and social justice.

In appreciation and recognition of the benefits of human diversity, constructivists are more holistic, subjective, and qualitative in the pursuit of knowledge. As previously noted, constructivists recognize that much knowledge that passes as objective and universal represents the Truth of only a minority group—the powerful within the population (Gilligan, 1982; Habermas, 1975; Harding, 1991; Miller, 1991; Restivo, 1988; Rixecker, 1994). The elite group's inability to know the realities of others outside their group, or even to know that they do not know, has left them open to criticism. Constructivism represents the historical vehicle, within the social sciences generally and within social work in particular, through which submerged voices of diversity may emerge from the margins to be heard.

Sources for Further Study

Berger, Peter, & Luckman, Thomas. *The Social Construction of Reality: A Treatise in the Sociology of Knowledge.* Garden City, NY: Doubleday (1967). This classic details basic concepts of social construction and uses examples that illustrate ways in which social constructions limit our choices in making decisions for ourselves. At the same, it time points out ways in which we impact social constructions in one way or another.

Fadiman, Anne. *The Spirit Catches You and You Fall Down: A Hmong Child, Her American Doctors, and the Collision of Two Cultures.* New York: The Noonday Press (1997). This book serves as the case example in this chapter, but it should be on the required reading list for every social worker.

Freire, Paulo. *Pedagogy of the Oppressed.* New York: Continuum (1982). While recognizing ways in which oppression is constructed and maintained through the educational system, recommendations are made to socially construct an education that liberates.

Laird, Joan. (Ed.). *Revisioning Social Work Education: A Social Constructionist Approach.* New York: Haworth Press (1993). Applying constructivism to social work education, recommendations are made for incorporating this philosophy into the profession.

Rosen, Hugh, & Kuehlwein, Kevin T. *Constructing Realities: Meaning-Making Perspectives for Psychotherapists.* San Francisco: Jossey-Bass Publishers (1996). This book explores the use of constructivism in therapeutic settings.

Questions for Critical Thinking

1. What are at least five different ways that constructivism and constructivist frameworks can be used or understood? Discuss each approach.

2. What do knowledge and its construction have to do with diversity, oppression, and social injustice?

3. Why do constructivists make language, meanings, and dialogue such a focal point in creating relationships that are not oppressive? In fact, what do language, meanings, and dialogue have to do with oppression?

4. What are the four metaphors or meta-theories that were identified by philosopher Stephen Pepper, and how are social work theories categorized according to each?

5. What does it mean to have a sociological imagination?

References

Ballou, M. B. (1990). Approaching a feminist-principled paradigm in the construction of personality theory. In L. S. Brown & M. P. Root (Eds.). *Diversity and complexity in feminist therapy.* New York: Harrington Park Press.

Belenky, M. F., Clinchy, B. M., Goldberger, N. R., & Tarule, J. M. (1986). *Women's way of knowing: The development of self, voice and mind.* New York: Basic Books.

Berger, P., & Luckman, T. (1967). *The social construction of reality: A treatise in the sociology of knowledge.* Garden City, NY: Doubleday.

Carpenter, D. (1996). In F. J. Turner (Ed.). *Social work treatment: Interlocking theoretical approaches* (4th Ed.). New York: Free Press.

Chambon, A. S., Irving, A., & Epstein, L. (Eds.). (1999). *Reading Foucault for social work.* New York: Columbia University Press.

Cooley, C. H. (1964). *Human nature and the social order.* New York: Scribner's (Original work published 1902).

Davis, K. (1949). *Human society.* New York: Macmillan.

Dean, R. G. (1993). Teaching a constructivist approach to clinical practice. *Journal of Teaching in Social Work, 8*(1/2), 55–75.

Efran, J. S., Lukens, R. J., & Lukens, M. D. (1988). Constructivism: What's in it for you? *Networker,* 27–80.

Fadiman, A. (1997). *The spirit catches you and you fall down: A Hmong child, her American doctors, and the collision of two cultures.* New York: The Noonday Press.

Franks, V. (1986). Sex stereotyping and diagnosis in psychopathology. In D. Howard (Ed.). *A guide to dynamics of feminist therapy.* New York: Harrington Park Press.

Foucault, M. (1970). *The order of things.* New York: Pantheon Books.

Freire, P. (1973). *Pedagogy of the oppressed.* New York: Seabury Press.

Freire, P. (1982). *Education for critical consciousness.* New York: Continuum.

Freire, P. (1989). *Learning to question.* New York: Continuum.

Gadamer, H-G. (1975). *Truth and method.* New York: Continuum Press.

Gergen, K. J. (1999). *An invitation to social construction.* Thousand Oaks, CA: Sage Publications.

Giddens, A. (1978). In T. Bottomore & R. Nisbet (Eds.). *A history of sociological analysis.* New York: Basic Books.

Gilligan, C. (1982). *In a different voice.* Cambridge, MA: Harvard University Press.

Goffman, E. (1959). *The presentation of self in everyday life.* Garden City, NY: Doubleday.

Goffman, E. (1963a). *Asylums: Essays on the social situation of mental patients and other inmates.* Garden City, NY: Doubleday.

Goffman, E. (1963b). *Stigma: Notes on the management of spoiled identity.* Englewood Cliffs, NJ: Prentice-Hall.

Guadalupe, J. L. (2000). *The challenge: Development of a curriculum to address diversity content without perpetuating stereotypes.* Ann Arbor, MI: UMI company.

Habermas, J. (1971). *Knowledge and the human interest.* Boston: Beacon Press.

Habermas, J. (1975). *Legitimation crisis.* Boston: Beacon Press.

Harding, S. (1991). *Whose science? Whose knowledge? Thinking from women's lives.* Ithaca, NY: Cornell University Press.

Hartman, A. (1990). Many ways of knowing. *Social Work, 35*(1), 3–4.

Hutchison, E. D. (1999). *Dimensions of human behavior: Person and environment.* Thousand Oaks, CA: Pine Forge Press.

Jaggar, A. (1983). *Feminist politics and human nature.* Totowa, NJ: Rowman & Allanheld.

Jordan, C., & Franklin, C. (1995). *Clinical assessment for social workers: Quantitative and qualitative methods.* Chicago: Lyceum/Nelson Hall Books.

Kant, I. (1938). *The critique of pure reason.* Trans., N. K. Smith. New York: Macmillan.

Kelly, G. (1955). *The psychology of personal constructs* (2 vols.). New York: W. W. Norton.

Kelly, G. (1963). *A theory of personality: The psychology of personal constructs.* New York: W. W. Norton.

Kuhn, T. (1970). *The structure of scientific revolutions.* Chicago: University of Chicago Press.

Laird, J. (Ed.). (1993). *Revisioning social work education: A social constructionist approach.* New York: Haworth Press.

Lincoln, Y. S., & Guba, E. G. (1985). *Naturalistic inquiry.* Thousand Oaks, CA: Sage.

Lyddon, W. J. (1987). Emerging views of health: A challenge to rationalist doctrines of medical thought. *The Journal of Mind and Behavior, 8*(3), 365–393.

Lyddon, W. J. (1989). Root metaphor theory: A philosophical framework for counseling and psychotherapy. *Journal of Counseling and Development, 5*(67), 442–448.

Maher, B. (1969). *Clinical psychology and personality: The selected papers of George Kelly.* New York: John Wiley & Sons.

McCarthy, T. (1981). *The critical theory of Jurgen Habermas.* Cambridge, MA: MIT Press.

Mead, G. H. (1968). *Mind, self and society.* Chicago: University of Chicago Press.

Miller, J. B. (1986). *Toward a new psychology of women.* Boston: Beacon Press.

Miller, J. B. (1991). The development of women's sense of self. In J. Jordan, A. Kaplan, J. B. Miller, I. Stiver, and J. Surrey. *Women's growth in connection: Writings from the Stone Center.* New York: Guilford Press.

Mills, C. W. (1959). *The sociological imagination.* New York: Oxford Press.

Neimeyer, R. A. (1993). An appraisal of constructivist psychotherapies. *Journal of Consulting and Clinical Psychology, 61*(2), 221–234.

Pepper, S. C. (1942). *World hypotheses: A study in evidence.* Berkeley: University of California Press.

Restivo, S. (1988). Modern science as a social problem. *Social Problems, 35*(3), 206–225.

Richardson, F., & Franklin, C. (1998). In S. P. Robbins, P. Chatterjee, & E. R. Canda (Eds.). *Contemporary human behavior theory: A critical perspective for social work.* Boston: Allyn & Bacon.

Rixecker, S. S. (1994). Expanding the discursive context of policy design: A matter of feminist standpoint epistemology. *Policy Sciences, 27,* 119–142.

Rosen, H., and Kuehlwein, K. T. (1996). *Constructing realities: Meaning-making perspectives for psychotherapists.* San Francisco: Jossey-Bass Publishers.

Ryan, W. (1971). *Blaming the victim.* New York: Vintage Books.

Saleebey, D. (1990). Philosophical disputes in social work: Social justice denied. *Journal of Sociology and Social Welfare, 17*(2), 29–40.

Saleebey, D. (1994). Culture, theory, and narrative: The intersection of meanings in practice. *Social Work, 39*(4), 351–359.

Saleebey, D. (1996). The strengths perspective in social work practice: Extensions and cautions. *Social Work, 4*(3), 284–294.

Schriver, J. M. (2001). *Human behavior and the social environment: Shifting paradigms in essential knowledge for social work practice.* Boston: Allyn & Bacon.

Szasz, T. S. (1961). *The myth of mental illness: Foundations of a theory of personal conduct.* New York: Harper and Row Publishers.

Turner, F. J. (Ed.). (1996). *Social work treatment: Interlocking theoretical approaches* (4th ed.). New York: The Free Press

Van Den Bergh, N. (Ed.). (1995). *Feminist practice in the 21st century.* Washington, DC: NASW Press.

Watzlawick, P. (Ed.). (1984). *The invented reality.* New York: W. W. Norton.

Part VII

Curricular and Other Implications

14

Diversity Inclusion Models and the Social Work Curriculum

Dr. Santos Torres Jr.

The Council on Social Work Education (CSWE), the national accrediting body for undergraduate and graduate social work programs, in their Curriculum Policy Statement for Master's (and Baccalaureate) Degree Programs in Social Work Education establishes

> Professional social work education is committed to preparing students to understand and appreciate human diversity. Programs must provide curriculum content about differences and similarities in the experiences, needs, and beliefs of people. The curriculum must include content about differential assessment and intervention skills that will enable practitioners to serve diverse populations.
>
> Each program is required to include content about population groups that are particularly relevant to the program's mission. These include, but are not limited to, groups distinguished by race, ethnicity, culture, class, gender, sexual orientation, religion, physical or mental disability, age, and national origin. (CPS B6.4 & M6.6)

While the standard mandates content be included, CSWE does not dictate a specific approach a program must adhere to in delivering this important content. Additionally, there are various pedagogical interpretations on how to achieve the standard ranging from integration to infusion, where diversity content would saturate every aspect of the program in the former to some elements of a program being designed to act as a vehicle in the provision of this content in the latter. However programs approach the matter of interpretation, reasoned consideration of factors such as its capacity to provide diversity content in terms of faculty, student composition, field placement opportunities, etc., must be addressed as a program seeks to meet the requirement.

For purposes of this discussion, the term *curriculum* is broadly defined and includes subject matter and content areas of social work and training; a plan of action (written or unwritten) that includes strategies for achieving desired goals; learner activities directed by program personnel (in and out of the classroom); and an orientation that informs the content, goals, and the organization of the curriculum.

Like all professional education programs, social work is assumed to engage in an ongoing process of curricular development, implementation, and evaluation (Eisner & Vallance, 1974; Ornstein & Hunkins, 1988; Tyler, 1949). These curricular-related processes and activities are influenced by the accreditation standards of the Council on Social Work Education, which establishes the procedures of accreditation. Further, these processes are greatly influenced by the values, beliefs, and preferences of the personnel administering the social work programs. Such an assumption places the emphasis on a particular program's freedom to choose among a variety of curricular models toward the inclusion of diversity content.

Explanations for the Growing Interest in Diversity-Content Inclusion

That diversity-related content has enjoyed such a surge in interest can be attributed to at least three causes, among others. The first is a result of the changing racial and ethnic composition of the United States as well as the reciprocal effects of demographics with sociopolitical and socioeconomic changes (Deyoe, 1977; Horner & Borrero, 1981; Jackson, 1981). A second explanation points to changes in the focus of policies and programs of the human services system in the United States (e.g., the growth of community-based mental health agencies and the realization of financial and social costs associated with whole segments of society being left underserved (Bernall & Padilla, 1985; Jackson, 1981; Lonner, 1985; Wyatt & Parham, 1985). Finally, a third explanation emphasizes changes in the policies, curriculum standards, educational practices, and research interests of educational training institutions preparing helping professionals (e.g., growing diversity among faculty teaching and doing research on human diversity as well as standards of accrediting organizations such as the American Psychological Association, Council of Accreditation of Counseling and Related Educational Programs, and Council on Social Work Education) (Corvin & Wiggins, 1989; Mio, 1989; McDavis & Parker, 1977; Schlesinger & Devore, 1979; Wyatt & Parham, 1985).

Models for Inclusion of Diversity Content

There have been a number of scholarly efforts on educational approaches, models, and programs for the inclusion of diversity content. Corvin & Wiggins (1989), in their earlier review of the professional education approaches to diversity inclusion, identified some common factors.

As result of the increased awareness of multicultural concerns . . . numerous approaches for training effective multicultural counselors have been proposed . . . and . . . share the following characteristics:

1. A basic assumption that an individual's ethnic or cultural ground significantly influences his or her worldview and the way in which he or she experiences and understands life and its problems.
2. An emphasis on learning about various cultural groups (i.e., cultural worldviews) so that there is some understanding of how an individual from a particular group may experience life and its problems.
3. A focus on teaching helping skills and interventions appropriate for use with members of various ethnic groups. (p. 105)

This chapter has two goals. The first is to introduce a diversity-content-inclusion framework, comprised of four approaches particularly relevant to social work education. These approaches have been labeled Primacy, Equity, Dependency, and Enrichment-Only. They are conceptualized as points along a continuum suggesting distinct forms of diversity-content inclusion in social work programs (see Appendix A). The terms *primacy, equity, dependency*, and *enrichment-only* are used to emphasize the position of diversity framework and content relative to other components of the curriculum. The second purpose of this chapter is to suggest program goals and strategies for the inclusion of diversity content in social work programs.

The continuum was developed from consideration of existing social work programs as well as diversity-content-inclusion models found in the literature. This chapter presents information on all four approaches in order that social work programs and students are able to generate a profile of where a particular program is in terms of their current diversity-content-inclusion practices as well as the strengths and limitations of a given diversity-content-inclusion approach.

The Primacy Approach

This approach is labeled "primacy" since it is understood as having the dominant or lead influence over the form and substance of the other curriculum components. The inclusion of content and instructional activities on diversity are viewed as having central relevance in the preparation of the professional social worker.

Under the primacy approach, the program's organizational structure and processes are all geared toward graduating human-diversity social work specialists. A program following a primacy approach might position diversity content as a specialized area of study or concentration. All students would be required to successfully complete and master this specialized content.

This approach involves an organized sequence of academic and training experiences designed to provide students with a thorough grounding in theory and practice that is cast within a framework of knowledge, values, and skills associated with the delivery of culturally effective and sensitive services. Programs employing a primacy approach would extend this requirement to field instruction and/or practicum training which would, by design, involve learning opportunities and training sites where exposure to and supervision in culturally relevant and sensitive knowledge, skills, and values would be central to the student intern's learning activities.

The preferred orientation in this approach would view the goal of intergroup relations to be ongoing (multiethnic, multiracial, multisocioeconomic, etc.) interaction and transactional assimilation within and between society's subcultures. The program would prepare students to effectively operate as professional helpers by utilizing foundation diversity frameworks as well as utilizing both the intracultural and cross-cultural and etic and emic perspectives.

The program's own educational mission, objectives, requirements, and outcome measures would be highly congruent with that interpretation of diversity accreditation standards and reflect a clearly articulated commitment to advance a diversity-oriented philosophy of education and training. Variations on this primacy approach are programs that require student participation in aspects of a diversity specialization or as requirements to complete along with one or more specializations.

The Equity Approach

Programs utilizing an equity approach deliver diversity content through required course offerings such as theory and practice methods in working with diverse populations. These courses would actually be part of a core sequence (e.g., practice with individuals, families, and groups) that constitutes a larger non-diversity-related curriculum component. In this sense, diversity content represents a pivot point. While perhaps considered a component with equal importance in the program's foundation curriculum, these courses enjoy a superordinate status relative to elective course offerings, which are viewed primarily as optional enrichment learning experiences. Programs adopting this approach would likely emphasize the need for students to have diversity content learning opportunities as part of their field instruction or practicum training but not necessarily require or judge training sites as inadequate where such learning was not the primary emphasis.

The preferred orientation in this approach would view the goal of intergroup relations to be the maintenance of subculture groups within one common economic/political system. The program would prepare the student by emphasizing the development of knowledge, skills, and values that would best align with the cross-cultural and etic perspectives while simultaneously grounding the student's knowledge in traditional theory and research.

The equity approach would be informed by diversity accreditation standards focused on competence in the area of human diversity, rather than specializing in human diversity. The curriculum would reflect a more global commitment to exploration and understanding of diversity-related concerns and their implications for practice. Variations on this approach, but still in keeping with its central propositions, would be programs that utilize course offerings outside the discipline as required in fulfilling degree requirements.

The Dependency Approach

In the dependency approach, diversity-content inclusion is clearly subordinate to the more traditional social work foundation curriculum components or even individual course offerings in this approach. It is couched within the framework of traditional foundation courses and provided via learning modules or highly compartmentalized class sessions related to diversity concerns. Inclusion of diversity content under this approach assumes that traditional paradigms, theories, and practice methods used with the majority culture are adaptable and generally adequate, thereby making coverage of diversity content incidental and/or supplemental in nature. Field instruction and/or practicum training would not consider diversity-content-based learning opportunities essential.

The preferred orientation in this approach would view the goal of intergroup relations to be respect for the coexistence of distinct and separate societal subcultures. Students would be prepared for practice as professional helpers through the emphasis of the more traditional theory and research. Intracultural and emic perspectives would be introduced as auxiliary knowledge if deemed applicable.

The program's selection and implementation of the dependency approach would be informed by an interpretation of diversity-content-inclusion accreditation standards that is vague, ambiguous, or general at best. The program's mission, educational objectives, requirements, and outcome measures would reflect the assumption that diversity content is to be informed by and subordinate to the goals of a more traditional curriculum.

Variations on this approach, but still in keeping with its central propositions, might include elective courses within the program's curriculum or even outside program course offerings as a mechanism of supplementing the student's social work training.

The Enrichment-Only Approach

As the name implies, programs adopting this approach would either approach it from a strictly student-training enrichment-only perspective or omit this content as required for competent practice. Students might participate in workshops or seminars to obtain diversity content. Traditional paradigms, theories, and practice methods used with majority culture systems are not seen as requiring modification for use with culturally diverse populations. Further, such curricular or training adaptations would be presumed unnecessary since host culture knowledge, values, and skills are held as completely adequate or perhaps inherently superior; so, therefore, are to be assimilated by minority culture systems. Like the "dependency" approach, one operating assumption of programs employing this model is that diversity content is truly subordinate to any other curriculum offering. Field instruction and/or practicum training experiences, as well as site selection for them, would be based on criteria other than diversity content training opportunities they might engender.

The preferred educational philosophy or orientation in this approach would view the goal of intergroup relations to be host-society conforming. Neither intra/cross-cultural nor etic/emic perspectives would be viewed as particularly relevant to preparing students. Traditional paradigms, theories, and practice methods used with majority culture systems are seen as not requiring modification in providing service to diverse cultures. Further, such curricular or training adaptations would be presumed unnecessary since the host culture is viewed as inherently superior; therefore, other cultural systems are expected to assimilate.

The program's own educational objectives and outcome measures might give brief mention to diversity content; however, it would generally exclude this from serious consideration. Such a program would be at great risk of being out of compliance within diversity-content accreditation standards.

Variations on this approach, but still in keeping with its central propositions, might include regularly scheduled programmatic offerings or sponsorship of diversity-content-related workshops, seminars, and/or colloquia might be made available but would not be required of students.

A Curriculum Guide toward Diversity-Content Inclusion

This curriculum guide for the inclusion of diversity in the preparation of social workers identifies an educational philosophy, a set of educational goals, educational experiences and training activities, curricular organization, and system of evaluation, which is oriented toward maximizing the inclusion of diversity content in student learning.

The educational philosophy of the proposed model curriculum guide borrows from two of five curriculum orientations offered by Eisner and Vallance (1974). They labeled these curricular orientations self-actualization and social reconstructionalism. It is the emphasis on content and learner role that makes these perspectives particularly applicable in this chapter.

As an approach to planning a curriculum, the self-actualization orientation places great stock in what is being taught; or, simply put, the curriculum is used to deliver content. According to Eisner and Vallance, the learner is also an important feature of this particular orientation. Education is seen as a facilitative process that promotes growth, autonomous development, and personal liberation in the student and enters into the very life of the learner. The educational enterprise and its vehicle for realization, the curriculum, are validated through this process of learning in context.

The second approach to curriculum thought particularly relevant to the proposed model curriculum guide views the institution of education as an agency of social change. This social change refers to both personal and societal change. Personal change, part of what is termed "adaptive social reconstructionism," involves preparing students to cope with the vagaries and instability of society. Students are to be given, through the content and processes of the curriculum, the necessary tools to adapt and survive in an ever-rapidly-changing societal context. The other brand of social reconstructionism uses the curriculum to produce social change agents. Here the goal of curriculum is to prepare the students to directly impact the social context within which they must operate.

Both the self-actualization and the social reconstructionist curriculum orientations best match the general goals of diversity education as articulated by Banks (1981), which are (a) to familiarize members of various ethnic groups with the unique culture of other groups and to develop an appreciation of other cultures as possessing value and meaningfulness equivalent to their own culture, (b) to provide students with cultural and ethnic alternatives, (c) to provide students with knowledge, values, and skills for functioning within and across multiple cultural contexts including those of their own ethnic culture, other ethnic cultures, and the cultural context of the host culture, (d) to reduce the effects of oppression and discrimination faced by students from some ethnic and racial groups because of their unique racial, ethnic, and cultural characteristics.

These curricular orientations, or philosophies, also fit very well with the definition of an emerging curriculum (Ornstein & Hunkins, 1988). An emerging curriculum is one that is currently evolving or has done so in the recent past. It contributes new content and areas of study that are innovative and reflect current social and political changes. It takes a learner- and values-oriented approach in its implementation. Implementation of diversity content in social work programs necessitates innovative strategies that are educational, political, and relationship building in nature.

Educational Standards, Purposes, and Goals of the Ideal Diversity-Content-Inclusive Social Work Program

The central agenda of the proposed model curriculum presented in this chapter is directed toward maximizing the inclusion of diversity content and learning experiences in preparing social workers. This curriculum guide articulates two different sets of goals: student-oriented and program-oriented.

Student-Oriented Goals

Student-oriented goals are those curriculum goals that specify expectations that students would be required to meet as a function of the preparation they received in the model program. Students would be prepared to value human diversity, to suspend personal bias and prejudice when working with diverse populations, and to increase a sense of comfort when working with diverse populations. As a result of the curriculum, students would

- work with diverse populations in a variety of contexts and settings;
- make accurate analyses and handle complex information about diverse populations such as the role and impact of culture in the lives of clients;
- function as effective helpers despite limitations in their knowledge of diverse populations;
- recognize and use the client/social worker interaction as a vital source of information for learning about diverse populations;
- demonstrate their skills and knowledge in working with diverse populations prior to graduation; and
- recognize the dual nature of their role in modern society as encompassing membership in a group or groups of those who are oppressed as well as membership in a group or groups of those contributing to the oppression of others.

Program-Oriented Goals

Program-oriented goals are those that identify expectations to be met by the diversity-content inclusive social work program as a whole. The program would

- complete an honest assessment of its goals, theoretical orientation, and educational philosophy regarding the preparation of professional social workers and would clearly articulate these goals to prospective students;
- have a well integrated and complementary set of diversity-oriented educational goals that are held by cooperating agencies and organizations serving as internship sites for the program's students;

- select and utilize cooperating agencies and organizations to be used as internship sites for the program's students that are able to provide diverse client populations as a regular part of students' caseloads;
- provide a strong sense of community, inside and outside of the classroom, that encourages comfortable involvement and participation by every member, and groups of members, in the program environment;
- demonstrate responsibility for the inclusion of diversity content in the program through assignment of the monitoring function to a member of the program faculty in order to insure the inclusion of this content; and
- actively include language and symbols, reflective of diversity, in institution-wide communication to raise the consciousness and awareness of diversity of those coming in contact with the program and institution.

Learning Experiences and Activities of the Ideal Diversity-Content-Inclusive Social Work Program

A program's educational activities are the means by which the curricular agenda is achieved. The learning and training experiences recommended in this guide reflect a developmental approach to diversity knowledge, skills, and values. The experiences and activities are intended for both students and faculty. Students would be required to

- participate in pre-training and early assessment activities designed to (a) increase their understanding of natural helping skills they possess that brought them to the field of social work, (b) cause the students to assess their comfort with diversity, and (c) engage the students in a safe environment where they can interact with others in exploring their own values, feelings, and attitudes about diversity;
- develop a set of diversity learning activities of their own choosing and design;
- participate in a series of practicum and internship training experiences (a rotation of internships) over the course of their training;
- engage in summer field placements and experiential labs focused on development of diversity skills employing a learning-by-doing approach;
- be concurrently enrolled in diversity-oriented coursework and internships to facilitate the integration of experience with affective and cognitive development;
- be matched with community-based mentors and participate in community sponsored and organized cultural events;
- interact with representatives of various cultural groups from the community brought into the classroom as outside resources;
- be exposed to a real representation of diverse faculty and students;
- participate in cultural-immersion experiences involving students in both counseling and non-counseling related activities;
- enroll in didactic coursework taught from various cultural perspectives;
- participate in program-sponsored research to study what culturally effective practitioners do that makes them effective in working with diverse populations to help close the gap between theory and practice;

- be supervised in internship settings serving diverse populations by social work professionals representative of various ethnic/cultural groups; and
- receive training experiences with diverse populations in a university-created in-house clinic serving diverse populations.

Program faculty would be required to

- participate in cultural-immersion experiences, after which the faculty members would return to the program to share and process their learning with colleagues and students;
- participate in developmental workshops and training related to diversity issues as a means of helping them learn ways to include diversity material in courses they teach.

Both students and program faculty would participate in program-sponsored activities focused particularly on relationship and sense-of-community building within various diverse groups and between those groups.

Curriculum Organization of the Ideal Diversity-Content-Inclusive Social Work Program

The following are recommended options for the organization of the educational experiences and training activities of a model preparing social work students for diversity practice. The issue of curricular organization is seen as being comprised of (1) how to prioritize diversity content and learning experiences; and (2) how to position diversity content relative to the rest of the curriculum.

Prioritization Options

1. Educational experiences and training activities would be given equal importance, and both would be provided simultaneously.
2. Immersion experiences would be engaged in first, ahead of all other educational experiences and training activities.
3. Self-awareness and other-awareness educational experiences and training activities would be engaged in first, followed by cultural-knowledge development and then diversity-skills development.
4. A long-term plan for the gradual phasing in of educational activities and training experiences would include the following priorities:
   a) recruiting faculty who are diversity oriented in order to establish tone of overall importance of diversity in program;
   b) student recruitment involving a proactive and creative approach to bring under-represented students into the social work field;
   c) curricular modification that employs an add-on course, and diversity-content inclusion in existing courses;
   d) student and programmatic support efforts to directly address the needs and issues of minority students in particular;

e) faculty development in the area of diversity awareness and sensitivity, as well as support for including such content and knowledge in their courses;

f) continued support and recognition of diversity-oriented research being an acceptable and a legitimate area for faculty and graduate students in which to engage; and

g) an ongoing process through which social work programs initiate their own sense of what it takes to be successful.

5. Faculty diversity-awareness training would be engaged in first, ahead of all other educational experiences and training activities.

6. Program commitment to diversity and a diverse faculty would be engaged in first, ahead of all other educational experiences and training activities.

7. Development of a sense of community among all program constituencies would precede all other educational experiences and training activities.

8. Diversity courses would precede any advanced training coursework among the educational experiences and training activities.

Relative Position Options

1. *The Infusion and Saturation Approach:* Diversity content and training would infuse and saturate the curriculum to the extent that it would act as an important programmatic thrust, which would influence and be influenced by the rest of the curriculum.

2. *The Diversity-Content Centered Approach:* Diversity content and training would act as the program's theoretical and philosophical core and represent the central curriculum component that influenced all others.

3. *The Interdependent Curriculum Approach:* Diversity content and training would be one of many curriculum components that would have reciprocal impact on each other.

4. *The Diversity Specialist Degree Approach:* Diversity content and training would represent both part and parcel of this social work program's curriculum.

5. *The Diversity Menu Approach:* Diversity content and training would be included in the curriculum as a menu of courses along a continuum of curricular inclusion options.

6. *The Infusion, Free-Standing Courses, and Program-Monitoring Approach:* Diversity content and training would be offered in a combination of infusion into content of existing courses, the offering of specific courses on social work with diverse populations, and authority and oversight responsibility would be vested in the program faculty.

7. *The Specialty-Courses Approach:* Diversity content and training would be provided as independent courses within the traditional curriculum offerings of the social work program.

8. *The Coursework and University-Wide Diversity Experience Opportunities Approach:* Diversity content and training would be provided through the provision of an independent course on diversity social work within the traditional curriculum offerings, and there would be additional university-wide organized and sponsored diversity-related workshops or events.

Evaluating the Educational Experiences and Training Activities of the Ideal Diversity-Content-Inclusive Social Work Program

Evaluation of a program brings the proposed curriculum guide full circle. Evaluation is the means by which a program is able to assess the degree to which the goals, educational, and training activities and curricular organization of a program come into congruence and can be used in further refinements. The following are recommended general strategies for evaluating a social work program's diversity inclusion efforts. The reader should note that not only student progress and development on the matter of diversity are to be evaluated, but so, too, is the overall program. This means that while well-trained professional social workers are a desired end, the program must be evaluated for its efficacy as a means to that end. Diversity content inclusion educational activities and training experiences would be evaluated by

- using existing methods of evaluation such as examinations, standardized assessment tools, and other mechanical means;
- using qualitative methods such as formal and informal faculty interviews and journal writing;
- using methods of direct and indirect supervision;
- using multiple sources of data including client and consumer feedback;
- using the first year of the program as a probationary period;
- using both formative and summative evaluation methods;
- determining the degree to which faculty include elements of multiculturalism in courses they teach;
- interviewing graduating social workers;
- determining the extent to which student outcomes match with program expectations;
- determining the level of student participation in cultural learning activities outside the classroom;
- using student input in the evaluation process; and
- using existing standards of the social work profession.

Conclusions

Arguably, all social work programs should be held to a standard that requires graduates to be, at minimum, human-diversity aware, but it would be an unreasonable expectation that all programs produce graduates who are experts in human diversity. Therefore, the overarching goal of a social work program may range from producing graduates who are human-diversity specialists, or human-diversity competent, or at least human-diversity aware. Many of the proposed recommendations are presumably in operation in social work programs across the United States; many are probably not. The hope is that the information provided here would be useful in prompting open discussion and action on the part of students and faculty working toward the inclusion of diversity content and learning experiences in preparing social workers.

Questions for Critical Thinking _____

1. Considering the primacy, equity, dependency and enrichment-only models for diversity-content inclusion discussed in this chapter, which would you identify as the most applicable in characterizing your social work program? Discuss your rationale, and provide supportive evidence and examples.

2. Should accreditation bodies such as the Council on Social Work Education require social work programs to include more or less content on diversity? Discuss your position and rationale.

3. What impact do you believe a diverse student body and faculty would have on the quality of education social work programs are able to deliver?

4. How do you think social work programs should measure student competency in the area of working with diverse populations?

5. Identify two or three diversity-related learning experiences you would like to see as part of your social work program.

Sources for Further Study _____

Ben, David, A., and Dalia, Amit. Do We Have to Teach Them to Be Culturally Sensitive? The Israeli Experience. *International Social Work, 42*(3), 347–358, 1999. A study was conducted to investigate cultural sensitivity among students of social work education in Israel. Data were drawn from three hundred thirty-four social work students in two social work programs who were screened for prejudice and cultural sensitivity. Findings revealed that social work education in Israel does not orient students toward reducing prejudice or enhancing their cultural sensitivity. A weak association between prejudice, cultural sensitivity, and gender was found to emerge during the third year of studies.

Dungee Anderson, D., and Beckett, J. O. A Process Model for Multicultural Social Work Practice. *Families in Society, 76*, 459–468, 1995. The authors discuss the first three steps of an eight-step communication process model designed to help social workers become effective multicultural practitioners. Introduced are Type 1 and Type 2 practice errors that cause failed communication and unsuccessful multicultural intervention. The three steps of the model are (1) acknowledge cultural differences, (2) know yourself, and (3) know other cultures. A multicultural case is presented to identify and analyze Type 1 and 2 errors in the worker–client relationship and in supervisor–worker interactions.

Forte, J. A. Culture: The Tool-Kit Metaphor and Multicultural Social Work. *Families in Society, 80*(1), 51–62, 1999. Swidler "tool-kit" metaphor is a resource for understanding culture and its influence. Concepts and propositions related to tools, tool kits, strategies of action, social frameworks for action, the continuum of tool awareness, and settled/unsettled social circumstances are summarized. The approach is compared to the culture as a values framework. Farkas's application of this cultural resources model to at-risk, ethnically diverse students and their families is summarized.

Gant, L. M. Are Culturally Sophisticated Agencies Better Workplaces for Social Work Staff and Administrators? *Social Work, 41*, 163–171, 1996. Using the concept of cultural sophistication, data from two hundred eighty-five African American social workers and administrators were analyzed to demonstrate what effect the perception of agency cultural sophistication has on reports of psychological and work-related stress. Among African American workers, perceptions of cultural sophistication had a significant effect in many areas of work stress, but not with reported psychological problems. For African American supervisors and administrators, a moderate effect was identified between cultural sophistication and decreases in work-related stress. The usefulness of cultural sophistication as an explanatory variable in understanding staff perceptions of occupational and psychological stress in human services organizations is discussed.

Goldberg, M. Conflicting Principles in Multicultural Social Work. *Families in Society, 81*(1), 12–21, 2000. The starting point for social work approaches to multicultural issues is the principle of respect for human diversity. But practice issues concerning multiculturalism and the role of ethnicity in patterns of oppression have revealed that current interpretations and applications of the principle of respect for human diversity often result in self-contradictions and conflicts with other social work principles. This paper describes three of these conflicts, and, drawing on the literature of cultural anthropology, ethnic-sensitive social work, and constructivism, proposes several conceptualizations to eliminate or manage them. The conflicts discussed are (1) respect for the contents of all cultures versus support for basic human rights, (2) an inability to understand the needs and views of people from different cultural backgrounds versus a mission to practice social work, and (3) the social worker's right to ethnic preference versus the social worker's obligation to eliminate personal cultural bias and prejudice. Conceptualizations proposed to deal with these conflicts include unconditional ethnic esteem, qualified cultural equality, right to ethnic identity, and reality and limitations of multicultural competence. Reprinted by permission of the publisher.

Gould, K. H. The Misconstruing of Multiculturalism: The Stanford Debate and Social Work. *Social Work, 40*, 198–205, 1995. The article discusses how the current social discourse on multiculturalism represents one of the most acrimonious public exchanges on the subject. Even the social work field has been polarized. This article asks if the profession, with its long-term commitment to cultural diversity, has any better grasp of the complex and subtle dimensions of the concept of multiculturalism than the recent participants in the controversy at Stanford University. The article examines the definition of multiculturalism in the literature on intercultural communication that provides the rationale for an alternative model. The author uses this perspective to evaluate social work's history in implementing a multicultural curriculum. Similarities in conceptual dilemmas suggest that a first step in developing a meaningful dialogue might be a paradigmatic shift from viewing multiculturalism as merely a practice extension of a minority perspective to viewing it as a framework that can help all groups in society orient their thinking at a transcultural level.

Hyde, C. A Model for Diversity Training in Human Service Agencies. *Administration in Social Work, 22*(4), 19–33, 1998. The need for diversity has been widely embraced in human services agencies. A variety of strategies are used to help make organizational diversity a reality. Largely missing from the literature, however, is a comprehensive model for diversity training in the human services. The author presents such a model, derived from interviews with thirty practitioners in and consultants for human service diversity. The model's core values, goals, and interventions, all of which are presented, reflect a synthesis of mainstream and social justice approaches to organizational diversity.

Lee, M. Y. A Constructivist Approach to the Help-Seeking Process of Clients: A Response to Cultural Diversity. *Clinical Social Work Journal, 24*, 187–202, 1996. The issue of cultural diversity presents clinicians with both dilemmas and opportunities. To deal with such a challenge, I have proposed a constructivist approach to the help-seeking process of clients from diverse ethnoracial backgrounds. A model of clients' help-seeking processes provides a useful and systematic frame for clinicians to understand clients' construction of their problem situations and possible solutions. It provides a useful key for clinicians to non-presumptuously understand clients' subjective experiences and to enhance clients' ability to resolve problems.

Potocky, M. Multicultural Social Work in the United States: A Review and Critique. *International Social Work, 40*, 315–326, 1997. The writer charts the history of multicultural social work in the United States, from early assimilation approaches in work with immigrants to the present emphasis on culturally sensitive practices. She contends that the current model is limited in the face of rising racism and neo-assimilation ideology, arguing that the model should be expanded to target racism, prejudice, and ethnocentrism among all members of society. In conclusion, she considers the national and international implications of such an expanded model.

Sachdev, P. Cultural Sensitivity Training through Experiential Learning: A Participatory Demonstration Field Education Project. *International Social Work, 40*, 7–25, 1997. The writer describes a pilot project involving four undergraduate social work students from an eastern Canadian university who spent eight weeks in New Delhi, India, in 1994 in order to gain knowledge and sensitivity toward cultural diversity in social work practice. He measures the learning outcomes phenomenologically using self-reports of the students, direct observation, and an attitudinal checklist administered prior to and following the sojourn. He reveals that all but one student demonstrated positive change in their attitudes and gained a better appreciation for the other culture.

References

Banks, J. A. (1981). *Multiethnic education: Theory and practice.* Boston: Allyn & Bacon.

Corvin, S. A., & Wiggins, F. (1989). An antiracism training model for white professionals. *Journal of Multicultural Counseling and Development, 17,* 104–114.

Deyoe, R. M. (1977). Theory as practice in multicultural education. *Educational Horizons,* 181–183.

Eisner, E. W., & Vallance, E. (Eds.). (1974). *Conflicting conceptions of curriculum.* Berkeley: McCutchan Publishing Corporation.

Horner, W., & Borrero, M. (1981). A planning matrix for standard 1234A. *Journal of Education for Social Work, 17*(1), 36–43.

Jackson, A. C. (1981). A model of social work education for multicultural practice in Great Britain. *Journal of Education for Social Work, 17*(1), 102–110.

Lonner, W. J. (1985). Issues in testing and assessment in cross-cultural counseling. *Counseling Psychologist, 13*(4), 599–614.

McDavis, R. J., & Parker, W. M. (1977). A course on counseling ethnic minorities: A model. *Counselor Education and Supervision, 17,* 146–148.

Mio, J. S. (1989). Experiential involvement as an adjunct to teaching cultural sensitivity. *Journal of Multicultural Counseling and Development, 17,* 39–46.

Ornstein, A. C., & Hunkins, F. P. (1988). *Curriculum: Foundations, principles, and issues.* New Jersey: Prentice-Hall.

Schlesinger, E. G., & Devore, W. (1979). Social workers view ethnic minority teaching. *Journal of Education for Social Work,* 20–27.

Tyler, R. W. (1949). *Basic principles of curriculum and instruction.* Chicago: University of Chicago Press.

Wyatt, G. E., & Parham, W. D. (1985). The inclusion of culturally sensitive course materials in graduate school and training programs. *Psychotherapy, 22*(2), 461–468.

Appendix A

Approaches to Diversity-Content Inclusions

Primacy Approach

Diversity content and training operates as the program's theoretical, philosophical, and practice core and represents the central curriculum component that influences all others. Diversity content would saturate the entire curriculum and be fully integrated throughout every aspect of the degree program.

Through this approach, diversity-content inclusion is achieved through a curriculum *saturation* strategy. Traditional curriculum components such as Practice, HBSE, Research, Social Policy, and Field Instruction would all be designed, implemented, and evaluated on the basis of how well diversity-content inclusion was addressed. The program would focus on the vertical and horizontal integration of diversity content.

Under this approach, the program might offer a diversity social work specialist degree.

Equity Approach

Diversity content and training would be one of many curriculum components, which have reciprocal impact and influence on each other. Diversity content would be infused throughout the curriculum to the extent that it would act as an important programmatic thrust in many, if not most, curricular areas.

Through this approach, diversity-content inclusion is achieved through a curriculum *infusion* strategy. Traditional curriculum components such as Practice, HBSE, Research, Social Policy, and Field Instruction would all be designed, implemented, and evaluated as potential areas for the inclusion of diversity content.

Under this approach, the program might have required course(s) on diversity and/or place special importance on reflecting diversity content across various areas of the curriculum.

Dependency Approach

Diversity content and training would be delivered in the curriculum through a choice or menu of course(s) offered through a range of educational options.

Through this approach, diversity-content inclusion is achieved through a curriculum *isolation* strategy. Traditional curriculum components such as Practice, HBSE, Research, Social Policy, and Field Instruction would all be designed, implemented, and evaluated as separate from the inclusion of diversity content.

Under this approach, the program might require independent diversity-related course offerings for a specific category of social work student and make them elective for others (e.g., practice- vs. policy-concentration students); or offer elective diversity-related course(s) that are not social work course(s) per se (e.g., Family and Culture, or History of Ethnic Minorities in America); or diversity-content inclusion is addressed through university-wide offerings such as special seminars, workshops, or events. The latter of these options might best be described as an enrichment-only approach.

Enrichment-Only Approach

Diversity content and training would be delivered in a strictly enrichment-only basis, and/or this content would be omitted entirely.

Through this approach, diversity-content inclusion is achieved through a curriculum *omission* strategy. Like the "dependency" approach, one operating assumption of programs employing this model is that diversity content is truly subordinate, if necessary at all, to any other curriculum offering. Traditional curriculum components such as Practice, HBSE, Research, Social Policy, and Field Instruction would all be designed, implemented, and evaluated as adequate without the inclusion of diversity content.

Under this approach, the program might encourage students to participate in elective social and non-social work courses, workshops, or seminars in order to obtain diversity content.

Determining a Program's Preferred Diversity-Content Inclusion Approach

Profile Criteria	*Primacy Approach*	*Equity Approach*	*Dependency Approach*	*Enrichment-Only Approach*
Status of diversity-content inclusion relative to other curricular components	Superordinate (Central)	Subordinate (Pivotal)	Subordinate (Supplemental)	Subordinate (Strictly Enrichment)
Structural characteristics of diversity-content inclusion in curriculum	Stand-Alone Curriculum Component	Subcurricular component	Course-by-course curricular inclusion	Non-existent or available as extracurricular option
Preferred educational philosophy toward intergroup relations	Multiculturalism	Cultural Pluralism	Structural Pluralism	Mono-culturalism
Interpretation of accreditation standards re: diversity content inclusion	Very Specific	Specific-to-General	General, Vague, or Ambiguous	General, Vague, or Ambiguous
Congruence of program accreditation standards re: diversity-content inclusion	High Congruence	General Congruence	Low Congruence	High Incongruence
Program variations but still in keeping with diversity-content inclusion approach of program	Multicultural Specialization	Interdisciplinary Courses	Elective Courses	Workshops and/or Seminars

Appendix C

Beginning a Diversity-Inclusion Dialogue

Instructions

Read the following Curriculum Policy Statement for Master's (and Baccalaureate) Degree Programs in Social Work Education.

> Professional social work education is committed to preparing students to understand and appreciate human diversity. Programs must provide curriculum content about differences and similarities in the experiences, needs, and beliefs of people. The curriculum must include content about differential assessment and intervention skills that will enable practitioners to serve diverse populations.
>
> Each program is required to include content about population groups that are particularly relevant to the program's mission. These include, but are not limited to, groups distinguished by race, ethnicity, culture, class, gender, sexual orientation, religion, physical or mental disability, age, and national origin. (CPS B6.4 & M6.6)

Please respond to the following questions dealing with the inclusion of diversity content in the curriculum of your social work program. You may assume that you have all the resources needed (e.g., staff, money, time, etc.) to design this ideal program. The goal is to construct a curriculum that provides the knowledge, skills, and values that students need to graduate from your program.

1. Discuss your views on diversity in social work education as an emerging issue in the field.
2. Given your perceptions of diversity, how would you specifically implement your view?
3. What educational experiences would the ideal social work program offer in order to maximize the inclusion of diversity content in its curriculum?
4. Of the diversity-content-related educational experiences offered by your ideal

diversity-content-inclusive social work program, how would you prioritize educational experiences in terms of effectiveness and importance? (Please provide rationale for the proposed ranking).

5. How would your ideal diversity-content-inclusive social work program organize its educational experiences to maximize diversity inclusiveness relative to the overall curriculum?

6. What curriculum goals and/or standards, directly related to diversity, would the ideal social work program possess in order to maximize diversity inclusiveness in the preparation of its students?

7. How would the ideal social work program evaluate student acquisition and competency in the areas of diversity knowledge, values, and skills?

15

Summary and Conclusions

Joseph Anderson
Robin Wiggins Carter

This book has covered some of the prevailing diversity perspectives and frameworks for social work practice. All of these frameworks have either evolved from within our profession's knowledge base or have been carefully adapted from other sources to the diversity-competence needs of the profession. As any theory for practice, they need to be understood in their historical and sociopolitical contexts and tested and refined in their current applications.

Many of the contributions to this book represent not just a description of well-known and much-written-about perspectives, but an analysis of the most effective use of the perspectives, their strengths and limitations, and their contribution to understanding diversity from a social work perspective. Many of these authors found new ways of examining existing frameworks, and therefore adding to an existing body of knowledge in significant ways.

Trends and Frameworks

As several authors have noted (Felin, 2000; Gutierrez, Fredrickson, & Swifer, 1999), the historical trend in our knowledge base has moved from an emphasis on cultural sensitivity, through cultural competence, to critical consciousness regarding oppression, status differences, and structures of inequality. The assumption of this book is that the products of all three of these trends—sensitivity to diversity, competence in the application of diversity knowledge and skills, and critical consciousness—are fundamental to social work practice with and on behalf of diverse populations.

The usefulness of these frameworks depends upon the differences that make a difference for specific people in specific contexts and the needs that are addressed in the service delivery situation. This position is most consistent with those who define a multicultural perspective as viewing others with "multiple cultures" with varying degrees of identification, affiliation, participation, and involvement and with differential influence on their expectations in different situations (Felin, 2000; Peterson, 1989).

A consistent theme throughout this book has been the recognition of the intersection of multiple cultural and environmental variables in the development of self-identity. Although some approaches may emphasize one variable more than others, each recognizes the multidimensionality of the individual in some way. Cultural identity, therefore, is not a static, rigid concept; instead, it is viewed as dynamic, fluid, and requiring ongoing reconceptualization based on ever-changing environmental influences as well as the inevitable development of the individual.

Multi . . . Dimensions

The intersection of multiple variables in the development of self-identity suggests that practice competence regarding diversity might best be based on a more multicultural grid. Such a grid would account for the differential relation of multiple cultural influences to particular client systems' needs.

Applying such a grid helps one to recognize that some of these cultural influences tend to be dominant for many people. This is especially so in regard to ethnicity (especially for people of color), gender, class, nationality, or religion. People within some groups, however, will have different levels of sociopsychological identity and participation with others in their group, as manifested in customs, language, social networks, kinship patterns, and organization memberships. For any individual, identity and participation are also likely to be influenced by a number of factors such as life-cycle stage, primary and secondary rela-

	Identity *High___Low*	*Participation* *High___Low*	*Resources* *High___Low*	*Obstacles* *High___Low*
Ethnicity/Race Gender				
Class				
Sexual Orientation				
Religion				
Ability/Disability				
Age				
Geography				

FIGURE 15.1 *Multicultural Dimensions*

tionships within and across cultures, length of time in the United States, residential segregation or integration, patterns of immigration and migration, and kinship patterns.

These variables also affect the cultural resources available to the individual and, conversely, the obstacles to meeting needs related to their cultural identification. Certainly historical and structural oppressions are major obstacles for members of particular groups, regardless of the individual's level of identification with and participation within the group.

This multicultural grid also suggests the importance of a variety of frameworks to inform our social work practice. Not only are there multiple dimensions to cultural influences, there are also differential influences from these in the multidimensions of most individuals' situations (family, friends, work, play, education, health, spiritual beliefs, etc.). In relation to some situations, ethnocultural frameworks may be more applicable. In others, a combination of ethnocultural and oppression frameworks may be more useful; and in others still, the frameworks that address and are responsive to vulnerability may best inform the social work practice.

Summary of the Competencies

This book's editors believe that a particular integration of the principles and concepts from a variety of frameworks is more efficacious for diversity competence. The more practitioners can learn about each framework, the better they can incorporate those that fit the practice situation they confront. At minimum, they need those that

1. Provide knowledge of specific values, beliefs, and cultural practices of themselves and those they serve;
2. Enable them to respect and appreciate cultural differences and to perceive others through their unique cultural orientation instead of the practitioners';
3. Help them be more comfortable and less anxious or defensive with diversity;
4. Control or change false beliefs, assumptions, and stereotypes;
5. Increase their ability to think flexibly and to recognize that their own way of thinking and behaving is not the only way;
6. Increase their behavioral repertoire in order to sort through general knowledge about diverse groups and to see the specific ways in which this knowledge applies or not to a given client situation;
7. Develop critical consciousness in order to understand the causes, consequences and dynamics of all forms of oppression;
8. Let others teach about the differences that make a difference for them;
9. Inform personal, interpersonal, and political empowerment; and
10. Envision and enable social and economic justice for the benefit of individuals, society, and the global community.

Summary of Frameworks

These skills require the use of aspects of Ethnocultural, Oppression, and Vulnerable Life Conditions perspectives as well as combinations of these. The Ethnocultural frameworks—

ethnic-sensitive practice and value orientation—contribute to social workers' achievement of cultural sensitivity and relevance. The overlapping Ethnocultural/Oppression frameworks—ethnic minority and dual perspective—place social workers' ethnocultural understanding in an intergroup context with specific attention to power differentials regarding ethnocultural groups of color. The Oppression frameworks—Ethnic-centric and Social Justice—deal more directly with the causes, consequences, dynamics, and solutions to institutionalized discrimination, marginalization, and oppression. The Vulnerable Life Situations/ Ethnocultural frameworks—ethnographic and communication—inform especially how to place those who are often disempowered in the center of focus and with the power to give their own voice to their contexts. The Vulnerable Life Situations frameworks—feminist and constructivist—deal specifically with the way power differentials affect and can be changed by social workers' constructions of reality in recognition of multiple perspectives and in practitioners' collective action toward social justice.

Conclusion

The editors and authors of this text deem it to be a source for further development of knowledge and skill pertinent to effective social work practice with and on behalf of diverse individuals and populations. Grounded in a strength-oriented empowerment foundation, such practice evolves from our conceptual frameworks for consciousness of, commitment to, confidence in, and competence for diversity practice. The continuous development of each practitioner's conceptual framework to inform this practice includes both substantial knowledge about diversity and the ability to "learn how to learn" about the meaning and consequences of diversity for those individuals, families, groups, organizations, and communities they serve. For the editors, authors, and readers, this text does not end. It begins a career-long journey to learn more about ourselves and others in our uniqueness, group differences, and commonalties. Bon voyage to us all.

Index